⚡ FROM
THE ASHES
OF THE OLD

BOOKS BY STANLEY ARONOWITZ

False Promises: The Shaping of American Working-Class Consciousness

Food, Shelter, and the American Dream

Crisis in Historical Materialism

Working Class Hero: A New Strategy for Labor

The Sixties, Without Apology (edited with Sohnya Sayres, Anders Stephanson, and Fredric Jameson)

Education Under Siege (with Henry Giroux)

Science as Power: Discourse and Ideology in Modern Society

Postmodern Education (with Henry Giroux)

False Promises

The Politics of Identity

Roll Over Beethoven: The Return of Cultural Strife

Education Still Under Siege (with Henry Giroux)

The Jobless Future (with William Difazio)

Dead Artists, Live Theories and Other Cultural Problems

Technoscience and Cyberculture (edited with Barbara Martinsons and Michael Menser)

The Death and Rebirth of American Radicalism

Post-Work (edited with Jonathan Cutler)

FROM
THE ASHES
OF THE OLD

American Labor and
America's Future

STANLEY ARONOWITZ

HOUGHTON MIFFLIN COMPANY

BOSTON   NEW YORK   1998

For Nona, a born negotiator

For information about permission to reproduce
selections from this book, write to Permissions,
Houghton Mifflin Company, 215 Park Avenue South,
New York, New York 10003.

Library of Congress Cataloging-in-Publication Data
Aronowitz, Stanley.
    From the ashes of the old : American labor and
America's future / by Stanley Aronowitz.
        p.   cm.
    Includes index.
    ISBN 0-395-88132-3
    1. Labor movement — United States. 2. Labor
policy — United States. 3. Trade-unions — United
States.   I. Title.
HD8072.5.A665   1998
331.88'0973 — dc21   98-18998
                                                CIP

Printed in the United States of America
QUM 10 9 8 7 6 5 4 3 2 1

Book design by Melodie Wertelet

In our hands is placed a power greater than
    their hoarded gold;
Greater than the might of armies, magnified
    a thousand-fold.
We can bring to birth the new world from
    the ashes of the old,
For the Union makes us strong.
Solidarity forever . . .

— Ralph Chaplin

Contents

Preface and Acknowledgments

THIS BOOK WAS PROMPTED by the potential reemergence of American labor as a force in American politics and culture as well as its work in behalf of the economic interests of working people. Having previously published several books on workers and their unions at a time when there were few grounds for hope, I was heartened by the election of John Sweeney and the other insurgents to AFL-CIO leadership and decided to offer an analysis of the movements that produced the first contested election for top posts since the merger of more than forty years ago. And I was moved to offer my views on the path ahead for labor. I want to thank my editor, Steve Fraser, for agreeing that this book was timely. He has been both encouraging and rigorous in his comments and criticisms.

Others have helped make this book better than it otherwise would have been. Ellen Willis read several drafts of the manuscript and sent me back to the drawing board many times. Lynn Chancer made valuable suggestions, and I have profited from Jonathan Cutler's comments on several chapters. Robert Heifetz read early versions of the chapter on professionals and managers and made many suggestions for improvement. I want to thank Bruce Raynor, executive vice president of UNITE-AFL-CIO; Maida Rosenstein, president of Local 2110 of the United Auto Workers; and Jon Kest of ACORN for their time and courtesy. The archivists at the Fletcher Library at

Duke University were generous with their assistance on archival material on Operation Dixie. I would not have had access to some important work on the South without the kindness of Professor Lawrence Goodwyn of the History Department at Duke. The advice of Manny Ness, an indefatigable researcher and student of movements of the working poor, was invaluable. Penny Lewis and David Staples dug up published articles and other documents. Finally, thanks to my agents, Charlotte Sheedy and Neeti Madan, who had faith in this book and spared no effort to see it through.

⚑ Introduction

NINETEEN NINETY-SEVEN, a summer of worker discontent, was, surprisingly, also an occasion that has been rare in recent years: a union victory over a large employer. Hobbled by internal divisions and the pending investigation of its president, the Teamsters union, after months of fruitless negotiations, prepared for a monumental struggle against its most important employer. The United Parcel Service (UPS) employs almost 185,000 union members. Never in its history had the company, the oldest and largest in the private mail business, been struck nationwide. Until the UPS strike and a recent series of smaller strikes against General Motors, it was the corporations, not the unions, that demanded concessions — and usually got them. During the recession years, unions bargained away many hard-won benefits and sometimes took wage cuts. In the last six or seven "boom" years, companies were able to keep wages at a below-inflation level. Certainly, there were few instances of clear-cut union gains.

The union demands on UPS were the first of their kind since 1982, when, on the heels of Ronald Reagan's unceremonious breaking of the strike by the Air Traffic Controllers, the Teamsters ignored labor's long-time principle of "equal pay for equal work" and granted the company a two-tier wage system and the right to hire tens of thousands of part-time workers, paying them half the wages received by full-timers. Under the leadership of its president, Ron Carey, a former UPS driver from Queens, New York, the union crafted a program of substantial raises for legions of part-time workers and demanded that the company create ten thousand new full-time jobs. After months of stalemate, the union's policy committee proposed a strike vote. In contrast to the membership's decision three years earlier, when it turned down a similar request, the rank and file overwhelmingly approved. Still, the company remained unconvinced.

UPS had reason to doubt that the Teamsters union was more than a paper tiger. By the time Ronald Reagan left office, in January 1989, the labor movement was inert. Although Carey won the Teamsters' presidency in 1991, on a program of renewed militancy, and John Sweeney followed suit with the AFL-CIO four years later, experts were skeptical that there had been an effective turnaround. The company wagered that if the workers walked out, they would soon return because the union's strike fund was broke, and, in many parts of the country, a UPS job, even at the part-time wage of between $9 and $11 an hour, was often the best in town. Lean and mean, the company had successfully tamed the union by offering high wages for its forty thousand full-time drivers in return for their submission to a draconian system of work rules. By building on efficiency and the two-tier wage system, UPS had grown to a $24-billion-a-year business, one of the nation's largest and most profitable.

But the company seriously miscalculated. For six months before the workers struck, on August 4, the union conducted an extensive educational campaign, explaining why the two-tier system hurt all workers, even those full-timers who worked at $20 an hour. Carey did much of the educational work himself, touring the barns and depots. Helped by a vigorous economy and tired of being humiliated, workers became convinced that the time was ripe to insist that the company close the gap between the 58 percent of its employees who worked part time and the full-timers. And the AFL-CIO pledged a loan of $10 million a week to supplement the Teamsters' modest strike benefits. Moreover, the company was entirely outflanked by the Teamsters' adroit public relations campaign, which convinced three quarters of the public that theirs was a just cause. Within two weeks the company estimated that it had lost $60 million. It caved in to the union's demands, including a pledge to create as many as twenty thousand full-time jobs if economic conditions permitted, and for a few weeks the victory electrified the entire labor movement.

But labor was not to be permitted to savor its victory. A court-appointed monitor found that Carey and some of his associates had grossly violated union campaign laws in his 1996 re-election bid, so the monitor vacated the results and a few days later ruled that Carey could not run in a new election. Carey took a "leave of absence," and in some respects union labor was back to square one.

■

The future of American labor is directly tied to America's future. In the last quarter-century, most of America's working people — blue collar, white collar, professionals — have taken an enormous hit. Corporate downsizing, technological change, and mergers and acquisitions have cut the workforce in some high-pay industries by half; in others, the best-paid employees have been replaced by part-time, temporary and contingent workers who often are given no benefits. Wages throughout the 1990s have been stagnant. Meanwhile, the government is stepping back from its responsibilities in health benefits, pensions, and the maintenance of safety and health standards.

In the 1970s and 1980s American unions, many of which had experienced steep drops in both membership and bargaining power, had almost ceased addressing the problems of all workers. Rather, they saw themselves as agents acting in behalf of their own members. But the election in 1995 of an insurgent AFL-CIO leadership, headed by John Sweeney, infused new hope among working people, their unions, and those sympathetic intellectuals who had been alienated from organized labor. Sweeney promised to put new energy into organizing and political action. This book is an investigation of the current and future prospects for American workers and their unions. I argue that unions, if they are to thrive, must overcome the complacency of the last fifty years and expand labor's influence throughout politics and culture. But first labor must overcome its image as the representative of a narrow segment of the working population. Unions urgently need to organize in four major areas: the South, now the growth region for manufacturing; among the working poor, many of whom are in the majority of services; professional and technical employees, who have traditionally spurned unions but are facing pressure on their salaries, job security, and work autonomy; and the vast number of low-paid white-collar, mainly clerical employees who remain outside labor's ranks. It is important to note that unions have become too close to the Democratic Party, which at times appears indifferent to labor's needs. Labor should strive toward an independent political and legislative program.

The last two decades seem an unrefutable rebuke to the idea of progress. Once, labor and progressives believed the global welfare state an irreversible achievement. If the American version was weaker than those of comparable European states, this lag would sooner or later be closed. Instead, it was the Reagan-Thatcher counterrevolution that held sway in countries such as France, Germany, and Italy, where the political compromise between labor and capital had originally been forged. The labor movement after World War II had renounced social rule in return for a powerful welfare state. Workers as well as employers had acknowledged the compact. But after 1973, the deal began to unravel. Although in the countries of continental Europe it would take longer to dismantle the welfare state, most conservatives expected to remake capitalism in the images of the free market. By the mid-1990s, for example, the right-wing French government planned to sell off many state-owned enterprises, reduce pensions, and chip away at universal health care. And while the center-left Swedish government was instituting modest cuts, its powerful labor movement mutely looked on.

At the same time a favorite target of the right — overpaid unionized workers — bore the brunt of the blame. In Europe high labor costs were held responsible for double-digit unemployment rates as whole sectors of capital pulled up stakes and fled for greener pastures, including the low-wage areas of the United States. For example, in 1995 German and Swedish wages were about $23 an hour, including benefits; the U.S. rate was about $17. As European joblessness hovered around 11 percent, American rates were officially about 5 percent. Many economists attributed the difference to the emergence of the United States as a model free-market economy, free of government regulation and of strong social benefits. Whereas for most of the first thirty years after World War II, American living standards towered over those of Western Europe and Japan, by the late 1980s the low-wage environment in the nonunion South and many rural areas became attractive to Japanese and European manufacturers seeking to escape high labor costs. The American labor market, in turn, became "flexible," a euphemism for the proliferation of part-time, temporary, and contingent jobs without benefits.

Now the idea of unionism as a fundamental right and protection for American workers was once more under siege. Many traditional U.S. manufacturing industries identified union-driven wage and benefit standards with low productivity and sluggish economic growth. In the 1980s, as talk of globalization littered the media, conservative commentators and politicians, seeking a scapegoat on which to pin rising unemployment, public deficits, and rising imports, pointed to the workers. And by the next decade, end-of-Cold War liberal hopes for revival, after more than twenty years of Republican government, were brutally crushed.

Persuaded by a business-led propaganda machine, the public has embraced eighteenth-century capitalism as the new ideal, and no public figure dares to utter a negative word against the free market. The American system of social insurance, never strong, has come under relentless attack from the right, and the administration in Washington, having lost the fight to establish health care for all in 1993, smarting from the rebuff of the 1994 congressional elections, and wary because of impending elections, gave in. In August 1996, President Clinton signed, over the objections of labor and of liberals, a bill demolishing one of the New Deal cornerstones of social reform, the principle of income guarantees for unemployed people — even though the amounts granted recipients were pitched to poverty standards.

✄

American history is routinely told as the story of exploited immigrants who, after they are assimilated into the mainstream culture and the workplace, move rapidly up the social ladder. According to this account, unions might have had something to offer the working poor, but since World War II, poverty has been considered a temporary condition and is ascribed to lack of opportunity because of racial discrimination, poor educational access, and personal disabilities. In short, poverty has been driven to the margins of a wildly successful American capitalism. Since the Great American Job Machine is still well oiled, sooner or later many of the "deserving" poor will acquire skills and education and will enter the mainstream job market. From there, they will move to the middle class. So, according to this optimistic story, unions were a product of the industrializing, urbanizing, and assimilating era. But now that capitalism has brought nearly all Americans into market capitalism, unionism has been rendered obsolete.

The deterioration of the social safety net accompanied the weakening of the trade union movement in many industrialized countries. But numbers do not tell the whole story. For example, although the U.S. labor movement suffered no steeper loss in membership than did, say, French unions, its political and social power has become far weaker. That is because the culture and the law of labor relations in the United States is tilted toward employers. Unlike employers in most European countries, corporate capital here never recognized the validity of labor's claim to *institutionalized* social justice. American labor had to fight for every inch of economic and political ground. The National Labor Relations Act grants bargaining rights only to those groups which choose them, yet in many European countries after World War II collective bargaining was established as a right, whether workers joined unions or did not. By 1990 the decline of American unions and the dwindling of effective collective bargaining in many industries made the chances of a labor revival almost unimaginable.

So why write about a movement that is fated to be consigned to memory? Isn't the labor movement a product of the age of reform, which is now nearly over? Weren't unions a response to the power inequalities of the industrializing era, which ended in the 1960s? Aren't the remaining victims harmed by technological and economic changes that require a different kind of labor force, not the one traditionally attracted to unions? And with the disappearance of the relatively small elite of skilled and semiskilled workers, who crowded the factories of the great cities, what role is there for unions in the workplaces filled with technically and professionally educated employees? They, after all, resemble their employers in background, culture, and training. What future is there for unions, which, in the classical mode, are movements of the dispossessed?

This book is not a postmortem, for I contend the reports on the death of the labor movement are not just premature but wrong. As C. Wright Mills once quipped, "The end of ideology is, of course, the ideology of endings."[1] If, as some believe, the unions created during the New Deal and its aftermath are destined by technology and globalization to be left to the nostalgia of historians, surely a new labor movement is destined to rise from its ruins. For the labor movement is a combination of workers in a trade, profession, or industry seeking to raise their wages and, at least historically, to reduce their hours. As long as people procure their livelihood by working for wages and salaries, they will recognize, sooner or later, the futility of appealing to their employers as individuals. Of course, the operative term here is "sooner or later."

A case in point. In 1981 President Ronald Reagan did not miss a beat when he swiftly fired more than eleven thousand striking air traffic controllers. For a time it appeared that unionism was dead among these controllers, because neither their association nor the AFL-CIO was able to retrieve their jobs. By 1983 the Federal Aviation Agency had trained and hired new controllers, but five years later conditions were so onerous that the replacement workers themselves organized a union and won recognition from their employers. This incident repeats a theme in the long history of American labor. In steel, textiles, auto, and many other industries, organizing drives and strikes have been soundly defeated by employers, and commentators have confidently announced the death of the unions. Five, ten, or twenty years later a new generation of workers takes up the cudgels and tries again, because, for most workers, there is no alternative to collective action. It's not that unions "organize" workers who would otherwise remain dormant. In many, perhaps most, instances, workers organize themselves.

ìì

Dickens's *Christmas Carol* may inspire some bosses to treat their employees fairly and with respect, but the "market forces" that propel most businesses make such accommodations unlikely. The famous "bottom line" — profits — is a reminder that the price of compassion may be bankruptcy, especially for small employers. Having won deregulation and lost exclusive control over their home markets, the big corporations are forced to seek cost-savings, and targeting labor remains their easiest means. In short, as the often rancorous history of American labor struggles demonstrates, the system's logic rather than greed may prompt the most civic-minded among the capitalists to cut wages and benefits and, in doing so, break labor unions. The same logic makes worker resistance likely.

But the labor movement has never been merely an attempt to redress the imbalance of power on the shop floor and in the labor market. With all its flaws, the movement remains the best hope for democracy, not only in the workplace but also in the public sphere. Civil libertarians may advocate free speech for individuals, but unions pioneered in obtaining the right of social groups to organize in their own behalf without the threat of legal repression. The right to organize, established at the turn of the century, was the result of mass strikes, demonstrations, and long court battles as well as the efforts of middle-class reformers. Labor's struggle for this right later became the inspiration for women, blacks, and other oppressed groups.

In the 1960s, for example, civil rights groups broke segregation in public accommodations and voting primarily through sit-ins and demonstrations, not just through political and legal redress. The civil rights organizers acknowledged their debt to the 1930s' sit-down strikers in auto, rubber, and other mass-production industries. Feminism got a boost from the 1973 Supreme Court decision granting women the right to abortion. But it was the demonstrations of the

1960s and early 1970s that produced abortion rights and the direct action by women and their supporters to defend abortion clinics that consolidated these gains through civil disobedience when they saw that feminism had lost its militancy. Ironically, antiabortion forces also learned from labor's tactics.

Some have called the new market-driven world order "the risk society," because the underpinnings of the old order — job security, guaranteed income for those unable to work, and Social Security for older Americans — have become shaky.[2] Polls show that many younger people don't expect to have a pension and do not believe the future augurs well for their children. Even official economic optimism fails to temper this anxiety. Confident that unions are too weak to push wages up and profits down, even as official jobless figures dip below the 5 percent mark, the stock market keeps rising. Despite indications of tight labor markets, wage increases have not surfaced. The answer to the paradox is that labor markets are tight for some occupations but not for most, and unions have been too weak to make a fundamental difference.

Although the right never ceased heaping invective on the labor movement, for the first quarter-century after World War II unions provided most of the political muscle for the welfare state and drove wages up, even for nonunion workers. More to the point, strong unions almost abolished workers' fears that they could be arbitrarily discharged for protesting management's policies. While craft unions always enjoyed considerable autonomy because their members' skills were difficult to replace, the widely accepted notion of production and clerical workers being interchangeable parts was reversed in many antiunion bastions. The new National Labor Relations law was accompanied by the growth of unions in the 1930s and the acceptance of collective bargaining in America's basic industries during the following decades. Many corporate opponents of trade unions, such as the Ford Motor Company, General Electric, and nearly all important steel corporations, altered their approach to labor, and for forty years after the 1930s, collective bargaining seemed to replace class war.

The rise of the labor movement in the twentieth century, then, marks the emergence of working people as a genuine economic and political force. But the labor movement also was the foundation of a whole new way of life. What became known as the "American" standard of living — the envy of the whole world — was a result, in large measure, of the astounding success of industrial unionism. Its gains raised the level of consumption of millions of unskilled and semi-skilled workers, who, until the 1940s, usually could not afford homes, appliances, travel, and higher education. Without the unions, the development of prepaid health care would also have been beyond imagination.

If industrial workers were the first beneficiaries of the new industrial relations system, millions of others — small-business men, clericals, professionals, and other service employees — were not far behind. Although union "density" — the term experts use to compare the percentage of union members to the total labor force — in the professions and the retail industries has never been deep, wages and working conditions for these largely nonunion groups have been measured by union standards. Employers were obliged to pay more than they wished if only to keep the unions at bay. In the more highly organized industrial sectors, nonunion workers made use of the union threat to improve their conditions. For example, where the union was often defeated, as in Southern textile factories, employers were careful not to overreach their wage advantage, lest the Textile Workers union mount a successful unionization drive.

In such key industries as auto, steel, electrical, and machine tools, unions created a virtual welfare state by means of collective bargaining. For example, when I worked in steel, our union-negotiated health plan provided 365 days a year of hospital care, free medicines, and free doctor visits for my wife, my children, and me. Although most workers in largely nonunion industries, such as textiles, and many unionized workers in competitive industries, such as hotels and retailing, did not enjoy these benefits to the same extent, the unions' progress allowed them to dream that one day they too would benefit. But by the 1980s, employers were taking back many of these hard-won gains. The typical health care package today contains co-payer provisions and hefty deductibles, usually 20 to 30 percent of the bill. Long-term hospital care has yielded to a new emphasis on cost-savings, leading to what one writer has described as "getting rid of patients."[3] Today a plan that allows as much as six months of hospital care, with appropriate deductibles, is considered quite good. Most plans are less generous.

■

As we approach the new century, organized labor has fallen on hard times. Once the force that encouraged government intervention in every aspect of economic life, the labor movement, over the last twenty years, has become a symbol of what many see as a surpassed system. Many younger people, who never experienced the Depression, World War II, and the days of postwar prosperity, are now mesmerized by the ideology of individual initiative and the promise of a gleaming high-tech future. Still, the young working poor do show an interest in unionism, and unions are catching on among many professionals who once believed collective action was only for those who were otherwise helpless.

The "death" of the American labor movement, as we saw, was one of the more popular journalistic themes of the 1980s and early 1990s. By 1990 some labor relations experts were predicting that by the year 2000 unions would represent no more than 5 percent of the private-sector labor force, and the labor movement was being reduced to public employees, some industrial workers, and a diminishing number of workers in the building trades.[4] And by 1995 labor had indeed been reduced to barely 10 percent of workers in the private sector. An influential work on labor relations, written in the mid-1980s, argued that it was the nonunion sector that now drove wages.[5] The authors asserted that unions had decisively lost the initiative: in effect, collective bargaining, for which labor had struggled for decades, was dead. Although unions still boasted a substantial wage advantage over nonunion sectors, real wages for everyone had been declining for twenty-five years.

Many Americans, even those who were the main beneficiaries of its successes, believed that the idea of a labor movement was as outmoded as the decaying factory buildings that littered urban landscapes. Where once the fearsome figure of John L. Lewis, leader of the United Mine Workers and first president of the Congress of Industrial Organizations (the federation of mass-production unions), the CIO, made many employers take heed, union leaders and their shrinking cohorts had diminished. Even the AFL-CIO, with nearly thirteen million members, was widely believed to be a leftover of a bygone era. Union retreats from many of labor's hard-won gains became a routine feature of collective bargaining. Many asked whether collective bargaining had not, in fact, disappeared. Management and labor still sat down periodically to negotiate a new contract, but give-and-take, the main component of the system, was less in evidence. Workers gave and management took; only in a sharply declining number of cases did labor get anything in return. The reason? Without a potent strike weapon or its economic equivalent, there was no reason for employers to bargain, and the last two decades have been marked by the effective disappearance of the strike as a labor tool. That is what caused so many to pay attention to the UPS strike.

One of the causes of the defeats of the 1980s was the company's legal right to hire permanent replacements for striking workers. Earlier regarded as only an occasional weapon to break strikes, replacing strikers came back into fashion in the 1980s. As the 1996 settlement in the auto industry shows, even the strongest unions are likely to accept a dual wage system in return for job security for its shrinking membership. Like longshoremen and printers in the 1960s, who allowed employers to automate production on condition that the current labor force continue to receive a guaranteed wage, many blue-collar unions have ceded the principle of equal pay for equal work in return for job guarantees.

In an arctic political climate, labor organizers encountered skepticism, if not hostility, where they repeated the familiar union message of higher wages, better working conditions, and fringe benefits. It wasn't merely fear that prevented the unorganized from heeding the call; few believed that the union could deliver. A labor movement in steady retreat before its adversaries could hardly present itself as a savior. Labor ran out of arguments to counter the intimidating and effective employer statement that a plant or office would move if employees joined the union.

The fear of losing jobs was heightened by an epidemic of plant closings, most of them due to globalization, mergers and acquisitions, and runaways to the nonunion American South. Technological changes, especially computerized production, further reduced the workforce. In the 1980s more than eight million factory workers lost their jobs, and most industrial unions, already depleted, lost 50 percent of their remaining members. The Steelworkers, Packinghouse Workers, Electrical Workers, Machinists, and other unions lost more than half, and the Clothing, Textile, and Garment Workers unions were reduced by two-thirds.

Computerized work processes have removed the imperative of *place* from the economic equation. For example, given the "smart" machine, auto parts manufacturers can produce in Mexico more efficiently than in the American South or in Detroit; back-office accounting and telemarketing can be done anywhere; and some engineering work can be performed in China and India. Plants, which need not be built next to water or to rail lines, no longer bring together thousands of workers in one place. Once concentrated in Detroit and Pittsburgh, auto plants and steel mills employing a few thousand or a few hundred workers are all over America's geography. Similarly, offices no longer require masses of clerical workers seated at typewriters and adding machines in big cities like New York, Chicago, and San Francisco. A relatively few people can perform the work in widely scattered workplaces located in rural areas or in their homes.

But unions' losses go far beyond those caused by the deindustrialization of America's Northeast and Midwest. Unions have faded among construction workers, once considered the core of skilled union labor. Unions have lost their grip on the booming sector of the industry, private construction, and retain a hold only on commercial and public building. In many sectors, deregulation of the transportation industries has reduced the once awesome Teamsters union to a shadow.

The popular perception that union members are among the fat cats of the American economy has not helped rally public support for some of the notable strikes of the last two decades — air traffic controllers, Peabody Coal's miners, Hormel's meatpackers, Boeing's aircraft machinists, Caterpillar's farm- and earth-moving-equipment workers. Public disaffection has grown so widely that one of the more militant labor groups of the 1970s and early 1980s, the public employees, has just about ceased using the strike weapon. The gains of the huge State, County, and Municipal Employees, the union of most public clerical and blue-collar workers, are being undone in many cities. As this is written, thousands of unionized teachers are working without contracts, and many more have extended their existing agreements without the prospect of pay increases.

Since employers have the upper hand, they freely violate the spirit of the laws governing labor relations and safety and health without fear of consequences, so workers who want union representation are not reassured by their formally legal right to form unions. In a time of job scarcity, those who might be union activists hesitate to stick their necks out. These days, getting action from the Labor Relations Board may take years. The complex legal proceedings do not inspire those who would like to join the union but feel that the cards are stacked against them. As a result, many unions have all but ceased their recruiting efforts.

Even at the hands of Democrats, unions suffered. Jimmy Carter and Bill Clinton lent only lukewarm support to labor's legislative program. Some centrist Democrats have even renounced the traditional alliance between unions and the party except on condition that unions demand little or nothing from elected officials.

It was a Democratic Congress that began, in the 1970s, the process of deregulating business. Trucking and airline deregulation wreaked havoc on transportation unions by putting labor in competition with itself. On the heels of this sea change, the Teamsters union, which had once ruled the trucking industry, was reduced in size and influence. Jimmy Hoffa may have been a scoundrel, but his prestige among the members of the organization he once dominated now makes his son a credible contender for its highest office.

Perhaps the most telling sign of the decline is the belief among union leaders and many activists that what they cannot achieve at the bargaining table may be gained in legislatures and by appeals to executive authorities. Because this belief has, over the years, tempered labor's militancy, the electoral arena has frequently governed bargaining strategy. For example, in 1981, when the air traffic controllers' strike was broken by Reagan, union leaders went to the White House to plead for mercy. Needless to say, nothing was done. The idea of calling demonstrations in every large city, even a one-day strike, was far from the minds of the union leaders. Some experts believe the union leaders could not entertain such tactics because they were afraid nobody would come. The AFL-CIO president, Lane Kirkland, ruled out even a symbolic strike on the grounds that most union contracts contain a no-strike clause.

Kirkland, the long-time lieutenant to AFL-CIO's founding president, the conservative and pugnacious George Meany, was not cut out to take on corporate heavyweights. Lacking Meany's hubris in remaining independent of the party's liberal wing, and staunchly supporting every element of the government's foreign policy, even when it hurt workers, Kirkland never risked provoking either of organized labor's ideological wings and did not veer from his middle-of-the-road political stance. When Ronald Reagan fired the controllers, members of an AFL-CIO affiliate, Kirkland refrained from attacking the administration. He concluded that an appeal to Reagan's union past and to his common decency was the best way to gain reinstatement of the eleven thousand fired controllers. It was only under great pressure from labor's progressives that he agreed to sponsor a Sunday outing, termed a demonstration, to protest Reagan's attack. When asked why he had not called a strike, Kirkland reminded his questioner that such a move would have violated the no-strike provisions of many contracts and risked heavy fines for some unions. When civil disobedience disappears from the vocabulary of active union people, the resemblance between the labor and the civil rights movement ends.

A second problem was that some in labor's hierarchy were not sure they wanted an active rank and file; after all, democracy brings potential political dangers. Unions, like other bureaucracies, are ruled by experts. Although they are dedicated to the union contract and to the services the institution provides, many of them view strikes and other forms of direct action with alarm. As the leaders extolled labor peace, the members watched their living standards decline. Despite the confident predictions by some that the 1990s would bring a new burst of liberal vitality, the first half of this decade showed that the conservative grip had been barely loosened, and that the Democratic Party, far from remaining true to its New Deal traditions, was fast moving to the right.

☙

The first signs that predictions of labor's death may have been premature was the fight over Senate approval of the North American Free Trade Agreement (NAFTA). In 1993, a severely weakened American labor movement put up a brave but losing fight against the treaty, which President Clinton had belatedly but warmly endorsed. The unions contended that NAFTA, which eliminated most tariffs on Mexican imports in return for substantial tax-free concessions to U.S. investors, would result in massive job migration. An unlikely alliance of Ross Perot, Ralph Nader, protectionist groups, and the AFL-CIO almost defeated the measure. Already dubbed a "new" Democrat, a euphemism for a politician who was something less than loyal to liberal traditions, Clinton worried that the unions, still part of his political base, might leave the fold or, more likely, sit out the next congressional election.

The stunning Republican victory in the 1994 congressional elections seemed to confirm the judgment. The progressive movement, of which unions had been the real muscle, finally seemed dead. Clinton, reading the election results to mean that his only strategy for re-election was to drift even farther to the right, became, in the second half of his first term the law-and-order, budget-balancing, poor-bashing, imperial president. Labor's only solace was the belated passage of the same minimum wage bill that had failed two years earlier. Like the Socialist Norman Thomas, who in 1936 complained that the New Deal had stolen his party's reform program, the Republicans were left to charge that Clinton was a conservative in centrist clothing.

Meanwhile, Clinton ended "welfare as we know it" by signing a bill that toppled one of the bases of the New Deal — the right of everyone to income support. Clinton heard only muffled murmurs of disapproval, except for a scattering of critics. As for the AFL-CIO, it pledged some $35 million to re-elect the president and restore Congress to Democratic leadership, hoping that a victory would be the first step on the road back to some kind of new deal.

The losses at the bargaining table and in legislatures, culminating in the 1994 midterm defeat, produced a wave of dissatisfaction with the established leadership of the AFL-CIO. By 1995 a majority of unions representing the federation's thirteen million members had declared their intention to contest the top offices. In rapid succession, Kirkland was forced into retirement, and John Sweeney, president of the million-member Service Employees (SEIU), declared his candidacy. He was immediately backed by the three major industrial unions — Auto Workers, Steelworkers, and Machinists — by the diminished but still big Teamsters union, and by the State, County, and Municipal Employees. In the AFL-CIO's first contest for top offices, the 1995 election of Sweeney to the federation's presidency gave hope that unions might once again play an important role in U.S. economic and political life. It was also a sign that most unions were profoundly discontented with the passivity of labor's leadership during the preceding fifteen years, which had seen a determined employer assault on wages and working conditions. Sweeney came to power as an insurgent, promising to bring a new militancy and new energy into the AFL. Early signs indicated the new position: that labor would distance itself from its postwar willingness to serve as an insurance company for a shrinking, even if highly paid, segment of the workforce.

Sweeney, arguing that task number one is to rebuild the ranks of the labor movement, has placed special emphasis on organizing the working poor, one of labor's most neglected constituencies. (The record of his own union, SEIU, in this regard is exemplary.) Sweeney's economic program is simple: reverse the long-term wage stagnation. At his inauguration he advanced the slogan "America Needs a Raise," which can be interpreted as a call for aggressive wage bargaining as well as for raising the federal minimum wage. In a remarkable display of the federation's legislative clout, political analysts acknowledged that the Republican Congress's capitulation, in the summer of 1996, to the bill to raise the minimum wage by ninety cents came about largely as a consequence of the AFL-CIO's efforts. But Sweeney has also recognized that workers have lost much of their voice in the long winter of labor's decline. Among the local leaders of SEIU Sweeney has a reputation as a "rabble rouser" who speaks the conventional union's language of cooperation and social contract but adds that "it has to come when unions are in a position of strength."[6] By the winter of 1996, Sweeney and his fellow officers had begun to make good on their promises. Taking a leaf from the book of the 1960s' civil rights movement, the AFL-CIO called for the recruitment of a thousand college students to participate in a project named Union Summer. At the federation's Organizing Institute they were to learn the techniques of organizing; perhaps half would become members of affiliates' organizing staffs.

The underlying assumption of this project is that working people may no longer be viewed as part of the privileged middle class of American society. Steadily falling wages and the explosion of part-time, temporary, and contingent jobs have begun to erode the belief that each generation is destined to do better than the preceding one. By placing a priority on organizing as well as on political action, the AFL-CIO has sent a message that now is the time for a new crusade for economic justice.

Since 1981, which marked the opening volley of the war against unions, the cause of labor has gradually taken on the aura of a civil or human rights movement. Where once most unions supported civil rights as a moral obligation, in the Reagan era the place of workers could have been likened to that of blacks, because they had been deprived of their most dramatic achievements, especially of industrial citizenship. The call for students to rally around the unions is a dramatic admission that labor was severely weakened by the events of the past fifteen years.

Yet the consequences of labor's crisis were even more far-reaching than economic and electoral. The crisis in democracy itself was evident in the expanding power of management to do what it pleased at the workplace, the unresponsiveness of government, and the court-sanctioned restrictions on workers trying to form unions. Sweeney has in some respects indicated his departure from postwar union reticence. When the Los Angeles Board of Supervisors announced, in 1995, a plan to cut eighteen thousand workers from its payroll, Sweeney threatened "a massive campaign of resistance and retribution" if the plan went through. Rhetoric? Maybe. But even such fighting words have been absent from labor's arsenal for decades. Of course, Sweeney is not about to make a U-turn in some of labor's cherished sentiments toward cooperation with employers. He hopes to forge a "new social contract" and to "build bridges" of labor-management cooperation. "But," he has said, "I believe in blocking bridges whenever these employers and those communities turn a deaf ear to the working families that we represent."[7] This statement reflects the profound sense of crisis experienced by many of his fellow union leaders.

What Sweeney recognized more than fifteen years ago, when SEIU spent 30 percent of its budget on organizing, remains the educational and political goal of the unions. Militancy and resistance are not symptoms of reflexive leftism; they reflect a growing perception, shared even by some fairly conservative labor leaders, that the "crisis" of American labor is not the warning of a few malcontents, but is a fair description of the current state of affairs. Sweeney's ascendancy indicates that there are some at the pinnacle of union power who are not prepared to lie down in comfortable graves. Coming from the ranks of the relatively staid trade unionists, Sweeney's new vocabulary is a sign that the days of trade union glory are certainly not ended.

Sweeney is a long-time loyal Democrat whose leadership style is entirely within labor's traditions. As SEIU president he presided over a tent large enough to accommodate a figure like Gus Bevona, the financially opulent president of the 110,000-member New York Joint Council and leader of its largest local, 32B–32J. Moreover, Sweeney settled intraunion disputes by imposing trusteeships over recalcitrant locals, most recently in Los Angeles. So it is not radicalism nor fervent loyalty to rank-and-file unionism that marks the insurgency; rather, it is an acute instinct for survival.

What separates Sweeney from his predecessor, Kirkland, is his recognition that labor is approaching the apocalypse and that its future is in doubt. So, just as John L. Lewis had invited radicals to join the CIO, Sweeney, aware that the labor movement suffers from tired blood, has invited intellectuals and idealistic students to join the labor movement. Shortly after taking office, he announced an organizing fund of $20 million to add to $35 million for the AFL-CIO political war chest in the 1996 elections. In addition, he chose Richard Trumka, of the militant Mineworkers union, and Linda Chavez Thompson, of the State, County, and Municipal Employees, to round out a slate against Thomas Donahue, the federation's acting president and long-time secretary-treasurer under Kirkland.

As encouraging as Sweeney's emergence is, the jury is still out on the fundamental questions facing the labor movement: can it overcome the far-reaching changes signaled by the words "globalization, technological revolution, restructuring"? Can labor overcome its internal problems, some of which are intimately bound to the conditions of its past success as a willing ally of the economic and political establishment? Can unions recover without flying ideological flags? And what about the historic patriotism of the American labor movement? Does the struggle against NAFTA and the Democratic Party's complicity with the end of New Deal reforms represent a potential political crisis for the labor movement? If not, how should it put forth its agenda?

I do not hope to find a golden mean. Rather, I look for tendencies in the movement and, more broadly, in society that may lead to an outcome different from the one suggested by the present conservative period in our history. For example, I suggest that if the labor movement broadens its vision to embrace the new class of knowledge workers employed in cutting-edge industries and occupations, those who in Europe are called "intellectuals," it may have a healthy future. If, as I claim, knowledge is the most important productive force in the growing industries of communications, media, and global finance, as well as cybernetically driven industrial production, then a thriving labor movement is obliged to find ways to attract those involved in these new processes. Similarly, I argue that, without forging an alliance with social movements, labor will remain isolated from the most dynamic currents in American society.

Still, there are questions about the revival of the impaired labor movement. How can the leadership arrest the hemorrhaging of large sections of American industry? How can it overcome a political and social climate that is unfavorable for organizing? How should it deal with the Labor Relations law, which has become an employer tool rather than a means to promote union organizing and collective bargaining? How should it address the Democrats' acceptance of the conservative social program of cutting out welfare, of balancing the budget, and of privatizing public goods? Perhaps most important, how can it mobilize labor's rank-and-file members to participate in its revival?

The new economic and political environment makes us question whether unions can survive if they remain committed to the belief that labor peace rather than class confrontation is in labor's interest. If labor is the heart of social change — a proposition I defend — then it can no longer be subordinate to political and social forces, least of all to transnational corporations whose loyalty lies elsewhere, or to a state whose interests are diametrically opposed to its own. To prosper, labor must take its future in its own hands.

1 ⊭ Riding the Wave of Postwar Prosperity

THE FALL OF 1945 was a heady and anxious time for America. Since most victors and vanquished had been equally devastated by the war, the United States became the most powerful nation in the world. Still, many Americans wondered whether the economy would be able to absorb eleven million members of the armed forces. Economists grimly predicted the return of the Great Depression. With a sense of foreboding, the Seventy-ninth Congress had, the year before, passed the G.I. Bill of Rights, to provide income and housing for veterans while the government figured out what to do with them. And workers and their unions braced for layoffs. They didn't come, nor were the problems of readjustment as grave as expected.

No section of American society seemed in a better position to gain from the economic, military, and political strength of the postwar United States than the labor movement. By the end of the war almost a third of paid employees were in unions, though few white-collar workers in the public and private sectors were organized. Labor's power had been acquired through hard struggle. The New Deal provided a legal framework for union organizing and collective bargaining. But from the 1933 apparel workers' and miners' strikes to the 1937 Supreme Court's decision on the constitutionality of the National Labor Relations Act, it took mass strikes, factory occupations, and demonstrations to convince large and small employers alike that the majority of industrial workers wanted unions.

Labor had come into its own during the war. Desperate to raise industrial production to supply the necessary quantities of military equipment, Roosevelt pledged to assist labor to overcome the resistance of many employers — especially Ford and some steel companies — to union organization. As it turned out, the wartime no-strike pledge to which, with the notable exception of the Mineworkers, nearly all of labor had agreed, was soon made permanent. Unions therefore insisted on a contractually mandated grievance procedure to address working conditions. To avert strikes, many contracts introduced the practice of impartial arbitration as the final step when the parties could not agree.[1]

After Japan surrendered, unions lost little time in putting their demands on the public agenda as well as on the bargaining table. Thwarted by the no-strike pledge, which had left their wages and benefits stagnant for four years, and, at the war's end, by inflation, which depressed their living standards, many workers were furious. And employers were reaping near-unrestricted profits. By the summer of 1946, workers staged strikes against most of the leading industrial corporations, strikes that represented the largest outpouring of militant workers in any one year in American history.[2] They were begun by longshoremen and oil workers, and they took on the aura of a crusade when the United Auto Workers demanded of GM a 30 percent wage increase. Soon the strike wave spread to the steel, electrical, and rubber industries.

The settlements fell short of the target: most employers agreed to 18 percent or eighteen-cents-an-hour increases, and Auto Workers' Walter Reuther's radical proposal that the increases be safeguarded by an employer agreement, to avoid price "pass alongs" to consumers, failed for two reasons. Despite some favorable public sentiment for the plan, General Motors and other leading corporations were determined to reassert the management "prerogatives" they believed had been eroded by wartime labor shortages and union power. And the Steelworkers union, next to the Auto Workers the most important force in the strike movement, permitted the industry to raise prices. Reuther tried another ploy: if General Motors insisted on price boosts to pay for the wage increases, he demanded the company "open the books" to union and public scrutiny to prove it needed the extra income. Again he was rebuffed.

Most union leaders drew different lessons from these struggles. The strikes demonstrated labor's power to improve the living standards of millions of members and, by example, the entire workforce. Some on labor's left read the signs to mean that the time was ripe for political independence and shop-floor militancy. But Reuther himself and the Steelworkers president, Philip Murray, who was also CIO president, were convinced that the well-being of American labor depended on its forging a new social compact with the largest corporations: the strike weapon and other confrontational tactics would be used only sparingly. Even though Reuther soon learned that, to ensure industrial peace, the government, even under a Democratic administration, was likely to be on the corporations' side, union leaders expected Congress and the president to enact universal health care and a massive housing program. What they did not foresee was that, after thirteen years of the New Deal, the Republican Party and its business allies were not about to roll over for a new wave of reform.

Riding the backlash against the unions' economic power, the GOP in the 1946 midterm elections took both houses of Congress and wasted little time in putting the brakes on labor's forward march. No sooner had Congress convened than it passed, with many Democratic votes, the Taft-Hartley amendments to the National Labor Relations Act. These restraints forbade sympathy strikes where a contract was in effect; enabled states to outlaw the union shop, which required workers to maintain union membership as a condition of employment; emulated the earlier Railway Labor Act by giving the president the right to ban strikes for eighty days if the administration thought the walkout would jeopardize the national interest; gave employers the right to hire permanent replacements for striking workers; and outlawed the so-called secondary boycott, that is, forbade workers to refuse to cross a picket line when they themselves were not directly involved in the dispute. Under that provision unions could be fined for directing their members to refuse to handle "hot cargo" — goods intended for, or emanating from, struck plants. Also, Communists were banned from holding elective union office. With an eye to the upcoming 1948 election President Harry Truman, who had publicly complained about labor's inordinate power, vetoed Taft-Hartley, but Congress overrode his veto and the bill became law.

Organized labor vowed repeal, but within a few years it became apparent that several factors made it unable to mount an all-out campaign. Perhaps the most important was that many labor leaders believed that building consensus in labor relations was more important than maintaining an adversarial stance. By 1948, Reuther and Murray were declaring a new era of labor peace, in return for which they expected companies like GM and US Steel to agree to higher living standards for workers. And, as the Cold War against the Soviet Union and the Communist bloc gained momentum, the anti-Communists in the labor movement were in no hurry to give aid and comfort to their internal adversaries — the American Communists, who emerged from the war stronger than ever in some industrial unions. In fact, they collaborated with the government to purge the Communists from their ranks. Finally, labor was still convinced that it had a reasonable chance to win an expanded social wage — especially universal health care — through congressional action and were wary of antagonizing lawmakers. Reluctantly, labor learned to live with Taft-Hartley.

By 1950 American labor was locked in an uneasy embrace with corporate America and the liberal state. In that year the postwar social compact was symbolically sealed when the Auto Workers signed a five-year agreement with GM and other auto corporations. The deal codified the wartime no-strike pledge, in return for which workers received regular annual wage increases and a cost-of-living hike to correspond to the consumer price index. In a period of substantial inflation, this "elevator" clause protected unionized workers against inflation-induced erosion of their living standards. Reuther's imaginative bargaining tactics were soon emulated by other unions, and the postwar pattern seemed set in stone. Labor agreed to give management the right to direct the workforce, invest in new labor-saving technologies, open new plants at the expense of older facilities, and set prices for its products at will. At the political level, labor was securely tucked in the folds of the Democratic Party and the bipartisan anti-Communist foreign policy. Perhaps most eventful was that Reuther and other leaders proclaimed their loyalty to capitalism as the best of all possible worlds.

☙

The New Deal's achievement went beyond the issue of workers' rights. Most trade unionists came to believe that the labor movement required government to secure workers' interests: labor needed a Labor Relations Act with full enforcement powers; collective bargaining, a symbol of cooperative relations with employers; and the protection of the Democratic Party to safeguard these gains. Far from being the radical break with the establishment that many in and out of the labor movement believed it to be, the rise of unions introduced a new level of industrial and political discipline. Labor, which had been an unwilling outlaw and cherished its independence from the state, began to enjoy the perquisites of political and industrial citizenship, which many of its leaders interpreted as bringing new responsibilities to maintain the status quo.

But even as wages were rising, all was not well on the shop floor. In many industries, management elevated delay to an art form. For example, under the "management prerogatives" clause — another wartime innovation — management retained the right to transfer workers from one job to another, install new machines or work processes, and impose discipline, including discharge, on workers who disobeyed direct orders. Discharged workers were deemed guilty until proven innocent. The aggrieved could do no more than file a complaint with a union official. The grievance process, encumbered by the management practice of piling up unsettled grievances, might last many months or even a year. Meanwhile, the workers were bound to stay on the job under what they believed to be unfair or onerous conditions. Labor's leadership may have determined that it was in their members' interest to cooperate with management by allowing the employer to set higher production norms and change work rules.

But in the first decade after the war many rank-and-file union members resisted such arrangements by staging walkouts over issues of productivity and disputed managerial prerogatives. Disruptions of production became, in the postwar era, the subject of numerous legal challenges. Employers sought — and often obtained — court injunctions ordering workers to return to work on penalty of heavy fines and being held in contempt. Because of Taft-Hartley, union leaders feared the so-called wildcat strike, because it almost inevitably resulted in legal sanctions that, if defied, could threaten the union's existence by imposing heavy fines.

Most unions, as a result, adjusted their practices to the no-strike rule. Many shop-floor leaders became de facto contract lawyers; now their main job was to interpret contracts and plead workers' grievances before management and arbitrators who were increasingly viewed as friendly adversaries. With full-time union representatives spending most of their time at grievance and arbitration meetings, the task of organizing the unorganized often became a marginalized occupation reserved for staffers to whom the leadership owed political debts. In the postwar era, "service" and organizing functions grew ever more distant from each other. While these arrangements did not prevent occasional acrimonious bargaining and militant strikes, most workers were tied to the unwritten "social compact" to safeguard production.

By 1953 union growth ground to a halt, but not before the labor movement completed what it had started twenty years earlier. Collective bargaining was in place for the majority of workers in key industries; the right to strike had been reinstated, even though it was restricted both by contract and law; trade union organizing had been fully integrated into the Labor Relations law, which relegated the "recognition" strike to second place in favor of a government-supervised representation election; and nearly all of labor became affiliated with the Democratic Party. Once the era of the New Deal was ended by Eisenhower's election, unions were clearly on the defensive.

With more than 40 percent of the factory labor force in unions by the late 1940s, even nonunion employees gained from labor's power.

There were still gaps in unionization, especially in the huge textile industry, and among white- and pink-collar employees, but American labor's strength was the envy of trade unionists in other industrialized countries. Mammoth corporations like IBM and Kodak, which kept their plants open shops, knew that in union-dominated electrical and metalworking industries they had to equal or surpass union wages and benefits. These corporations went so far as to guarantee lifetime jobs for their employees, a promise they could fulfill only in the era when labor costs were absorbed by relatively high prices for their products, many of which were underwritten by the military.

One of the changes in labor's philosophy was the replacement of the union commitment to solidarity with the emphasis on creating jobs by increasing consumer demand. Traditionally, equality was best achieved by shortening hours and thereby swelling the numbers of jobs, narrowing the wage gap between skilled and semiskilled workers, and fighting race and sex discrimination in hiring, promotions, and upgrading. Solidarity was a prerequisite for strengthening a movement that could contest social and political power. It was the UAW's Walter Reuther who broke with this tradition by fervently advocating full employment and higher labor productivity as unions' two guiding principles. With jobs and worker productivity acknowledged as essential to ending poverty and discrimination against racial minorities, the traditional labor demand for shorter hours was all but jettisoned. Reuther saw paid work as basic to both human redemption and American prosperity.[3]

To combat racial inequality, postwar labor put much of its legislative clout behind policies to promote economic growth rather than behind possibly divisive programs to end discrimination in hiring and promotion. Even though Reuther was a member of the NAACP's national board, he argued tirelessly that expanding the number of jobs was the way to overcome the exclusion of many minorities from postwar prosperity. It was government that could best provide paid work for all. One of the major lessons learned during the war was that federal military spending was the shortest distance between mass joblessness and full employment. Few labor leaders, therefore, were willing to oppose the permanent war economy. By the 1950s, most production unions were firmly in the hawks' camp and supported Truman's proposal to make peacetime military preparations the basis of economic as well as foreign policy. Mainstream labor, opposing all efforts to reduce military spending, was subsequently thwarted in its quest for social reform by the conservative argument that America could not afford both "guns and butter." Unions supported their (unionized) employers against arms budget-cutters.

Rather than fighting labor's postwar legislative defeats in housing, universal health care, and labor law reform, labor hunkered down in the face of conservative attacks portraying workers as selfish. Although some trade unionists understood that labor had to persuade the "general public" that its cause was their cause, the old narrow mentality of the crafts — which industrial unionism seemed to have buried during the 1930s — came back to dominate postwar labor's political culture. Nor did industrial unions take their picket-line victories as signals to launch organizing campaigns to recruit new categories of workers. When it did take such a step — the ill-fated Southern organizing drive of 1946–1948 — internal tensions and sheer incompetence hobbled the effort.

From 1945 through the early 1950s, many unions were embroiled in a civil war. Pressed by anti-Communists like Reuther and by traditional "right-wing" progressives like the Textile Workers' president, Emil Rieve, in 1947 CIO president Phil Murray seized the opportunity to break with the Communists. For their part, the Communists and their allies and other Cold War critics began to work for the election of Truman's opponent, Commerce Secretary and former vice president Henry A. Wallace. The third-party movement gave Murray and his new allies the excuse they needed to drive Communists out of the CIO in 1948.

Notwithstanding Harry Truman's spectacular come-from-behind victory that year, it was plain that the New Deal was over. The right had obliterated the image of labor as victim, and the unions, having accepted their place as junior partner in the political and economic power bloc, refused to look back at the millions of workers who were excluded from the postwar compact. Although many in the CIO had been disappointed during Truman's first three years by his half-hearted pursuit of the unfinished elements of the New Deal, they threw themselves into his 1948 campaign. Labor had been allied with Roosevelt since 1936, but it did not perfect its electoral machinery until Roosevelt's 1944 bid for a fourth term. By 1948, the CIO Political Action Committee had an efficient apparatus in place, and the AFL was also reversing its traditional antipathy to active participation in national politics. But despite labor's importance to the Democrats' electoral chances, conservatism had, perhaps irrevocably, gained the upper hand. By the time Truman left office, in 1952, two successive Democratic Congresses had not been able to deliver a single major item on labor's reform agenda.

American unions interpreted Eisenhower's election in 1952 as a signal to turn inward. After losing crucial congressional legislative battles in 1949 for a national health insurance bill and public housing, workers and their unions spent the next two decades using collective bargaining to obtain benefits for veterans, including low-interest loans to buy houses. Collective-bargaining agreements set the norm for what may be termed a "private" welfare state: company-paid health insurance, pensions to supplement inadequate Social Security, paid holidays and vacations.

≠

The model of American exceptionalism to the European model of class-based politics was never true but it felt true after the war. The Depression came to be regarded by many celebrants of American capitalism — and a fair number of its critics — as a ten-year interlude in the long wave of American economic progress. And because the working class and its organizations had not embraced socialist and labor parties to advance their interests, those who did were viewed as little short of unpatriotic. The formation of unions as industry-oriented institutions that primarily served the interests of their dues-paying members corresponded to the anti-ideological orientation of most of their leaders. They saw themselves as a powerful interest group within a pluralist society. Labor did not place itself in opposition to capitalism, nor was it prepared to form alliances with other social movements to extend rights and freedoms beyond their legal dimension. Reuther never hesitated to inveigh against "poverty, hunger, and disease," but, on the whole, labor placed little importance on reaching out to the dispossessed and the disenfranchised.

The pattern of accommodation was dramatically illustrated by the union(s) of longshoremen on both coasts and by the newspaper-printing unions in the early 1960s. Mindful of their obligation to address the job security of their members, these unions responded to management's introduction of labor-saving technologies by demanding a guaranteed annual wage for existing workers. Given the enormous reduction of labor entailed by automation, the unions took care to protect at least a single generation of members from income loss, regardless of whether they worked. In fact, most of them did not, but were required to report for work and be available when needed. Harry Bridges, the once fiery leader of the left-wing West Coast Longshoremens Union (ILWU), remarked ironically, after his retirement, "I sold out the working class to save my members." The older practice of protecting industry- or corporatewide equality of wage levels — the principle of equal pay for equal work — gave way to the idea of taking labor out of competition with itself in order to gain job security, but not equality, for the existing workforce. To safeguard its senior members in the 1960s, the ILWU established a two-tier classification system for workers; the lower tier did not have the guaranteed wage. The pioneer agreement was emulated by the East Coast Longshoremens Union, which, despite its conservative and corrupt reputation, actually negotiated a better deal than Bridges had done.

These powerful unions did win a fairly substantial share of the cost savings produced by automation, but their deals do much to explain why wages and salaries have declined steadily since the early 1970s. Many sons and daughters of union members can no longer follow their parents into the well-paid union job; instead, they are obliged to seek work in low-wage, nonunion retail and service jobs, which typically pay half what factory and transportation jobs pay. Thus many families require two wage earners to bring home the income formerly brought in by one.

Steelworkers, telephone workers, and many auto workers, with ten to twenty years of service, have lost their jobs since the early 1960s, when corporations began to introduce sweeping changes in the work process: automated relays resulted in tens of thousands of layoffs for telephone operators; automation in basic steelmaking wiped out many jobs; auto companies installed the transfer machine, replacing thousands of workers in their engine plants; a decade later, they introduced to assembly plants computer-driven robots, numerical controls, and laser processes, which reduced the workforce by half. Detroit lost its pre-eminence as Motown when, with the union's tacit agreement, the big three auto corporations decentralized investment. Although the union eventually negotiated a transfer program for displaced workers, many were reluctant to go South or to rural areas, sites of new plants.

To be sure, the Auto Workers and Steelworkers unions negotiated such innovations as an employer-paid supplement to state unemployment benefits for up to two years and a limited retraining program for laid-off workers. But, in the main, guaranteed income, shorter hours, and other work-sharing arrangements were taken off the bargaining table. Indeed, at a 1961 Steelworkers union convention, President John F. Kennedy made the case against a proposal to reduce the work week to thirty-two hours. "The Communist challenge," he said, "requires this nation to meet its unemployment problems by creating abundance rather than rationing scarcity."

Some have argued that racial, gender, and ethnic divisions among workers and within the unions account for much of labor's weakness. Clearly, only a labor movement dedicated to overcoming race and gender inequalities in the workplace can hope to rectify the unequal balance of power between workers and large employers. But some unions are mainly white labor monopolies that systematically exclude blacks from many of the best industrial and craft jobs. Blacks and other racial minorities have been effectively barred from union membership in many of the high-wage sections of construction crafts and are only marginally represented in the skilled trades in the auto, electrical, and machine tool industries. In the machinist and tool-and-die trades, for example, blacks and Latinos hold fewer than 2 percent of the unionized jobs. They are somewhat better represented in the nonunion shops, which, of course, pay less.

What is puzzling about the resistance of unions to adopting a workplace civil rights program is the labor movement's position in the forefront of legislative fights for these very rights. But unions are political institutions, and many leaders who seek re-election by the rank and file have hesitated to support black hiring and upgrading in industries where jobs are awarded on the basis of family and community connections. Even in instances of labor shortage, white workers have often resisted opening membership rolls to qualified minorities, even on a temporary basis. Their memory of joblessness and their fear of losing control to outsiders have discouraged many of them from accepting inclusion. Instead, government coercion has been called on to break the race barrier. Yet, sadly, court orders and federal sanctions have failed to improve the situation, because the law barring discrimination in employment is, except in rare instances, simply not enforced unless organized civil rights and community groups make a public issue of the closed door.

The Auto Workers, Packinghouse Workers, and other industrial unions did support, with funds and public statements, the Southern civil rights effort. For example, linking arms with King and A. Philip Randolph, the black leader of the Sleeping Car Porters union and a major civil rights advocate, Reuther walked at the head of the 200,000 participants in the 1963 March on Washington, even as the AFL-CIO refused to endorse the event on the grounds that it was being run by left-wingers, thereby embarrassing the Kennedy administration. Some unions sent representatives to Mississippi Summer, a SNCC voting-rights project in 1963, and vigorously lobbied for the Civil Rights and Voting Rights Acts of 1964 and 1965. But even as Reuther openly defied George Meany and gave a ringing speech at the March rally, the emergence of a new generation of black activists within the UAW and other Northern-based unions became a vexing problem for labor liberals.

In the late 1960s, in some of Detroit's larger auto plants, an organization called the League of Revolutionary Black Workers agitated for upgrading of its members to supervisory and skilled positions, and pointed out that blacks occupied most of the heavy, dirty jobs in the plants. These workers were little impressed by the union's support for civil rights in the South and in state legislatures. From their perspective, the UAW mirrored the worst of American society by failing to fight the auto corporations for better jobs for blacks and failing to agitate against the racist policies of plant and corporate managers. In 1968 and 1969 the organization's affiliates at Dodge Main, one of Chrysler's premier plants, staged a walkout that stopped production for several days. In other locations, such as Ford's Mahwah, New Jersey, plant, black workers protested a union-company alliance to exclude them.

Race trouble also brewed within the UAW leadership itself and in other former CIO unions. Black trade unionists, most of whom were staff officials, formed caucuses demanding integration at the middle and top levels of the union hierarchy. Although Reuther tried to head off this rebellion by meeting some of the caucus's demands, he reserved the choice of which black officials to elevate to top office. In the UAW, the leader of the black caucus was Horace Sheffield, a Reuther loyalist who tempered some of his colleagues' fire. Nonetheless, he was a vocal critic of union racial policies, so when Reuther finally supported a black member of the union's International Executive Board, he chose Nelson Jack Edwards, a staffer who was not involved in the caucus movement.

The suspicion between blacks and the labor movement echoed the alienation between labor and the social movements of the 1960s. The peace movement was, perhaps next to the civil rights movement, the most important. In the late 1950s antinuclear weapons activists had won broad public support for the ending of weapons testing and counted on their side the 1956 Democratic presidential candidate, Adlai Stevenson. Organizations were campaigning to transfer a substantial portion of the military budget to a fight against poverty and an expansion of other social programs. But under the leadership of George Meany, the AFL-CIO took every opportunity to criticize these proposals. And when the antiwar movement became bolder, in the wake of Lyndon Johnson's escalation of American military involvement in Vietnam, the AFL-CIO stood firmly behind the administration. It warned its affiliates not to give aid and comfort to the Vietnamese Communists and their domestic supporters. Some top leaders of affiliated unions, notably Frank Rosenblum, secretary treasurer of the Clothing Workers, and Patrick Gorman of the Meatcutters, sponsored the organization of Labor For Peace, a group of middle-level and local union leaders. The organization was mercilessly red-baited by the AFL-CIO leadership; in some cases, staffers who joined the effort were discharged.

▰

Labor did not distance itself quite so far from the feminist movement. In the early 1970s the AFL-CIO supported the organization of the Congress of Labor Union Women (CLUW), whose membership is composed almost exclusively of staff and local leaders rather than wives of male unionists, as was the old Ladies Auxiliaries. Within the labor movement and in Congress it has advocated more equality for women. As women's participation in unions rose during the 1960s, the attitude of male leaders underwent a definite turn. They spoke out for equal pay and the urgent need to integrate women at all levels of the labor's leadership. But in the wake of a fierce attack on abortion rights after 1973, the AFL-CIO has refrained from taking a stand on that issue and has been silent in the face of right-wing attacks.

With the important exception of public employees' unions whose relation to social movements was exemplary, labor paid dearly for its refusal to establish connections with the civil rights, antiwar, and student movements. It also lost standing because of its failure to reconsider its relation to the bipartisan foreign policy and to the

Democratic White House. As a consequence, many intellectuals and professionals have developed an adversarial attitude toward the postwar labor movement, thus depriving organized labor of one of its most precious resources: the support for its struggles by public intellectuals and by the young. It also lost the contributions these people could have made to its political and economic knowledge, a contribution highly valued in European labor movements.

The dominant image of American labor in the postwar era was that of a prosperous and conservative white working class, with somewhat complacent unions, for whom social change had become anathema. By the late 1960s the American public had come to believe that the iconic union worker was a male fat cat who owned not only a house and a late-model car but an expensive boat. To some, labor's demands seemed unworthy of public support.

Labor's history in the postwar era, while not identical with the more celebrated events of the period, was part of its time. There were rank-and-file rebellions on the shop floor against long-term contracts and management's arrogance; insurgencies against established leaders in such unions as the Steelworkers, which in 1959 shut down almost the entire steel industry for 116 days; a California farmworkers' movement of the dispossessed, who saw themselves as part of the contemporary radical upsurge; and a minority of national and local union leaders who expressed their discontent with the AFL-CIO leadership. By the late 1960s there were some notable and noteworthy defectors. Walter Reuther, the long-time Auto Workers president, was the most prominent. A vigorous opponent of the Communist influence in the labor movement and, following World War II, a leading supporter of the permanent war economy and of the Cold War, Reuther had sharp disagreements with George Meany, especially over the nation's foreign policy and labor's collaboration with U.S. intelligence agencies. In 1968 the UAW withdrew from the AFL-CIO and openly contemplated leading a new union alliance with the controversial, independent Teamsters union.

In the turbulent Democratic presidential primaries of 1968, Reuther, having taken his leave of Johnson's circle, supported the candidacy of Robert Kennedy. It was the West Coast regional director of the union, Paul Schrade, who was wounded as he stood next to Kennedy at the moment of his assassination. Although, after Kennedy's death, Reuther was loyal to Hubert Humphrey in the general election, it was clear that, at least ideologically, Reuther, an architect of labor's postwar social compact with corporate America, was reconsidering his position.

It is impossible to predict how unions might have changed if Reuther had lived; his death in a plane crash in 1970 marked the end of an era. No other labor leader's articulate statements on a wide range of social, political, and economic issues had been so avidly sought by the press. Indeed, in the first quarter-century after the war, the auto industry was a true barometer of the U.S. economy, its workers serving as cultural and economic ideals of the working class. Had Reuther lived to lead the American labor movement in resistance to the corporate offensive against labor in the 1970s, the entire history of the last twenty-five years might have been different.

As the UAW approached the 1970 auto negotiations with GM, Reuther was cautiously moving away from traditional Cold War politics. Animated by social responsibility in 1967, he had led the UAW in one of labor's earliest negotiated concessions. The union agreed to a cap on cost-of-living increases and a wage settlement that, for the first time in two decades, failed to match the inflation rate. But in the next three years, pressure mounted from discontented local unions to lift the cap, and an irresistible movement arose in the ranks to establish the so-called thirty-and-out pension, allowing a worker of fifty-five, with thirty years of service, to retire with $500 a month until Social Security kicked in. This was a solid indication that thousands of workers on auto assembly lines and parts plants were less interested in high wages than in the prospect of freedom from what they considered lousy jobs.

A fervent proponent of the work ethic, Reuther at first resisted the demand for early retirement, as he had rejected shorter hours in the 1950s. At sixty-three, Reuther was slated for retirement in 1972. Since the 1970 auto contracts were his last, Reuther wanted to go out preserving his reputation — and securing a smooth leadership transition. He embraced the thirty-and-out demand, but did not live to see it come to pass. After a two-month strike, one of the industry's longest since 1945–1946, the union won an agreement for early retirees to receive about two thirds of their regular wage until, at sixty-five, they would have their pension adjusted to Social Security.[4]

Reuther's death coincided with the beginning of the steep descent of the American labor movement. With his quintessential Brooklyn cadences, Meany was colorful, but in his long tenure at the helm of organized labor he rarely offered a clear and compelling labor commentary on political events. Nor did the leaders of most of the federation's affiliates. All were exemplars of the new breed who had emerged from the trials of postwar America. They became career trade union politicians, which meant they were frequently more in touch with business people and elected public officials than with the rank and file or the public. The labor leadership became a corps of anonymous functionaries whose lack of public visibility corresponded to organized labor's metamorphosis into a series of insurance companies and, politically, a pressure group.

This gradual change was accompanied by the perceptible erosion of labor's power. From a 34 percent union density in 1953, twenty years later unions represented about 25 percent. Since this figure included millions of public employees who were newly organized, the decline was, in fact, even steeper. Yet unions in mass-production industries and some others remained effective in delivering on wages and benefits. In the end, it was the vaunted bargaining power of American unions that became a linchpin in the restructuring of U.S. capitalism to address economic globalization.

⚓

The year 1973 is acknowledged by many to be a crossroads. It marked the end of thirty-five years of economic dominance that brought Americans the highest living standards in the world. After 1973 most Americans watched their incomes decline as prices for most necessities went through the roof and wages and salaries stagnated. The decline is illustrated by the following statistic: in 1980, hourly compensation in U.S. manufacturing was $9.87, second only to that in Germany, where welfare benefits were much more extensive. By 1995 U.S. compensation had advanced to $17.20, but it was behind the European average of $21.25 and exceeded only those of Britain and Italy. Even France's $19.34 was ahead, although in 1980 French workers earned about 14 percent less than their American counterparts.[5] The ferocity of the American corporate war on workers and their unions was partly the result of the limited scope of the social compact. But capital was determined to break what it perceived to be a powerful labor movement.

After 1973 union bargainers could no longer rely on the growth and stability of the nation's economy to justify their wage and benefits demands; European and Asian competitors and a number of transnational corporations prompted employers to insist that labor become competitive with itself by renouncing its traditional objective of equalizing labor costs across the country and internationally. The needle trades and textile unions, which had bitterly complained that the government was indifferent to their demands for rigorous enforcement of import quotas, were joined by the auto and steel unions, which devised schemes to control such items as foreign-made auto parts, raw steel, and fabricated metal goods. For example, the Auto Workers sponsored in Congress "domestic content" legislation requiring a certain proportion of U.S. labor in every automobile sold in the United States.

The early 1970s marked the beginning of the partial replacement of the nation-state by a new global metastate. Transnational capital forged its own networks outside the framework of the nation-states and operated as a series of close-knit autonomous entities. These corporations were relatively indifferent to the fate of the workers and communities affected by their decisions; the major consideration in where to locate a plant or facility, whether to modernize or close an older plant, was the bottom line — profits. And labor also suffered job destruction because of automation, computerization, and organizational shifts that undermined workers' shop-floor power. This was not unintentional. Companies that had once bargained job-security deals with strong unions began to engage in flagrant outsourcing — sending work to nonunion or low-paying companies at home and abroad — in violation of the agreement. In many cases, employers made their right to outsource a leading demand at subsequent contract negotiations and provoked some of the most important strikes of the 1990s.

The transnational corporate business class has told national governments that the conditions for maintaining any degree of corporate citizenship are (a) taxes that are low but education levels that are high enough to provide them with a trained labor force, a Catch-22; (b) removal of most federal regulations that restrict the right of business to unlimited production and trade autonomy; (c) abandonment of regulations that provide workers with occupational health and environment protection, prevent child labor, and ensure rigorous enforcement of wage and hour legislation; and (d) the rescinding of antitrust laws and financial regulations, freeing them to engage in mergers and acquisitions without regard to traditional protection. The Supreme Court ruled that considerations of free enterprise should take precedence over these protective regulations and has permitted formerly restricted local communications companies to do business anywhere in the United States. With the relaxation of antitrust regulations in the 1970s, mergers and acquisitions across national borders became the big game for investors and managers, and caused unprecedented job losses among middle managers as well as factory and office workers.

In the early 1970s, the United States, which had largely been a self-sufficient energy producer, started its journey down the long road to dependence. Oil imports rose from 5 percent of America's consumption in the 1960s to more than 50 percent by the mid-1980s. And, after more than fifteen years of importing American goods, foreign countries began to flood the U.S. market with clothing and shoes, basic and fabricated steel products, autos, and machine tools, which eventually cost American workers more than a million jobs. Of course, many of these imports flowed from plants owned by United

States–based transnational corporations, but were widely seen as unfair competition perpetrated by "foreign" capital. With the growth of
imports of some basic industrial commodities, such as cars and steel,
consumers began to feel the inflationary pinch as the dollar took a
series of plunges against foreign currencies.[6]

The immediate cause of the decline of the dollar was President
Nixon's "repeal" of the 1945 Bretton Woods agreement, which had
fixed the prices of foreign currencies against the dollar. That agreement was predicated on U.S. world economic dominance, but as
the economies of Europe and Japan recovered, their basic industries
began to supply their own domestic needs, substantially reducing
imports from the United States. Moreover, their production of consumer goods, especially autos, electronics, and appliances, was sufficient to satisfy their domestic markets and also create a substantial
export market, most alarmingly in the United States. The American dollar could not be expected to retain its strength under these
circumstances, so it started to "float" against the much stronger German and Japanese currencies.

During the 1970s many U.S. corporations were responding to
competition by investing in developing countries and the nonunion
American South rather than putting their money in older, high-wage
plants in the Northeast and Midwest. In fact, by the early 1970s they
were already shutting down many of these plants. The big three auto
corporations, which already had a significant stake in the European
and Japanese car industries, built plants for parts and assembly in
Tennessee, Alabama, and Mississippi. By the 1980s, auto, electronics,
and appliance corporations were building plants on the Mexican side
of the border and in Brazil.

These sweeping changes spelled the beginning of the end for the
great manufacturing complexes of Pittsburgh, South Chicago, and
Akron. By the mid-1980s these major industrial cities and dozens of
secondary centers were almost completely stripped of their large industrial plants. In the steel industry, computer-based technologies led
to the construction of new mills in the South and in border states;
today they are operated largely on a nonunion basis. Where the older

mills employed thousands, the new mills could produce equal quantities of tonnage with hundreds. In the 1990s, U.S. mills produced more steel than ever before. But where, at the time of the 1959 strike, the industry had employed 600,000 workers, by 1995 there were fewer than 200,000 in the basic steel industry. The rubber industry was also reduced to a shadow of its former glory. The big four rubber companies — Goodyear, Firestone, U.S. Rubber, and Goodrich — merged with European and Japanese competitors, such as Michelin and Bridgestone.

From the closing of Kaiser Steel's mill and GM's assembly plants in Southern California to the shutdown of Butte's huge metal mines, the decimation of steel towns, the emptying of Pennsylvania's coal regions, the virtual demise of textile production in New England, New Jersey, and Pennsylvania, and the migration of nearly three quarters of a million factory jobs from the leading production center of the nation in terms of jobs, New York City, the fate of urban, industrial America seemed forever sealed. New York and Pittsburgh survived as financial centers, but did not train and hire for clerical and administrative tasks the workers who had been the heart of the old industrial workforce. Factory workers had to take low-wage construction or light manufacturing jobs, leave the region, or, if they were old enough, retire.

Everybody knows that New York was the world's fashion center in production as much as design; more than 200,000 needle trades' workers were employed in making men's and women's clothing, hats, fur, and leather goods. But New York was also the third largest U.S. metalworking center, a major producer of pharmaceutical and cosmetic products, and one of the leading centers of plastic and paper products. The New York metropolitan area was, as well, an important supplier of electrical and electronic products. For example, in the 1950s it was the world's leader in television and radio production, first in lightbulbs and in small electrical parts. To transport this enormous output, New York was the country's top port and truck terminal. And New York was a union town. Not only its manufacturing but many of its retail and wholesale establishments were unionized. Because of federal legislation mandating "prevailing wages" for government contracts, commercial and industrial construction was nearly 100 percent under union agreements. And transportation, public as well as private, had strong unions that could use their potential power to make economic gains.

In the three decades before 1995 only the dramatic expansion of public employment staved off utter urban disaster. Thousands of left-behind workers were absorbed in New York's and Chicago's vast health care, education, and administrative systems. In the 1960s publicsector expansion drew from welfare rolls as well, but the conservative political triumphs, combined with the cities' shrinking tax base, slowed and finally reversed the growth. According to the sociologist William Julius Wilson, by the 1990s more black adult male city residents were out of work than were actively engaged in the labor force.[7] Full-time jobs had disappeared for all but a layer of highly educated and trained professional and technical employees. And, once buoyed by labor shortages and consequent high salaries, the occupations of computer programming, engineering, accountancy, and law are beginning to feel the loss of jobs, a decline accelerated by technological change in the professions.

Economists and corporate leaders once told us that the restructuring of the U.S. workplace was necessary to make it competitive in the new global marketplace. They insisted that the U.S. production system would have to become meaner and leaner. Workers and their unions would have to cede greater flexibility to management. Rules designed to protect workers' health and safety would have to be relaxed; voluntary overtime would have to yield to a compulsory regime; management's right to introduce new labor-saving technologies and to set the pace of work would have to be unconditionally granted. In the late 1960s and early 1970s, many workers resisted management's efforts to achieve higher productivity by speeding up the line, but by 1980, threatened with capital flight, union leaders and many rank-and-file auto workers were convinced that their future lay in cooperating with management in "quality of work life" programs designed to quell resistance, make more high-quality products, and give up work rules. In order to save the tottering Chrysler corporation, the union actually agreed to a temporary pay cut in order to secure government bail-out funds.

Led by the Auto Workers, most industrial unions agreed to the new policy of flexible specialization, by which companies do not stockpile parts but instead make them "just in time" to fill an order. Flexible specialization, robotics, and other computer-based technologies and outsourcing resulted in the loss of a third of the workforce in the auto industry and similar employment losses in the other Auto Workers' plants, such as farm equipment and construction machinery. By the 1990s leaders of corporate paternalism, like IBM and Kodak, which had long boasted that their employees held lifetime jobs, were rewarding employee loyalty by laying off tens of thousands from their plants and their offices; ATT announced it was eliminating forty thousand jobs.

At stake in labor's decline is, in addition to its economic character, nothing less than the political and social climate of American society. That we have growing inequality in America — income differences are greater than in any advanced industrial society — may be ascribed mainly to the erosion of trade union power rather than to some mysterious market mechanism. The rightward drift of the Democratic Party attests to organized labor's waning strength. Labor was hard pressed to hold the line against erosion of its hard-won social wage: the panoply of government-paid benefits such as unemployment insurance, workers' compensation, Medicare, and Social Security. And, at least until the 1996 elections, when labor once more flexed its muscle, public perception of the irrelevance of the AFL-CIO to national politics and to the economy contributed to the labor movement's difficulties, especially in recruiting new members and keeping many of the old ones.

What provoked labor's fall from power and influence, even in the period of its members' greatest gains? There are two explanations, one emphasizing "objective" factors, that is, those forces deemed beyond labor's control; the second focusing on the historical transformations of the labor movement itself. According to the objective explanation, unions and their leaders are, in essence, held blameless for the current state of affairs. According to the second, labor's fall was by no means inevitable. Labor made its own bed.

The main idea of the objective explanation is that the old social compact — the close regulation of wages and prices with high levels of mass personal and social consumption — was no longer economically viable. Nor was the persistence of worker-enforced shop-floor practices that held down production. For example, it was a staunchly prounion Democrat, Senator Ted Kennedy, who in 1978 sponsored the deregulation of transportation industries, where unions were strong. Labor's failure to enact labor law reform in the late 1970s, even when the Democrats controlled both houses of Congress and a Democrat occupied the White House, prefigured its disastrous loss of political power in the 1980s, as the Reagan administration swept away all possibility of reform.

Proponents of the objective explanation generally argue that the Wagner Act of 1935 was, in AFL president William Green's uncharacteristically flamboyant phrase, "labor's Magna Carta." They are convinced that the decline of unions may in part be traced to the weakening of the act by courts, its evisceration by Congress, and its subversion by successive Republican administrations. Few claim that the Wagner Act remains an effective mechanism for dealing with workers' rights. Even Lane Kirkland once called for repeal of the National Labor Relations Act on the grounds that, under conservative administrations, it is useless for American workers. There were too many loopholes for employers. In fact, many students of industrial relations argue that today any large employer can defeat union-organizing campaigns by firing union activists, using the delays available under current administrative law, and employing intimidating propaganda, which, in recent years, courts have deemed within the bounds of the employer's "free speech" rights.

Yet even if many organizers admit that the cards are stacked against them, most unions still rely on the procedures specified under the act to increase their ranks. They still choose the election route rather than strikes for recognition of union representation, even though obtaining a contract often proves next to impossible, especially in the South and in volatile low-wage labor markets. Moreover, under the law employers are required only to bargain, not to conclude an agreement. When, after months of fruitless negotiations, a union files a complaint that an employer is deliberately stalling, the procedure will allow even longer procrastination. The union's back may be broken, and the campaign may, and frequently does, fail. To be sure, labor protests the letter but not the spirit of the laws. Under the terms of the unwritten postwar social compact, labor accepts its subordination to the legal structure within which unionism once prospered but now has fallen. This structure is shaped by legislation that goes well beyond organizing; it embraces the whole tradition of contract law. As a legally executed document that regulates the sale of labor with respect to wages or salaries, benefits that have been termed by courts "in lieu" of wages, and conditions of work, the contract has become both the end and the means by which most unions live.

By law, unions become liable for infractions committed by those within its jurisdiction. As we have seen, unions may suffer severe financial and legal penalties for violation of the terms of the agreement, especially the standard provision to maintain continuous production, or violation of court injunctions by its members. Under these coercive implications lies a deeper loyalty. Labor harbors deep respect for the law's authority, including the authority of the labor agreement. The burden of its legislative and bargaining programs is to uphold what it regards as hard-won agreements and necessary postwar compromises. This is the double bind that drives contemporary American unionism. Most union leaders recognize that the law doesn't work, but the law remains, in their view, labor's best hope.

There are two closely related questions raised by the explanation that relies primarily on "external" factors to account for labor's recent decline. The first is whether labor's expansion in the 1930s and 1940s can be traced to the Wagner Act's recognition of workers' rights to form unions. The second is whether the contract itself is what holds the employer to certain rules. According to this explanation, the law, political relations, and the political will that underlies them are held to be sovereign and routinely obeyed by its subjects. When capital broke the social compact, especially by its flagrant abuse of the Labor Relations Act and of the labor agreement in the 1980s, it was engaging in lawlessness, which for many trade unionists is the cardinal sin but over which they have little control. Although few would deny the efficacy of the sit-down strikes and other manifestations of mass support for industrial unionism, the New Deal gets the main credit for the relatively powerful labor movement that existed during the Depression and the war. Conversely, according to this wisdom labor has fallen on hard times because of changes in the White House and in Congress and business's discovery that it could pretty much do what it pleased under Republican administrations in the 1950s and especially in the 1970s and 1980s.

The other view is that the upsurge accompanied or even preceded the Roosevelt administration's agreement to enter into a compact with organized labor. Key events in 1934 — two citywide strikes led by radical transportation unions in Minneapolis and San Francisco, and the nationwide textile strike — and similar events in Toledo and elsewhere forced Roosevelt to address workers' problems. Although Congress passed the Wagner Act and the president signed it, the legislation faced a series of court challenges in 1936 and early 1937. Until the Supreme Court upheld the act, in mid-1937, workers seeking independent union representation had few legal protections. When a company proposed to restore the eight-hour day after five years of six hours, twelve thousand Goodyear rubber workers in Akron staged a dramatic factory occupation. After five weeks, the fledgling United Rubber Workers won restoration of the six-hour day and union recognition. Thousands of Cleveland and Flint auto workers followed with their own factory occupations. In 1937, the small Auto Workers union was able to win recognition at General Motors, and Chrysler soon followed. Even after the Supreme Court decision, many trade unionists overcame such aggressive antiunion tactics as company intimidation, blacklists, and discharges by means of direct action. They remained skeptical about the ability of legal measures, even collective bargaining, to address company domination of the workplace.

The rapidity of the decline of union power may be traced to the history of labor's loss of independence in the wake of the social compact, the erosion of its militant origins in favor of a kind of social-work model of unionism, and the subsequent change of unions as democratic institutions in which the rank and file had genuine sovereignty. Some writers have cited the experience of European and Canadian labor as proof for their claim. While denying neither the virulence of employer opposition to unionism in the United States nor a political culture that fully accepts the divine right of capital for most of its history, critics point to the relative success of the European and Canadian labor movements in holding the line against employer offensives, including the attempt to dismantle the welfare state. Many ascribe European labor's greater political power to its political and ideological independence.

For example, the French labor movement, divided among three major and several smaller federations, represents some 6 percent of private-sector workers but a considerably larger portion of public employees. Despite its relative numerical weakness, the labor movement has thwarted the attempt by a conservative government to make deep cuts in the welfare state. Led by railroad workers, public employees have taken to the streets on several occasions, beginning in 1995, and have received broad public support among the French population for their demonstrations.

The Canadian situation is by no means identical with that of the United States, especially with respect to its political culture. But more than three quarters of its production and commercial industries are in the hands of United States–based corporations, and key elements of its popular culture, especially television, are shared with the Americans. Nevertheless, economic restructuring, which has produced far more mass unemployment than in the United States, has not decimated the unions. In fact, union membership has doubled in the past twenty-five years while that of U.S. unions has been more than halved. Among other differences, since the 1960s the Canadian labor movement has decisively broken with the Liberals and formed its own party, the New Democrats. This group has had a decisive influence on social legislation, including labor relations. Under the union-sponsored federal labor law, Canadian employers must bargain with unions that display a majority of signed representation cards. Further, whereas U.S. employers face mild penalties for law violations, the Canadian law imposes severe penalties on recalcitrant managements. And while U.S. union leaders are unknown to most of the general public, in Canada many union leaders are public figures. Consistent with their wish to speak to the general interests of working people and, therefore, of all Canadians, labor leaders are free to comment on a whole range of public issues. The labor movement, then, is a credible candidate for social and political power and for this reason is taken seriously by other political forces and by the employers.

Since the Depression, unions have been less than staunch defenders of the interests of the working poor, even though many of its members earn little more than the minimum wage. The AFL-CIO did oppose Congress's 1996 abrogation of income guarantees for any legal resident who requires them, but it did not mount a strong protest, as it had during debates about NAFTA in 1993. The most overt explanation for the AFL-CIO's relatively weak response to ending "welfare as we know it" was that it did not choose to promote controversy in the midst of President Clinton's re-election campaign. But the labor movement's public silence has deeper roots.

The reluctance of most unions to identify themselves with the economically abject may stem from the rift in the American working class between high- and low-paid workers and from racial and gender divisions. But the development of a labor force with three or four tiers of income was not solely an impersonal economic trend, especially the difference between wages in the industries dominated by a few giant corporations and those owned by smaller employers. Segmentation was as much the result of labor's postwar organizing failures among low-paid workers, especially in the South and in the cities.

In the past twenty-five years, waves of immigrants have swelled the ranks of the poor; many of them are undocumented and are forced to work in the recently revived underground economy — so named because it flourishes outside the law — especially in the needle trades and in other light manufacturing industries.

To a considerable degree unions have constructed a barrier between their members and the rest of the working people. There are social differences that signify the gulf between the skilled and unskilled, men and women, black and white, immigrant and native-born workers. Many in mass-production industries, unionized construction, and most government jobs consider themselves to be middle class, sharing the consumption patterns and neighborhoods of salaried professionals and low-level managers. One may ascribe their disdain for those who depend on welfare to mass media or conservative propaganda, a disdain fostered by conservative dominance of the national polity. The point is that unions have done little to disabuse their own members of the view that most welfare recipients are lazy and "cheats." It is the unions that should make clear that many full-time workers collect some public assistance because their wages are below the poverty line; many others are on the public assistance rolls because there is a real job shortage, especially for older people and for single parents. For those faced with the high cost of child care, staying at home is a rational calculation. Most states do not subsidize day care; if, like New York, they do, there are long waiting lists for these services.

Unions should see themselves as educational institutions responsible for endowing their members and the general public with a broad understanding of the economy and a broad vision of America's future. Why aren't union leaders staples on Sunday-morning talk shows, television programs such as "Charlie Rose" and "Nightline"? Why have they not undertaken an offensive, using magazines and videos? Union leaders and many activists may argue that labor's waning power is tied to the unions' numerical decline, but it may well be that unions are weaker and labor's cause muted for reasons not directly linked to membership losses. Perhaps membership eroded because organized labor did not present itself as a tribune of the popular interest at a time when millions were suffering from slipping wages, periodic joblessness, and a sense that the future for themselves and their families had grown dark.

Perhaps equally important is the consolidation of the social position of union leaders as men and women "in the middle" between management and membership. As administrators of large, often prosperous organizations, many union officials value the continuity of production and the well-being of the employers with whom they do business. They want their "own" employers to succeed, because they believe their members' interests coincide with those of successful companies. And there are other causes of the sustenance of business or contract unionism. Many trade unionists are convinced that the contract is the worker's best friend and that its negotiation and enforcement is the main task of them, the leaders.

Just as unions bargained away elements of worker shop-floor power and conceded management's unilateral right to make investment decisions during the postwar boom, they have responded to the end of the compact by making further concessions in return for a measure of job security for senior employees. Equally important, unions have adopted a defensive posture in order to retain the basic right of representation in the new plants many companies have established far from the bases of union strength. From the leadership's perspective, negotiating the right of laid-off workers to transfer to other company plants took precedence over keeping older plants competitive or to sharing the work by reducing working hours. By the 1970s, union transfer rights were effectively substituted for demands that older plants in traditional industry centers be modernized rather than being closed. Among other reasons, the leadership was strengthened by decentralization. After all, its opposition was concentrated in traditional industry centers such as Detroit, Chicago, Cleveland, and Pittsburgh. The outlying locals were easier for the central office to control.

Many union officials continue to insist that concession bargaining is unavoidable, given the erosion of the production industries in the United States. Yet wages and benefits for workers of America's main competitors are higher than those in the United States. Foreign competition for basic goods comes, for the most part, from high-wage countries. Nor does that argument for concession bargaining account for the failure of unions to organize the unorganized. In fact, by demanding job protection, even some of the more progressive unions have accepted the permanent existence of a large nonunion sector of the industry, which explains their acceptance of a two-tier wage system.

Thus, in the 1996 auto industry negotiations union leaders proposed, and members approved, the two-tier wage system in parts production. A parallel agreement in New York City's Transit Authority, which permitted welfare recipients to perform union jobs at welfare income, was narrowly approved by the membership. The strength of the opposition, more than 45 percent of the vote, was due to strong rank-and-file opposition within this 30,000-member local. Similarly, after its executive director failed to convince the mayor of New York to declare a moratorium on workfare, the leadership of Public Employees District Council 37 agreed to permit thousands of welfare recipients to work at jobs in parks, hospitals, and public facilities formerly done by union members. By the fall of that year, as a price for keeping their benefits, 35,000 welfare recipients were working for $120 every two weeks, which, combined with benefits, equaled the federal minimum wage. DC 37's concession on workfare, in return for the Republican mayor's protecting higher categories from displacement and layoff, was handsomely rewarded in the fall of 1997. The union, once a bastion of the city's Democratic voters, endorsed him for re-election.

The struggle to take labor out of competition with itself by insisting on equal pay for equal work would not necessarily be a cure. Public sector workers would have to convince the larger electorate, inundated with high taxes and antiwelfare propaganda, of the justice of their position. In the private sector, unions would have to devote most of their money and staff to the difficult task of organizing. And taking a stand against employers' outsourcing to nonunion plants might well provoke strikes and lockouts. But the recent choices made by unions have had profound economic and political consequences. The labor movement is disarmed, outflanked, and bewildered.

Despite a few union successes in fighting new cost-cutting policies, the price for many of keeping a job is painful. They experience shrunken benefits, speed-ups, and long-hour schedules. And, since most union-negotiated health and pension agreements are controlled by employers, it is not uncommon for workers to discover that their pensions and health insurance have been used by employers for other purposes. During the 1980s employer contributions to benefit plans rose more slowly than health costs, which forced reductions in coverage. Where many workers once enjoyed full hospital, physician, and surgeon coverage, the typical "co-payment" agreement now requires workers to pay 20 percent or more of these costs. And many contracts do not provide for long-term and catastrophic care.

Fearing even worse losses, union leaders reacted strongly against worker resistance. For example, the 1985–1986 strike of the Hormel packinghouse members of the Food and Commercial Workers against a wage cut was opposed by the international union on the grounds that it disrupted an industrywide agreement. Airline workers rarely achieved their goals because their unions were willing to compromise in order to maintain union recognition. Most attempts to hold the line failed, and the strike weapon appeared to union leaders, let alone labor relations experts, to be a relic. Indeed, between 1980 and 1990 the annual number of strikes shrank from nearly four hundred, a substantial decline from an annual average of four thousand during the first decades after the war, to fewer than fifty.

The corporate offensive of the past twenty-five years has accelerated the decline of union membership and union power. Although membership never again reached its high of 34 percent of the labor force, attained in 1953, it was still 25 percent in 1970 and much higher in the intermediate technology industries, such as auto, steel, oil, chemical, machine tools, and electrical. Since then, union membership has stayed at about sixteen million, a figure reached in the mid-1950s, even though the labor force nearly doubled in the same period. Consequently, unions now represent only about 15 percent of the workforce and less than 10 percent of private sector workers. In the same period, most industrial unions lost half or more of their members, not so much because of disaffection as because of plant closings and the lack of aggressive efforts to recruit new members.

Besides the successful public employees' organizing campaigns, there were several important exceptions to the general lethargy of organized labor in the 1960s and 1970s. Against all forecasts, a tiny union of New York drugstore employees audaciously organized more than 100,000 employees of the region's nonprofit hospitals. The story of Local 1199's achievement is testament to a politically militant and savvy leadership, a mobilized and dedicated membership, which, in its 1959–1970 organizing phase, was prepared to engage in mass strikes under conditions of extreme sacrifice for workers. It is also a compliment to a local labor movement that overcame its reservations about the political coloration of 1199 and invested both its political clout and its financial resources in the struggle of low-paid black and Latino workers.

In 1959 the union was a strange fish in a sea of complacent New York and national trade unions that bestirred themselves on very rare occasions, mostly when other unions sought to invade their jurisdiction. From the beginning of 1199's organizing efforts, its key figures — the president, Leon Davis, and the organizing director, Elliot Godoff — made clear that, though it would agree to a no-strike deal, it would conduct a determined wage drive and not accept small increments. As Davis said, his proposal to forgo strikes was a tactic directed at the public; it was not a matter of principle. He was aware that, given the hospital trustees' intransigence, the workers would probably have to strike to reach their goal. When the trustees of the six hospitals where workers had signed union cards rebuked Davis, thousands of union workers stayed on strike for three months. In order to support them, the leaders sought and received considerable help from the Central Labor Council, led by Harry Van Arsdale, the leader of the city's electricians' union. Tens of thousands of dollars in cash and food contributions were donated by nearly every major union in the city.[8]

And 1199 adroitly made the cause of the hospital workers a civil rights struggle. Backed by A. Philip Randolph, Adam Clayton Powell, and eventually Martin Luther King, Jr., the union effectively reached out to other sections of the New York community. The subsequent organizing of nearly 100,000 metropolitan area hospital workers was an exemplary instance of a labor-community alliance. After attempting to derail the strikers' demands for union recognition, Mayor Robert F. Wagner and an initially skeptical press came around to the union's side. Within twenty years, the union had branched out from its start in Jewish hospitals to Catholic and Protestant hospitals as well.

Local 1199 — and the national union of hospital employees it helped create — has a proud record of achievement. Within a few years it increased salaries for low-paid employees from less than $40 a week to $100, and by the 1990s housekeeping, dietary, and patient-care entry-level employees were earning more than $30,000 a year. High labor costs, reduced government funding, and the persistence of high doctors' fees have threatened many of the union's gains. But by the late 1990s New York's health care system and the systems of many other regions were bowing to managed care. Hospital administrations that once had met union demands for a living wage were reversing themselves. As in private corporations, the technological changes, work reorganization, and managed care were causing layoffs of the most vulnerable: the least skilled and the lowest paid. Nevertheless, the administrations were no longer able to make unilateral decisions but were required to consult the union over changes.

This exceptional achievement in an otherwise dismal period of labor organizing could not have occurred without a leadership dedicated to what some have described as social movement rather than business unionism.[9] The union never wavered from three fundamental commitments: it would conduct mass strikes as well as elections to gain recognition; it would take issues of race and gender into consideration of the demands it advanced and the composition of its own leadership; it would participate in solidarity struggles with other workers and with the civil rights movement. All major national civil rights demonstrations and many antiwar rallies were strengthened by thousands of 1199 members wearing the union cap. Since the retirement of its initial corps of officers, in the 1980s, who were mostly white and Jewish, the leadership has reflected the racial and ethnic composition of its varied membership.

The remarkable union-building efforts of 1199 inspired hospital organizing in nearly every part of the country. Under the aegis of the National Union of Hospital Employees, workers in Boston, Philadelphia, Milwaukee, and Newark organized unions. On the West Coast and in the Midwest, unionism was assumed by the Service Employees (SEIU), which, under John Sweeney's leadership, had become the largest union of hospital workers by the 1980s. But Teamsters, Hotel and Restaurant workers, Teachers, and public employees' unions also organized in the health field. The State, County, and Municipal Employees, which had first tried to compete with Local 1199 in the voluntary sector, finally concentrated its efforts in New York City's municipal hospitals. And SEIU's Local 144 focused on private nursing homes and eventually unionized some thirty thousand workers in the New York metropolitan area.

At a time when many unions, especially in goods production, were shedding members as a cat sheds hair, the Service Employees was growing exponentially. During John Sweeney's fifteen-year presidency the union nearly doubled its membership, largely on the strength of an organizing fund that claimed 30 percent of its budget (most unions spend 5 percent or less on organizing) and Sweeney's policy of hiring dedicated young organizers instead of relying on the old guard. Sweeney rewarded with staff and money the locals that started effective organizing campaigns, and the results have justified his administration's dedication and single-mindedness. In addition to its long-time base of janitors and maintenance people in big city-building services, SEIU, having merged in 1997 with 1199, is today the largest hospital and nursing-home workers' union and has many members among state and local public employees. SEIU has led the way in organizing among private sector, mainly low-wage workers in an era when, in the main, only public employees' unions have added members.

Bill Clinton entered office just as the economy, which had been in the doldrums since the 1987 stock market crash, began to show signs of life. The recovery was by no means vigorous, at least by postwar standards, but several industries, particularly autos and computers, revived. And new housing starts, which had slumped under high interest rates, resumed a fitful but generally upward movement as banks, brimming with uninvested money, relaxed credit and the Federal Reserve Board moderated interest rates. But the recovery was peculiar in other ways. While the big picture was optimistic, many firms kept up their relentless drive to boost profits by merging, downsizing, and stretching the physical limits of the existing workforce rather than hiring new full-time workers. In many industries and occupations the part-time and temporary job replaced the full-time job. And, most distressing of all, wages stayed in the basement, so people were working harder for less.

Weary of fifty- and sixty-hour workweeks with no respite, in 1994 GM workers at Flint and Lansing struck against the widespread industry practice of enforced overtime. Claiming the pressure of severe foreign competition, especially from Japan, the big three auto companies got the United Auto Workers to reverse its historic position against forced overtime. The new management work regime requires workers to work ten- or twelve-hour shifts, six and even seven days a week, and, since the union has agreed to this arrangement for many plants, workers who refuse overtime are subject to discharge. Still, much to the surprise of the company and the UAW, the locally sanctioned strike succeeded in loosening the employers' insistence that their employees submit to work without end. Coming during a period of a boom in auto production, the strike forced the company to reduce hours and make overtime voluntary. Workers had found that, even though they made a lot of money (sometimes in excess of $70,000 year), in their own words they "had no life." GM hired nearly eight hundred new workers in Flint and undertook new hiring in other company plants. Of course, the company continues to find ways to reduce its labor costs. As the 1996 negotiations began, GM announced its intention to ask for concessions on its outsourcing agreement. In March of that year, 3200 workers at the brake-producing

factories in Dayton struck in protest against the company's announced intention to outsource some of the work to low-waged
plants. Because GM had instituted just-in-time, the system that dispenses with the conventional practice of stockpiling parts, virtually
the entire U.S. chain was shut down within days, and 166,000 workers
were idled. After suffering more than $50 million in losses in only a
few weeks, the company backed off from its demand.

The irony of the union victory is that it depended on a production innovation that GM had instituted to save money by cutting back
on labor and space. Had the company retained the old methods, it
might well have won the day, because the stockpiles could have kept
its other plants working for months. And, since under most circumstances workers are forbidden by law to strike during the life of a
contract and are enjoined from conducting sympathy strikes, the
Dayton workers would have been left twisting in the wind. Instead,
eager to resume production, the company did not exercise its right to
seek a court injunction or to sue the union for damages.

But because outsourcing is a company demand that doesn't go
away, the big three made it the central issue in the auto industry
negotiations of 1996. The Auto Workers, by permitting the companies to pay less to workers in parts plants not under the master agreement and to those employed in new factories, were, in effect, sanctioning a two-tier work system. In return, Chrysler and Ford agreed to
job guarantees for 95 percent of its workforce, although a provision
of the agreement gave the companies numerous reasons to renegoti-
ate this commitment.

The renewed power of the unions on the picket line and in Congress slowed labor's downward slide and brought a new generation of
young organizers and intellectuals to assess the labor movement.
Many questioned their former indifference to the "labor bosses" and
decided that the labor question was once again on the national
agenda. Also, some workers considered it time to drop their own
reservations and seek union organization to redress their grievances. Doubts remained, but the dominant mood among many was
renewed hope.

2 ✄ The Rise and Crisis of
Public Employees' Unions

ONE OF THE BEST-KEPT secrets in the story of postwar labor was the astounding success of public employees' organizing, an achievement that rivaled in numbers the industrial workers' victories in the 1930s. Like industrial workers, public employees were aided by laws that granted them organizing and bargaining rights. As in earlier times, the law restricted some rights and went into effect after the initial organizing moves. And like industrial unions, eventually public employees' groups were perceived by the public employers as "too costly." Public workers had barely enjoyed their gains before conservatives launched a massive campaign to turn back the clock. The center of their design was privatization.

Blaming public employees' incomes and low productivity for the budget deficits and high taxes, the conservatives combined their attack with proposals to privatize public goods. But despite their success in convincing many Americans that "big" government was a major source of their economic ills, most people remained in favor of the specific services that constituted the welfare state: Social Security, Medicare, public schools, and clean, safe streets. These were, after all, middle-class benefits. But with few exceptions such services are highly labor intensive. People, not machines, were the key providers — teachers, physicians, nurses, and millions of maintenance, house-keeping, dietary, and administrative employees in hospitals and clinics. That the people who delivered these services deserved decent living standards rarely entered the public debate. Although some unions conducted vigorous campaigns to remind the public of these considerations, most public employees' unions were not strategically committed to influencing the public conversation. As a result, the right dominated the battle of ideas, and by the mid-1980s, the power of the public employees' unions had passed, at least for the time being.

☙

The rise of public employees' strength had come as a surprise to many experts and political leaders. Daniel Bell, a leading writer on labor, claimed that unions had reached the zenith of their power. As the 1950s wore on, younger employees became restive, but many older civil servants lost their gratitude and humility as they experienced the wartime and immediate postwar periods as years of decline in their relative status; like most Americans, their earnings increased, but they were falling behind unionized factory workers, who, for the first time in American history had higher incomes. In the early postwar years, union gains had reversed the historic income advantage of white-collar over blue-collar work. As late as 1939, before the era of extensive collective bargaining in many manufacturing industries, average weekly earnings for white-collar workers were $33.04, compared with $25.44 for blue-collar workers, a differential of about 30 percent. Five years later, blue-collar earnings had overtaken white-collar earnings. In 1944, abetted by labor shortages in defense plants, blue-collar workers earned $45.83 weekly compared with $43.63 for white-collar workers. In the early postwar years white-collar workers regained, briefly, a slight advantage, but by 1952, the height of union power, blue-collar wages averaged more than white-collar by about 5 percent. From 1929 to 1952 blue-collar earnings increased two and a half times, while white-collar earnings less than doubled. This is precisely the period of intense industrial union activity.

Yet in 1955, the labor movement, most white-collar workers, and expert opinion did not believe the moment had arrived for mass

unionism in public or private sector services. The prevailing view —
that labor's forward march was destined to be circumscribed by blue-
collar production and service occupations — was based on the idea
that unions were too closely identified with blue-collar workers' interests and their culture. Media accounts had successfully painted industrial and transport workers as strike-happy and unconcerned with
the effect of wage increases on prices. Many white-collar workers
viewed unions as anti-consumer, and since many consumer organizations appealed to the salaried middle class, whose members were on
relatively fixed incomes, these groups were considered immune to
union appeals. And traditionally skilled and semiskilled manual workers sought to win their demands by imposing monopolistic control
over labor markets, and excluded others, especially minorities and
women, both groups growing sectors of the public and white-collar
workforce. As we have seen, by 1950 most of the new unions had
ceased to be social movements and instead became stakeholders in a
triumphant corporate order.

Writing in 1958 in *Fortune,* Bell predicted that "union membership has reached the upper limit" at about 30 percent of the labor
force, a "saturation mark; they have organized as much of their potential as they can".[1] Just before the rise, most trade unionists, as well as
labor relations experts, saw little hope for public employees' unions.
Given the publicity of congressional investigations into union corruption, the public was more hostile to labor than at any time since the
1920s. Yet twenty years later, these very unions had organized more
than a third of workers in the public sector and by 1980 were the
largest department in the AFL-CIO. In face of most of organized
labor's stagnation after World War II, how did four million public
employees confound opinion between the late 1950s and the late
1970s?

The ebb and flow of private sector unionism depend, to a large
extent, on market fluctuations, but in the public sector the political,
social, and ideological environment has a more potent effect. Even as
they share many common concerns with craft and industrial unions,
public employees' unions have different characteristics. In the public

sector, unions must worry about whether settlements reached at the bargaining table will be funded by legislatures. And public employees' salaries and benefits are directly dependent on the party in power. Although industrial workers often reach for public support during strikes and organizing campaigns, public employees must mobilize both union membership and important segments of the public. When public employees permit politicians to pit their interests against those of the public, they are likely to lose.

Unions do not wax and wane in a social vacuum. In conservative times they are likely to retreat; in times of hope for broad social change, labor will often grow and, in turn, stimulate some of those changes. Signaled by the 1955 Montgomery bus boycott and by the Army-McCarthy hearings the preceding year, changes began to take place in the latter part of the 1950s, culminating in the civil rights, feminist, and peace movement victories in the 1960s and 1970s. America was transfixed by the television spectacle of a scholarly and gentlemanly attorney taking on the most feared public figure of his time, Wisconsin senator Joseph McCarthy. Not that virulent anti-Communism disappeared at this bold stroke. But Joseph Welch, Esquire, succeeded in clearing the air of the hysterical anti-Communist venom of McCarthyism.

The contribution of Martin Luther King, Jr., and the Montgomery movement was no less powerful. If the Army-McCarthy hearings invited many Americans to reclaim their right to voice grievances against the political and economic system, King showed that legal remedies were only one way. Millions of citizens, especially blacks, took heart from his message that ordinary people could achieve social justice by direct action. The fight for civil liberties and for civil rights defined the generation that had reached its majority in the shadow of political and social repression. Although many who had suffered the economic deprivations of the Great Depression compromised their better judgment and came to cherish economic security above any other value, those born around 1940 — their children — took unparalleled American wealth for granted. Consequently, when these younger people discovered that democracy and prosperity were reserved for the few and that many were being left out, they were determined to redress the wrongs.

The rise of public sector unionism is inextricably linked with the rise of social movements. Even as most industrial unions were settling in to fulfill their new role as insurance and service organizations, the fledgling public labor unions were taking on the characteristics of a crusade. They used, sometimes illegally, the traditional labor movement weapons of strikes and demonstrations. But what made them a social movement was the combination of self-interest with a broad vision. They sought salary increases and greater benefits, but they also articulated the goals of a changing America. They strove to eliminate gross inequalities based on race and gender, and where the New Deal had argued for a larger public sector only as a temporary remedy for the failures of the market, they boldly advocated the public good as a value in itself.

The dramatic growth of the public sector spurred by the Cold War and the continuation of the Depression-era government intervention in the economy seemed a permanent feature of American life. Reflecting a broad public consensus that government's role was to regulate business, ensure full employment, and provide social welfare for those neglected by the market, public jobs grew twice as fast as those in the private sector. Public-sector employment rose from three million in 1941 to almost fifteen million by 1960, from about a twentieth of the labor force to more than a sixth.

A common explanation for the enormous expansion of public workers' unions is President John F. Kennedy's celebrated 1962 Executive Order 10988, granting bargaining rights to federal employees, a stroke of the pen copied by many state and local governments.[2] Under this executive order, public workers were deprived of the strike weapon even though some workers did resort to strikes to win their demands. The close alliance of the AFL-CIO with Kennedy, which had been crucial to his victory over Nixon two years earlier, played an important part in this extraordinary gesture. Kennedy's order remains to this day one of the AFL-CIO's major postwar achievements. There is no denying that legislation and executive fiat encouraged this most vulnerable group of workers to seek redress through unionism and collective bargaining rather than through "collective begging."

But this assessment underestimates the gains unions made at the local level through demonstrations, job actions, and strikes before federal and state labor relations laws were in effect. Management frequently resorted to private-sector methods of intimidation, like firing union activists or denying them promotions, and to the laws that forbade strikes and imposed severe financial penalties on unions. But many experts ignore the role of social awareness in bringing millions into organized labor's ranks. Because many state and local governments were reluctant to follow Kennedy's lead, it took the determination of union organizers, especially among teachers and poorly paid employees in public and nonprofit hospitals, to establish unions. Not until these organizations mobilized a substantial segment of the workforce did the larger labor movement respond to their appeals that lawmakers and state executives recognize unions of public employees.

Within a few years, many governors issued orders, and state and local legislatures enacted legislation, granting bargaining rights to public employees. (The South did not follow suit, and to this day a number of Southern states grant unions no bargaining power except the right to "meet and confer" on employee grievances.) The American Federation of Teachers (AFT), its rival, the National Education Association (NEA), State, County, and Municipal (AFSCME), and the Service Employees (SEIU) have gained most from the introduction of state and local collective bargaining. Today these unions together represent an estimated five million public employees. Others, such as the Government Employees, Postal Workers, and a number of state-based independent civil service employee associations, became unions in the wake of challenges by AFL-CIO affiliates and also made substantial gains. For example, after years of weak independent representation, in 1982 New Jersey state employees chose the Communications Workers to represent them. New York's state employees, who until the mid-1980s had been represented by a battered 200,000-member independent Civil Service Association, have since affiliated with AFSCME. And tens of thousands of members of the Police Benevolent Association and Firefighters union got collective bargaining under these laws, although their power over salaries and working conditions predated the laws' enactment.

Plainly, the laws provided a framework for union power, but not substance. That came when, for example, municipal employees' unions in New York, Chicago, and Philadelphia became allied with the black community. In San Francisco, Seattle, and San Jose, the unions joined with feminists and presented themselves as a movement.

There were other reasons for the burst of union organization. One was the smoldering discontent of relatively underpaid employees who felt bypassed by the union train. Traditionally, government administrations expected that employees would, in return for fairly secure employment, sacrifice their voice on the job. Moreover, some argued, wasn't public service a calling that entailed vows of poverty? Although this ideology of sacrifice was powerful among older employees who had experienced the Depression, the postwar boom in public employment brought younger people into the workplace. They saw higher prices and stagnant salaries, and they protested.

▬

After the surge in production jobs generated by the war and the postwar boom, factory employment had leveled off. Most of the millions of new jobs were created in public and private services, especially administration. Clerical and professional employment in the private sector expanded, too. But, as we have seen, the most explosive growth was in public employment. Teachers and other education employees tripled between 1941 and 1955; public higher education, once much smaller than private colleges and universities, rapidly overtook the private sector. By 1965 the public sector accounted for 70 percent of all students in these institutions. Another important cause of the spurt in public employment was the policing and care of the many poor people who had been left outside the prosperity era.

Contrary to popular impressions, most of the poor worked. But the minimum wage chronically lagged behind living costs, so many still depended on government programs — like food stamps and partial checks — rather than on collective organization, which was denied to them by organized labor's neglect. The full-time working poor, the fully unemployed, the short- and long-term jobless constituted perhaps 20 percent of the adult labor force, so federal and state governments were obliged to continue Depression-era relief programs. While the federal government provided most of the funding, the state and local authorities retained administrative control over welfare and unemployment insurance. In the first fifteen years after the war, local governments hired social workers and administrators to determine recipients' eligibility for benefits and to police their behavior. Other employees provided counseling, job referrals, and therapy services. In the 1960s, under the federal government's antipoverty programs, job creation and job training were added. Soon, those who provided services to the poor and unemployed were among the fastest growing sectors of the labor force. In sum, blue-collar employment advanced by inches, and white-collar employment grew by yards. By 1960, those providing nonprofit services accounted for 20 percent of the labor force. Most of them were nonunion.

At first, lagging wages and rising employment were not sufficient to produce a new wave of public-sector union organizing. In part, this was because the economic and social conditions of the service sectors were fundamentally different from those of the blue-collar workplace. In the 1950s the United States, despite its vast industrial base, was on the path to becoming a knowledge-based economy. Entrance into these growing sectors often required not only a high school diploma but also a college degree. Moreover, in public employment the rules were different for salaried employees: many did not punch a time clock; when they were sick, their pay was not reduced; they were not as vulnerable to the ups and downs of the economy as were workers paid by the hour. In an era when white-collar employees were in short supply, employers were eager to placate them with almost any amenity — except higher salaries. What kept many underpaid public employees on the job was the promise of advancement, not the satisfaction of their current conditions.

But as union-driven real wages continued to rise and inflation fears intensified, labor's enemies found another way to thwart the unions, especially the white-collar groups. A coalition of business organizations, Southern Democrats from right-to-work states (where compulsory union membership was outlawed), and the Republican Party began to beat the drum against union corruption. "Big" labor, it was claimed, was dominated by a self-perpetuating bureaucracy that ignored the rights of the rank and file and espoused legislative programs that drained members' dues — and sometimes pocketed those dues. In 1957 Senator James McClellan, a Democrat from Arkansas, conducted hearings into trade union corruption. The real target was the controversial leader of the nation's largest union, James R. Hoffa. A year and a half after the widely publicized hearings, Congress enacted antiracketeering legislation, the Labor-Management Reporting and Disclosure Act, popularly known as Landrum-Griffin. Although the law contained many vital protections for union members against the worst practices of some labor unions, the hearings dealt a huge blow to labor's image. The AFL-CIO expelled the Teamsters and several other unions that had been tarred. It forced others, like the International Longshoremen's Association, to clean house. But the damage had been done. Labor had barely absorbed the Taft-Hartley blows when it was hit by the new barrage of accusations, followed by onerous legislative restraints. The right's one-two punch failed to achieve its intended knockout, but it did harm to the cause of white-collar unionism, particularly in the public sector.

☛

The story of public-sector unionism has aspects of the Cinderella story. Like the famous fairy tale's protagonist, the interests of public employees were brushed aside by leaders of older, more prosperous unions. At best, some trade unions tolerated their weak sister unions; at worst, they questioned whether the poor ones belonged in the House of Labor. Many outstanding figures, like Samuel Gompers, had accepted the prevailing concept that unionism was for the skilled segment of the working population. Others, influenced by the views of their forebears, including Gompers, thought that white-collar workers' interests were actually opposed to that of wage workers. Nor were the experts more enlightened. Most believed that, like other white-collar and professional employees, those who worked in the public services would not heed union appeals. After most government jobs were removed from the patronage system by the civil service reforms of the 1920s and 1930s, many public employees passed the required examinations and achieved tenure, a perquisite of the civil service system; others were protected by their educational credentials. Equally powerful was the doctrine that public servants should not be partisan or self-aggrandizing. Congress even passed a law barring federal workers from engaging in political activity. In short, the idea of public "service" seemed to preclude unionism.

Despite these obstacles, a small band of true believers beat the drum for public employees' unionism. Formed in 1916, the American Federation of Teachers was unable to make much headway until the 1930s, the same period that saw the American Federation of State, County, and Municipal Employees (AFSCME), a number of federal employees' groups, and some active but underfunded CIO unions, struggle for survival. By 1941 the combined memberships of these unions reached perhaps 200,000, but no recognition was forthcoming from any major federal, state, or local government agency. The members were concentrated in a few large cities where unionism, especially its left wing, was relatively strong. The left-led United Public Workers had established a solid base in some state labor departments and social service agencies. But they fell victim to the CIO's civil war and, by the early 1950s, disappeared, its members dispersing into competing organizations.

Perhaps the most important of the public employees' organizations were the postal unions, which together had enlisted nearly a quarter of the half-million employees in various crafts of this huge agency. But the public unions' power to deliver on salaries was almost exclusively confined to lobbying Congress and state legislatures, where, with the help of the national and state AFL-CIO organizations, they were sometimes able to persuade elected officials to grant wage and benefit improvements. To add insult to injury, they worked under an authoritarian managerial system that was rarely willing to address their grievances, even when state law provided them and their unions with "meet and confer" rights. Under these laws agency heads often were required to discuss, but not to settle, grievances. Most states did not provide "meet and confer" rights until organizing gained momentum in the mid-1960s.

But in the early 1950s, blessed with a coterie of dedicated organizers, most of them recruited from radical movements, several unions embarked on an organizing drive in New York, America's preeminent "union town." AFSCME and the Teachers were blessed with a few gifted organizers, such as Jerry Wurf and David Selden, who possessed the vision, the stamina, and the talent needed for this sustained unionization effort. For despite the prevailing Democratic administrations in most large cities, it had been clear since the 1930s, when the quintessential progressive local politician of the New Deal era, New York's Mayor Fiorello La Guardia, blocked city employee unionization efforts, even as he championed the cause of unionism in the abstract, that most of his successors were hostile to public employees' unionism, even as each sought the support, at election time, of the powerful New York labor movement.

Then a combination of circumstances caused one of these successors, Robert F. Wagner, Jr., the son of the famed sponsor of the National Labor Relations Act, to break ranks. For some years, Wagner's political fortunes were tied closely to his alliance with Harry Van Arsdale, leader of New York's million-member Central Labor Council. But it wasn't until the Teachers, Municipal Employees, and Hospital Workers mounted major campaigns that Van Arsdale was moved to intervene with the mayor. In each case "Van" proved that he was a trade unionist first and a politician next. In 1958, as city workers demanding recognition marched through the streets of the city, around the mayor's residence, Gracie Mansion, and down to City Hall, Van Arsdale urged Wagner to seek a solution to the crisis. At the center of the movement was Jerry Wurf.

Born and raised in New York, Wurf had his early training in the socialist youth movement. Like many of the generation that reached young adulthood during the Depression, he believed that the labor movement held the key to social change. He joined AFSCME in 1948 but, until the mid-1950s, found the going rough. Only eight hundred members were affiliated with the newly formed District Council 37. Wurf was a one-man band from 1948 to the early 1950s and received some support from AFSCME only when the council president, Henry Feinstein, departed to become president of Teamsters Local 237, and John De Lury of the city's Sanitation union also left.

Wurf, at last at the helm, had only a handful of hospital workers and assorted categories of city employees. But with the AFL-CIO merger in 1955, District Council 37 held the franchise to organize most categories of nonuniformed municipal employees in America's largest city. The well-financed Teamsters local presented a significant challenge, so Wurf desperately needed a "rabbi" in the city's official labor movement. He found him in the Seafarers' union boss Paul Hall, who feared that the Teamsters, one of his chief waterfront antagonists, had its eye on public employees. Hall, seeing DC 37 as a way to head off the Teamsters' campaign among city employees, put money into Wurf's organizing drive and provided bodyguards to protect Wurf against the threat of physical assault. Even in the absence of substantial support from the national union, the Wurf-Hall alliance was able to pave the way for future victory.

For nearly a decade, the struggle between Teamsters Local 237 and DC 37 to represent almost 150,000 nonuniformed city workers was among the most dramatic events in New York's labor scene. Beyond its importance for the city, it became the inspiration for a renewed effort by many unions around the country to organize public employees. By the use of militant job actions, Wurf consolidated his base among the largely blue-collar Parks Department workers and gained support in the sprawling municipal hospital system. In the mid-1950s, Local 371, the social service employees of the Welfare Department, grew substantially. Aided by Wurf's taste for confrontation and by the interunion rivalry, DC 37 claimed 25,000 members by 1958. The Teamsters had also recruited nearly 20,000 to its ranks.

The combined strength of the two unions amounted to less than a third of city employees, but what DC 37 lacked in numbers, it made up in political noise. Wurf was especially adept at getting the union's name in the newspapers and on the eleven o'clock newscasts. The union was poised for a political breakthrough. Recently elected for a second term with organized labor's support, Wagner was induced by pressure from organized labor to issue Executive Order 49. (This was four years before Kennedy's order.) Wagner's order recognized unions for the purposes of collective bargaining, established a grievance procedure, and set procedures for determining bargaining units and representatives through the city's Labor Department. Following the tradition of the National Labor Relations Act, Order 49 provided that the winner of an election would have exclusive bargaining rights. But Wagner's order, which covered only about half the city's employees, excluded some large groups, such as the Transit Authority, the Board of Education, and the city's colleges. And because Wagner did not wish to favor one contender over another, unions were forced to fight "inch by inch, title by title," the biggest prizes being citywide clerical workers, hospital employees, those in social services, and workers in the housing authority.

The outcome of the struggle was a qualified victory for Wurf and District Council 37, qualified because the Teamsters were able to win in the large Housing Authority and the citywide blue-collar craft workers. But DC 37 took Parks, which became Wurf's source of volunteer organizers; the huge 35,000-person clericals, the union's largest local; the 17,000 members of social service employees, the largest unit of college-educated professionals; almost 6000 engineers and draftspersons in all city agencies; and cafeteria workers in the Board of Education, a 12,000-member local. And it won in the hotly contested municipal hospitals. By the late 1960s, nearly all of New York's eligible public employees had selected union representation, including police and firefighters. Within a decade the example of New York and Philadelphia, which had experienced a similar explosion, rapidly spread to state and local governments throughout the country.

A paradox of the 1960s was that even as young radicals and intellectuals bitterly complained that the labor movement had gone over to the establishment, many of the same people were caught up in the public-sector organizing drives. In the heat of the civil rights, antiwar, and feminist movements, millions of young, black, and female public employees joined unions to redress a myriad of grievances, especially low salaries and the lack of a voice on the job. They not only voted for unions in representation elections but also mounted picket lines and staged mass demonstrations at city halls and the statehouses all over the country. In the two decades after 1955 more than four million public employees became union members or were represented in collective-bargaining agreements. By 1980 two of every five public employees were represented by unions, compared with just one in seven private-sector workers. Many were black and Latino workers at or near the bottom of the pay scale; they worked in hospitals, parks, on sanitation trucks, and in road crews. But clerical workers — white and black — perhaps the largest segment of public employees, and those who worked in the public and voluntary nonprofit hospitals, also flocked to unions. And professional and technical employees, most visibly teachers, swelled labor's ranks. By 1975 the combined teachers' unions numbered nearly three million members, the largest in the labor movement, and had the largest union density of any occupation, about 80 percent. In many cases, radicals were key organizers, especially at the local level, of the State, County, and Municipal Employees and of the Service Employees. Some who learned their trade in the student movement, community, and antiwar organizing projects became leaders of large local unions and, in a few cases — like Paul Booth, organizing director of AFSCME — found themselves at the headquarters of major national unions.

The astounding rise of public employees' unionism after World War II is inextricably bound up with the rise of "new" social movements. The resentment shared by this neglected sector of the American workforce was the true impetus behind the organizing explosion, but its wide scope and its social-liberal and militant nature cannot be explained by economic influences alone; after all, white-collar workers in the private sector suffer similar wage lags but to this day have not joined unions in significant numbers. The brilliant move of many who led the organizing drives was to link traditional union appeals to public issues, especially civil rights and the feminist movement. In the post offices and many state and municipal agencies, blacks and Latinos invoked the iconography of these movements — Martin Luther King was the patron saint of the New York Hospital Workers and, more fatefully, of the Memphis Sanitation Workers — integrated minority and women's issues into bargaining, and encouraged members to participate in peace, feminist, and civil rights demonstrations. For example, AFSCME's secretary-treasurer, William Lucy, was the organizer of the Memphis strike and an activist in the civil rights struggle. Many young men chose to become schoolteachers rather than risk being drafted to fight in Vietnam. Some, especially in New York and Los Angeles, were caught up in the union organizing efforts that built the American Federation of Teachers, and many others threw themselves into a more unlikely effort, the transformation of the National Education Association from a lobby and advocacy group for teachers' professional interests into the largest labor union in the United States.

Perhaps the most dramatic early example of a New Left union was the 17,000-member Local 371, the Social Service Employees Union (SSEU) of New York. Following the growth of welfare recipients, between 1962 and 1966, New York City's Department of Social Services doubled its number of caseworkers. In a time of severe shortages of qualified workers, many who had been involved in the civil rights and antiwar movements, and who were not interested in graduate or professional school, became caseworkers.

But caseworkers' jobs are not easy. Under the old system they had welfare "clients" whom they regularly visited, called, and met with in their offices. Their task was to make sure that the clients were spending the public assistance income properly: that they and their children had enough food and clothing; were not abusing alcohol and drugs; were not living illegally with employed lovers or relatives; and, if able-bodied, were looking for work or were in a training program. Caseworkers complained about horrendous caseloads and low salaries, and, given their political sympathy, regarded the policing aspects of their jobs with contempt. Moreover, they considered the welfare system degrading to clients.

By 1964 the union was infused with new leadership. In a sharply contested election, the membership elected a slate led by a former student activist, Judy Mage. She had been a student leader of a small radical socialist group. The vice presidential candidate on her slate, Bernie Cacchione, although by no means an old leftist, was the son of a popular former Brooklyn Communist city councilman. The elected executive board included young radicals like Stanley Hill, later to become executive director of DC 37. Enraged by Wurf's autocratic leadership style, SSEU seceded from the council and remained independent for the next five years. During this period Mage and her associates led two major strikes for higher salaries and better working conditions, especially reduced caseloads. Among the union's most important innovations was an alliance with client groups, especially the city's welfare rights organization. The second strike was waged in part around an unusual demand: increased client benefits. Facing a chronic shortage of caseworkers, the city administration was prepared to deal on wages and conditions but stonewalled demands that involved client interests, alleging that these were outside the purview of collective bargaining. The 1966 walkout won widespread support among unions, but when the social service union vigorously took up client issues, trade union support melted away. Most union leaders, even the progressives, believed that the local was wrong to bring welfare rights to the bargaining table. This disregard of the problems of the unemployed and the poor foreshadowed the inability of some of them to address issues of workfare thirty years later.

Similarly, SEIU in California employed a large number of antiwar and other activists as organizers and staff in its drive to unionize state and Los Angeles city employees. Its statewide local of social service employees was mainly under the leadership of people who had cut their teeth on the student movement, like their New York counterparts, newly radicalized college-educated workers. We have already seen how black and Latino hospital workers constructed their struggle as a civil rights movement as well as a labor movement. AFSCME, West Coast Service Employees locals, and the AFT were no less aware of the importance of forging links to other movements and framing their demands in social as well as economic terms. Attentive to its young, left-leaning, and largely female membership, particularly in big cities, AFSCME allied itself with the progressive wing of the AFL-CIO. It was an early war opponent and was especially active in the feminist movements of the late 1960s and 1970s, which, at the local as well as the national level, made an enormous difference in its organizing and bargaining strategies during this period.

In the 1970s and early 1980s one of the more innovative feminist-oriented bargaining demands was that of "comparable worth." In Washington State, Minnesota, and the city of San Jose, the predominantly female AFSCME membership waged an effective campaign to evaluate "women's" jobs in relation to those of men. They used such quantitative measures as degrees of responsibility, physical or mental stress, and skill. To objections that men would lose income, proponents of comparable worth argued that all employees would gain from this method of raising the bottom. Their predictions proved correct. In San Jose the union had additional help from a newly elected mayor, who ran on a feminist platform and pledged to implement the comparable worth program. In the early 1980s Minneapolis, Washington State, and several California cities passed laws sanctioning comparable worth approaches to achieving pay equity.[3]

Comparable worth was a direct consequence of the emergence of women as leaders in important sections of AFSCME and the Service Employees. But it was also among the more controversial wage-equity strategies in these unions. It departed from the traditional practice of relying on across-the-board increases by targeting the wage inequality between men and women. Soon local governments realized that comparable worth was far more effective in raising salary levels for all employees, and took the issue to court. In a famous decision a Washington State court struck down the state's comparable worth law on constitutional grounds. Combined with the emerging fiscal "crisis" of local governments and the conservative backlash against union gains, the promise of this innovative approach to wage justice was temporarily set back.

Comparable worth was perhaps the leading indication that many public employees' unions were more than bargaining agents for their members: they adopted many of the features of a social movement that recalled the 1930s and bonded with the spirit of the 1960s. They aimed at nothing less than changing the lives of their members, not only by raising living standards but by providing the means by which many of them could, through education and training, reach beyond their backgrounds. But some were also dedicated to broader changes in American society, especially racial and sex equality. While the rest of the labor movement was formally committed to equal pay for equal work and for broad access of minorities to economic opportunity, some of the new unions became among the country's leading forces in preserving and extending the welfare state — not only through income guarantees for the poor, but also by public-sector job creation, the program promoted by Kennedy and Johnson for overcoming poverty. From the late 1960s through the early 1990s, the years of the fiscal crisis inflicted by the tax revolt and by conservative legislatures on many states and local communities, public employees' unions, especially the Service Employees and AFSCME, were bastions of resistance to service cuts and layoffs. They formed coalitions with community groups, welfare rights organizations, and civil service associations to oppose referenda, legislation, and executive orders that mandated what we now called "downsizing" of public goods. As one observer wrote, these unions became the main "state builders" in a conservative age.

But the public employees' unions made use of another element drawn from the intellectuals' criticism of the mainstream labor movement. In the main, these unions were, at least in their infancy and youth, fiercely democratic and participatory. Rank-and-file nurses aides and street cleaners spent many hours after work attending meetings in the union hall and going to education classes; many donated their mornings and evenings as volunteer organizers. Others formed committees in the local union to plan events like Black History Month celebrations, conferences, and, perhaps most important, informal caucuses within the union to lobby leaders for more action against job discrimination, especially upgrading, and for bringing minorities and women into union leadership.

The concept of public employees as workers was undoubtedly a major shift in the strategy of postwar white-collar unionism. If some were confused by the images of white-collar workers as underpaid, overworked victims of their pitiless employers, public employees rallied to the new spirit. Perhaps the most startling transformation was among teachers. The militancy evinced by New York's 45,000 public school teachers had immediate effect among the ranks of public employees, particularly teachers themselves. As with the CIO in the 1930s and 1940s, the emergence of the AFT prompted other associations, notably the three million-member National Educational Association, to revisit their traditional professionalism and antiunionism. And, as when the AFL outstripped the CIO, the NEA, once on the union path, became bigger than the AFT.

The experience of the teachers' unions reveals the complexity of public-sector organizing. The AFT leadership aligned itself with the AFL-CIO's foreign and domestic programs and, despite a strong commitment to racial integration, remained an exemplary craft union. At the same time its key organizers — among them David Selden, who led the momentous New York drive — were pioneers in applying some industrial union strategies to the public workplace. These strategies have had enormous implications for the relationship of the union to community groups, especially racial and ethnic minorities, because the union has, in the interest of protecting its own members, often found itself in alliance with city administrations and boards of education, the very institutions it was at first obliged to fight in order to gain recognition.

Sensing that bargaining rights would extend to teachers, in 1958 the AFT president, Carl Megel, sent David Selden to beef up its scrawny New York affiliate, the Teachers Guild. Although the Guild's rival, the left-led Teachers union, was crippled by the state's Feinberg Law, barring Communists and other suspected subversives from public school teaching, the Guild was unable to take advantage of the union's weakness. The Guild was more like a debating society than a union and seemed more concerned with its anti-Communist credentials than with organizing teachers. Selden's ambition was intense. He had been a teacher in the New York City schools, but his heart and mind were devoted to building the labor movement through the use of the strike. He set about to persuade the many professional organizations among the city's teachers to surrender some of their autonomy to a strong union. But, in a time when public schools were places of social and intellectual conformity, any union, even one that was plainly anti-Communist, was regarded with suspicion.

The Guild president, Charles Cogen, made no secret of his antipathy to Selden's proposal to use militant methods. Despite these disagreements, however, the two unionists shared the conviction that the AFT should become the union of choice for the underpaid and administratively subordinated teachers. Together with two other active organizers — the junior high school math teacher and socialist Albert Shanker, and the high school teacher George Altomare — the Guild made its way in one year from an anemic fifteen hundred members to a respectable twenty-five hundred by 1959. But if the cause of teacher unionism was to prevail, it would need a bold gesture to convince teachers to break from the past.

That gesture came from the much stronger independent High School Teachers Association, which in 1960 called a strike protesting the decision of the Board of Education to eliminate the differential between high school and elementary school salaries. After some hesitation prompted by its solidaristic ideology, which opposed differentials, the Guild backed the strike, which failed. But the main outcome was that the Guild and the High School Teachers had formed an alliance. In 1961, with audacity entirely unjustified by its relatively modest size, the AFT local called a citywide teachers' strike for pay increases and union recognition. Some five thousand teachers mounted picket lines, and the public nature of the walkout forced school closings in most districts, a result of Selden's public relations. Facing re-election and labor's pressure, Mayor Wagner, whose earlier order had opened the floodgates, literally panicked, and he granted the teachers their bargaining rights. In the subsequent campaign for representation, the newly formed United Federation of Teachers, of which the Guild and the High School Teachers Association formed the core, swamped its opponents.

The New York experience transformed public employees' unionism throughout the country. Wurf and Selden had decisively broken with the older professional models by relying on direct action and overt political pressure. If Selden was the true pioneer of this approach, Shanker refined it to an art form. When, as Cogen's successor to the UFT presidency, Shanker went to jail in 1965 in defiance of the state's Condon-Wadlin Act, prohibiting strikes by teachers and other categories of public employees, his courage electrified his own membership and teachers throughout the country. From 1965 to 1980 teachers' unionism was marked by frequent strikes; Shanker's line was that it was disgraceful that teachers earned less than truck drivers, and that until they acted like other trade unionists, they would continue to fall behind. For the time being, teachers were to lay aside their professionalism and act like workers. Their concerns should be salaries, hours, and working conditions. Later, he led the almost-million members of the national teachers union back to professional concerns.

Similar changes were under way at the federal level. President Kennedy's Executive Order 10988 severely restricted the scope of bargaining, both by barring the right to strike and by a "management rights" provision that gave unions little room to negotiate. More, the order prohibited bilateral negotiations over wages and salaries; these issues could be resolved only by civil service and congressional action. Nonetheless, Kennedy's order galvanized federal employees, especially postal workers and the growing force of clerical and professional workers in various federal agencies. In the decade after its issuance, the largest federal union, the American Federation of Government Employees, had won representation rights for 700,000 employees, the combined postal unions bargained for 500,000, and independent unions won elections for some quarter million more. Yet except for postal workers, union membership among federal employers hovered around a third of the workforce or less, largely because the meaning of "bargaining" in that context was extremely narrow. Recognition did not bring substantial changes in the power relations in the federal workplace. Lobbying rather than direct action remained the main tactic for improving conditions.

The major difference between postal and other federal employees' unionism can be summarized by a single event: the unauthorized 1970 postal strike, which involved a majority of the post office workers. The effect of the strike was immediately felt by the government and by the entire country. Even under threats of discharge and other reprisals, the workers did not obey President Nixon's order that they return to work, so he sent the National Guard and armed forces to try to move the mail. That became one of the great jokes among postal workers. The conclusion of the strike was a victory for the workers and their unions. Where average annual salaries for clerks and letter carriers were $8500 in 1970, ten years later workers earned about $25,000 a year, an increase of nearly 250 percent in a period when inflation rates rose by about 90 percent. Clearly, it was the postal workers' bold and unexpected use of the strike that made the difference. And leading the fight were a large number of black postal clerks, who worked on the loading docks; many were Vietnam veterans, especially in New York, Chicago, and Washington, D.C.

The economist John Maynard Keynes argued that government should fight depressions by raising the demand for goods. One way to do so was to put the jobless to work at government-funded projects. When asked what kind of work, he answered that, from the perspective of economic policy, digging holes might be just as effective as more socially productive activity. Scandalized, conservatives took pains to attack public jobs as "boondoggles." Building roads, providing postal services, running schools and other public functions would be better performed by private companies. For years, no one paid heed, but as public employees' unions drove labor costs to the level of the private sector, what had once been regarded as a quaint notion inherited from the discredited doctrines of Adam Smith gradually became a credible alternative public policy. By the early 1970s proponents of public-sector growth were on the run.

The success of unions in the public sector had radically changed the cost of public services, the tax system, and the politics and economics of government. With each wage and benefit increase, the costs of education, health care, and other basic public goods rose. As long as American prosperity was sufficient to absorb union gains, the corporate and political establishments were relatively quiet. But with the painful economic restructuring in the late 1970s, public employees became a major target of the advocates of austerity. Perhaps the New York City fiscal crisis of 1974 to 1976 was the start of the war against public goods and public employees. Some leading banks announced that they would no longer extend short-term loans; without them, the municipal administration could not function. The mayor capitulated, and after the administration surrenders its fiscal autonomy to a board consisting of the heads of financial institutions, extensive negotiations began. The city's major public employees' union agreed to a permanent layoff of 50,000 workers, about a sixth of the workforce. In 1978, California's Proposition 13, limiting public spending, became law. That curtailed the power of public employees' unions, which was widely believed to be necessary for addressing some of America's economic woes.

Although union gains were not solely responsible for the rising costs of public goods, it is true that wages and salaries for employees in the public sector more than tripled between 1955 and 1975. In that same period, prices doubled. Even taking into account that a substantial portion of these increases simply made up for discrepancies between private- and public-sector wages in the first decades after World War II, their effect on local tax structures was devastating. Many states cut income taxes, and then, in order to maintain schools and other services, local communities were forced to raise property taxes. At a time of growing business political activism, politicians preferred to raise revenues by hiking sales and other nuisance taxes, which were relatively hidden, rather than increasing business and income taxes of those in top brackets.

Although the public-sector unions mounted some response to these assaults, they felt obliged to adapt to the changing political and cultural climate. Since city and state agencies have, in the past quarter-century, resolutely privatized services, many have become sympathetic to privatization proposals, like the use of vouchers to enable students to choose among a number of public and private schools.

Public-sector organizing was significantly stalled during the

1980s, as it was in the nonprofit agencies, such as those in health and human services, which depend on public funding. Only the two large education unions continued to make some membership gains, but in other respects they had run out of steam. President Ronald Reagan's firing of eleven thousand federally employed air traffic controllers, in the summer of 1981, and the visible economic stagnation of the early 1980s help explain why the social direction turned rightward as employers and their conservative allies mounted an assault on public goods, income assistance to the unemployed and indigent, and the very idea of unionism and of collective bargaining. What was revived was the once discredited doctrine that workers' wages were responsible for America's economic ills.

Taken aback, most unions were unable to counter these charges and began looking for protection in the Democratic Party, which was happy to take labor's money and campaign assistance but had moved away from many of its cherished legislative and political goals. Many unionists responded with even more fervent support, but by the 1990s, even with the election of a Democratic administration, labor was on the defensive. Even with their impressive memberships, public employees' unions were hanging on for dear life. In education, the fiscal crises of state and local governments made contracts harder to conclude as teachers lost confidence in militant action to bring major gains. In many ways AFT and other unions reverted to the old strategy of legislative lobbying to achieve key contract objectives and to protect their past gains. After several court decisions declaring comparable worth agreements illegal, the strategy was abandoned, and in some of its most formidable strongholds, AFSCME district councils found themselves negotiating to minimize layoffs instead of making advances.

In New York and Chicago, business groups and budget-conscious politicians took pains to enlist top municipal labor groups in their crusade for fiscal "responsibility." Increasingly separated from their own rank and file, some leaders found themselves conceding hard-won gains. Where in the past DC 37 and the UFT leaders had little difficulty winning membership approval for bargaining deals, the situation was reversed in 1995 and 1996, when leadership got its five-year contracts — which provided no pay raises in the first two years — only with great difficulty. The UFT rank and file turned down the contract at first but finally accepted nearly identical terms. When DC 37 submitted its proposals to its 100,000 union members, the results were mixed, but the leadership had its way. Several large locals did turn the agreement down; still, public employees' unions no longer proclaim militant resistance to the cutbacks of government and its services. Instead, even as John Sweeney leads an organizing crusade at the national level, public union leaders in the largest cities have tended to adopt policies like those of industrial unions: retreat to protect the core of long-time employees, even if it means sacrificing the bottom. These are some of the contradictions of organized labor.

▶

The Service Employees are an exception to this general pattern of retreat. Bucking the trend toward labor's downsizing, throughout the 1990s the union continued to grow in size and scope both by organizing and by merging with other unions. In December 1996 the union's executive board voted to add more than $8 million to its 1997 organizing budget and committed 45 percent of its budget to organizing, a funding level that, according to the union newspaper, was "unequaled in the labor movement since the 1930s." By mid-1997 it had organized more than 22,000 new members, though its unionizing efforts among state workers in Georgia were not at first successful. It did enlist the support of several religious groups and won an important election among nearly two hundred community agency employees in Tennessee. And in the past several years there has been an acceleration of organizing in the health sector, especially affiliations by physicians, nursing-home workers, and nurses groups. After the affiliation of the 8500-member New York area–based Committee of Interns and Residents in 1997, Service Employees union president Andy Stern announced a $1 million fund to organize interns and residents.

Now, after almost a decade of slack organizing, there are signs that AFSCME, the AFL-CIO's largest affiliate, is coming alive. Most impressive is the union's drive to organize nurses and other health care employees of Columbia/HCA, the nation's largest health maintenance organization (HMO), which has fiercely resisted the effort. In 1996 its California affiliate won a big victory in San Diego for 2600 nurses employed by Sharp Professional Nurses Network. In 1997 it won a sweeping victory in four large units of Maryland State employees. Like the Service Employees, the Teamsters have shifted considerable funds and staff to new organizing. In the public sector they have made gains among prison guards in county and state facilities and among other law enforcement officers.

These results are heartening and partly vindicate the change in AFL-CIO leadership. But SEIU's efforts to organize Georgia State employees and AFSCME's thus far unsuccessful drive at Columbia/HCA indicate the how difficult is the path ahead. In both cases, the issues behind these campaigns is the consequence of the relentless drive toward privatization of public goods. In the name of efficiency and cost containment, Georgia's Democratic governor, Zell Miller, adopted privatization as public policy. And the whole HMO concept — and its concomitant managed care — is becoming identified with the transformation of nonprofit health care into private enterprise. Leading health care organizations, such as California's Kaiser Permanente, New York's Blue Cross, and many others, are, like Columbia/HCA, now for-profit organizations. Or they use cost-accounting criteria to drive their service regimes. The bottom line is to reduce jobs and union protections in the interest of cost containment. That is how they intend to cut state taxes and hold the line on insurance premiums. As we shall see, the crowning feature of welfare reform, workfare, may be viewed as the outsourcing of union jobs.

While privatization has proved a good organizing issue, the evidence thus far is that most unions are reacting defensively and have not yet proposed bold alternatives. Will public employees' unions remain fervent state builders, or will they adapt to the new era of privatization? The future of the whole idea of public goods is in their hands, because they are the only politically powerful force capable of reversing the current trend. But, as always, they will have to form alliances with other labor organizations and with religious and community groups. And they must show that the privatizers are robbing the public of its legacy and the people of their incomes. They will have to be public participants in the debate over health care and privatization. The question is, are they up to it?

3 ✍ The South, Labor, and American Political Culture

SOUTHERN LABOR AND AMERICAN POLITICS

Some years ago a prominent labor historian warned us to avoid at all costs the temptation to engage in "what if" thinking.[1] Tracing what actually happened was the correct way to grasp history's course, not imagining what could have been. Perhaps. But consider the consequences for the country's political culture of the long, sad, and often bloody history of Southern workers after the Civil War. In this era of Southern-based conservative dominance of both the White House and the Congress, it is hardly idle speculation to ask how national politics might be different had labor made inroads into the burgeoning Southern manufacturing industries. During the upsurge of the 1930s and in the postwar boom, some unionists hoped for success in organizing the South, but in both periods their efforts yielded only meager gains. Instead, the South became a magnet for Northern employers seeking high profits on the basis of low-wage labor. The South's role in a national two-tier wage system had implications not only for this once predominantly agricultural region but for the rest of the country. A century after union efforts to organize workers, the South remains an antiunion bulwark. It would be inaccurate to say that unions' efforts have had no impact on the region, however. Union pressure has forced Southern employers to make some changes in wages and working conditions.

Twentieth-century Southern politics is geared to keeping farmers and workers in their place, making the South good for business investment. It is true that the populist, labor, and middle-class liberal movements have contested the politics of popular subordination.[2] But the oligarchy revived after Reconstruction has managed to hold on to power in part because the South regularly delivered votes to Democratic presidential candidates. The rise of Southern conservatism and the decline of its once considerable populism must be attributed in a great measure to the weakness of the labor movement. If, for example, the Textile Workers union had secured a more significant beachhead in North Carolina after World War II, perhaps Jesse Helms would not have been elected in successive close races with moderate Democrats. Similarly, Mississippi has regularly sent some of the most reactionary politicians to Congress, a symptom of labor's weakness in its auto parts, cotton, and wood industries. But no Democratic president before the South's own Lyndon Johnson was willing to buck the oligarchy, especially on the explosive race question.

There are places in the South where unions do make a difference in electing legislators who challenge entrenched conservative incumbents. The successful 1996 re-election of several black members of Congress would have been unlikely without backing by Southern-based unions and the funds provided by the national AFL-CIO. And the strong showing in North Carolina of Harvey Gantt, a black Democrat, against Jesse Helms was aided by the state's largest union, the Union of Needle Industries and Textile Employees (UNITE), as was the success in defeating Oliver North's 1994 senatorial bid in Virginia. On the whole, however, unions have not built effective coalitions against the conservative legislators, governors, and local officials. Increasingly, these office holders are influenced by groups like the Christian Coalition. Unless labor can find a way to shift the balance of power in the South, hope for even modest legislative gains at the national level remains dim.

Since the late 1960s, the center of economic as well as political gravity has moved from the Northeast and Midwest to the Southeast and the Southwest. Nixon's Southern strategy was bolstered by a massive population shift to the South after World War II. People moved because of disappearing factory and transportation jobs in the North and because of the growth of high-tech industry in the South. Drawing on the scientific resources of the region's universities — Duke, the University of Texas, and the University of North Carolina — many electronic research and production companies have located in Durham, Raleigh, and several Texas cities. Similar shifts have been made to Georgia and Florida. Then, too, major production corporations, such as General Motors and General Electric and foreign companies like Mercedes-Benz, Bavarian Motors, Honda, Nissan, and Toyota, were welcomed by local governments. While General Motors plants, like the Saturn facility in Tennessee and the Oldsmobile assembly plant in Oklahoma City, came with union organization, labor was much less successful where companies like Nissan and GE, whose union contracts do not cover newly built plants, actively opposed unionizing efforts, even though nearly all of GE's dwindling Northern plants are unionized and Nissan deals with Japanese unions.

Many regions, especially the Northeast, have suffered from slow growth and job losses. The Southeast and Southwest are booming. Southern plants and service industries do pay below the national average, but their work is more or less steady. For example, although wages at the nonunion Nissan assembly plant in Smyrna, Tennessee, were $3.50 an hour behind the industry norm of $17.50 in 1994, workers who had never seen a pay envelope much above legal minimum found $14 an hour and plenty of overtime a fortune. They would not risk their jobs by joining a union. In 1991 the workers rejected the Auto Workers for the second time, and prospects for unionization in the future are not promising.

Since World War II, textiles have experienced a concentration of ownership in fewer hands. The industry is marked by several multiplant chains — Burlington, J. P. Stevens, Fieldcrest (which recently acquired Cannon), Deering Millikan, and Lowenstein. Although in 1996 none of these had more than 5 percent of the market, fewer than twenty firms accounted for more than 60 percent of investment, production, and employment. Since these firms had the capital resources to automate production, they were the survivors in a once fiercely competitive industry. Moreover, even when unions did make inroads in one or more plants, organizing was hampered by the company's ability to transfer work to nonunion plants.

Despite these setbacks, the last twenty years have seen a revival of labor activity in the Southern textile and clothing industries. The recent record of UNITE and one of its predecessors, the Clothing and Textile Workers, counters the belief that the labor movement has been wholly unable to organize in the South.

EVENTS BELIE FORECASTS

For textile corporations the two lessons of labor's history in the South were (1) that if they could find a patriotic, Anglo-Saxon labor force, they would avoid industrial conflict; and (2) when choosing locations in the South, they would find rural areas more amenable than urban areas, because city workers, having more job options, might be rebellious.

> We have often boasted, in sincere pride [wrote David Clark, of *The Southern Textile Bulletin,* on the occasion of a Southern textile strike wave], that the cotton mill operatives of the South were of pure Anglo-Saxon blood and that they were far superior in character to the "scum of Europe" which operates the mills of New England. We have thought in years past that we understood the mill employees of the South, but events during the past two years have made us wonder at the traits of character that have been shown.

These sentiments revealed more than prejudice against immigrants. Many mill owners genuinely believed that Southern textile workers would never engage in strikes and other forms of collective protest unless they were provoked by "outside agitators." This theme, repeated with numbing frequency throughout American history, is predicated on the belief that absent union agitators, native-born workers are loyal to their employers. Needless to say, the history of the Mineworkers union in the South, most of whose members are descendants of Anglo-Saxon settlers, belies the nation that when collective organization occurs among "truly" American workers, there must be foreign influence, especially by European-inspired radical ideologies.

The story of the 1934 textile strike was, until recently, one of the most blatant examples of the suppression of memory in the annals of Southern labor history. The culmination of more than thirty years of Southern labor struggle, the strike was joined by 400,000 workers — about half the industry's operatives, 171,000 of them — in the South. It was not so much that the strike was lost; defeat was almost a routine of textile unionism. What made the outcome of particular significance was the way it embodied the hopes of an entire generation of workers eager to free themselves from the employers' paternal social order; how much these hopes were buoyed by the belief, encouraged by union leaders, that their cause would be supported by President Franklin Roosevelt and the New Deal; and how these expectations were completely dashed — some believed betrayed — by the federal government and the United Textile Workers.[3]

Rural and urban workers joined the walkout, scorned eviction notices from company-owned houses, and, though many were hungry, stayed solid for three weeks. As the walkout spread throughout the Carolinas, strikers invented a new tactic, the "flying squadron," which a few years later was adopted by the Auto Workers to great effect. Workers from striking mills piled into cars and pickup trucks and drove into nonstriking mill towns. Sometimes they blocked passage into the mill; more often they stood outside the gates and urged workers to join the strike. In response, employers set up "machine guns on factory rooftops, hired armed guards, and petitioned the governor for National Guardsmen."[4] Nonetheless, workers by the thousands responded affirmatively to the squadrons. It was not uncommon for workers to walk out on the spot when a squadron appeared at the mill gate.

Roosevelt appointed a commission to make strike-ending recommendations, but none addressed the reasons that the workers had taken to the picket lines. One especially infamous reason was the stretchout, where workers were forced to operate more and faster-running machines. Nevertheless, convinced that the strike was on the verge of collapse, the union leadership quickly accepted the report, and the strike leader, Francis Gorman, hoped the Roosevelt administration would eventually facilitate union recognition. Even with a substantial financial gift from the Amalgamated Clothing Workers and lesser amounts from other organizations, the union's treasury was depleted and its staff stretched to the breaking point amid reports of back-to-work movements, especially in the South, most of which proved to be exaggerated.

"The sudden termination of the strike was like the opening of a leaky dam, unleashing retaliation by textile manufacturers on an unprecedented scale. . . . No sooner had the President told textile workers to go back to work than the repression began. Hundreds of mills quietly but firmly refused to take back strikers."[5] After weeks of turmoil, during which some mills were closed completely, management declared it would not reopen until workers openly renounced the union. In Georgia, military personnel prevented strikers from returning to work. Some strikers were rehired while many others remained unemployed and were evicted from their homes if they remained true to the union. Most workers had only two alternatives: stay loyal to the company or leave town. It seemed that the long journey had come to an ignominious end. More than four thousand were permanently fired; employers established a blacklist of union activists; and even when some union locals held on to their local charters and met regularly, they finally returned to the skeleton national union. Some UTW representatives later declared that they had done their best to take care of fired workers, but for many workers the experience merely proved that years of effort to build a textile union in the South had come to naught.

The participants chose to erase the strike, its consequences, and unionism from memory. In the aftermath of the strike, working conditions grew worse, and the federal government did little to heed workers' pleas for action on their grievances. But it was the psychological defeat that was most devastating: workers felt that the union had lighted a fire and then snuffed it out. In later Southern campaigns, organizers reported that the "1934 factor" remained a major impediment to unionization.

A GREAT CRUSADING MOVEMENT
ON BEHALF OF HUMANITY

Like public employees, Southern workers benefited little from the industrial union movement's Depression-era successes. Formed in 1937, under Sidney Hillman's leadership, a CIO Textile Workers Organizing Committee made significant inroads in the industry's Northern sector, but organizing gains in the South were few, apart from the Carolina-based Cone Mills' six thousand workers and wartime unionization of the sprawling Dan River, Virginia, Mills. Unions needed a whole new approach in the South. They would have to solve their own disagreements, donate a great deal of money, and supply organizers for a coordinated drive. Besides, the campaign would have to confront the classical Southern obstacles: the color line, which in 1946 remained powerful in cotton textiles and many other industries; a hostile political environment; and the legacy of 1934. CIO organizers did recognize that the war had created yet another barrier: the industry's growing concentration and the emergence of a handful of large, multiplant chains that dominated the industry.

At its March 1946 convention, the CIO boldly formed a Southern Organizing Committee (SOC), popularly known as Operation Dixie. The international unions contributed some $1 million; paid for more than a hundred organizers to work in twelve state groups; and agreed to surrender autonomy to the committee until each plant was organized. The Organizing Committee included many unions, so it had a commitment to recruiting workers in lots of industries. But Operation Dixie was defined, in great measure, by its decision to concentrate on cotton textiles. One of its goals was to shrink the North-South wage gap by raising Southern wages and thereby prevent the migration of Northern plants. A second goal was to establish a permanent presence in some of the big textile corporations in the South.

Operation Dixie's director, Van Bittner, made use of social movement rhetoric to announce the campaign — he called the effort a "great crusading movement in behalf of humanity" — but he made it clear that it he was leading a trade union movement, pure and simple, and had no designs on social change, especially with regard to the problems associated with race. On the contrary. Operation Dixie's official strategy was to reassure the prevailing political structure that the labor movement did not aim at upsetting the applecart. There may have been another reason for the decision to keep the drive in the narrowest channel. The two camps within the CIO — the left and the mainstream liberals — disagreed on the best way to address race. The left-led unions participating in Operation Dixie pursued an organizing strategy in which racial equality occupied a prominent place. Bittner, CIO president Philip Murray, and other leaders were convinced that the incendiary race question could be circumvented. They believed the left was raising the race issue to embarrass them in the internal fight.

Nine months after it began in January 1946, the textile campaign appeared to hit a brick wall. Having met most of the conditions for success, the CIO could find no strategies to surmount formidable obstacles. Bittner and the CIO leaders planned staff and money reductions. The drive was hampered by the left-right conflict within the labor movement; it broke out into the open in 1946 and defined the internal life of organized labor for the next seven years.

Instead of pursuing a diverse industrial agenda, especially in industries where support by black workers might have established a base for industrial unions throughout the region, the leadership concentrated on the virtually all-white textile industry and went after North Carolina's Cannon Mills as a typical big corporation. Of the twenty-five organizers assigned to North Carolina, fifteen were in textiles — ten in Kannapolis, the site of the huge Cannon complex of twenty-one thousand workers. Similarly, the major effort in South Carolina was in textiles around the Rock Hill area, a center of dye houses and textile mills, and the textile-rich Greenville-Spartanburg area. Organizers reported to the state director in each of the twelve states, but the real test, the leaders knew, would be in the Carolinas, particularly the Cannon drive.

By March 1947, the new coordinator, Joel Leighton, based renewed optimism on the fragile sign that workers accepted the leaflets they were handed instead of throwing them away. The committee staff succeeded in organizing taxicab drivers but few textile workers. Everything the organizers tried seemed to make no impression, especially their attempt to show that Cannon wages were below those of the North and that textile workers' wages were generally behind those of steel and auto workers. One reason for worker unresponsiveness was that Southern textile employers had, early in the war years, fearing labor shortages and union campaigns, increased wages. One Cannon organizer complained that his road was hard because management was relatively benign and the owner, "Charlie" Cannon, was popular among the workers. That the union's appeal was almost entirely devoid of shop-floor issues showed that the campaign had purposes beyond organizing the unorganized. Perhaps its aim was to slow the migration of Northern mills to the South. At Cannon, the organizing staff was aware of stretchout, but did not focus on it. Its first mention was by Leighton in a report, but not in a leaflet. Nor was it raised at organizing meetings. And specific instances of managerial authoritarianism, such as arbitrary discharges, transfers, disciplinary action, and the entire question of health and safety, were completely absent from reports as well as from union literature. In sum, the organizers were unable to seize on any incident, nor were they tuned in to the shop floor. The campaign at Cannon was stubbornly fixed on the wage question, which, given the new prosperity of many large mill employers, could be quieted by raises. Organizers who had known the 1934 general strike story often said that its legacy was hurting the campaign in textiles.

There was in effect a general policy of asking those who signed cards to pay a dollar as a sign of commitment to the union cause. Organizers, however, frequently promised card signers that they would pay "no initiation [fee] until a contract is secured," a pledge that drew Bittner's anger. He told the staff that "a worker who can't pay $1.00 to belong to a union is not much benefit to our organization."[6] To the organizers, knowing the history of textile unionism in the early 1930s, it seemed better not to strongarm workers into joining up. Bittner was from an older tradition, in which paying dues showed commitment to the union cause. These clashing principles were not resolved during the Southern drive.

As the Cannon drive trudged along, organizers were unable to form in-plant committees and offered reasons for why workers were reluctant to sign up or become active, including the weather, the company's use of the "negro issue," and workers' fear of strikes. The official policy of the Southern Organizing Committee was to steer clear of local and national politics and focus instead on "trade union" issues, like wages. For example, the Political Action Committee, one of the CIO's most effective groups, was barred from the organizing drive. Bittner made clear that Operation Dixie was to be devoted to "winning one thing, and that is elections," a policy that seemed to contradict his own emphasis on collecting dues.

The campaign did try to reach out to local communities through radio broadcasts and talks with ministers in the hope of neutralizing church opposition. Yet the brazen use of local civic leaders and state officials by companies went unopposed. The organizers defended themselves by emphasizing the nonpolitical nature of the campaign, which, of course, utterly failed to stem the open hostility of many prominent citizens. Even the work of the staffer Lucy Randolph Mason, a noted Christian layperson, and the presence on the union's staff of several ministers, such as the South Carolina director Franz Daniel, did not mitigate the charge that the union was not only a Northern import but was filled with "godless" Jews and socialists. Shortly after opening the Kannapolis drive, the coordinator Dean Culver, a Southerner and former aluminum worker, reported "the reluctance of women to responding may become the greatest impediment" to its progress, because "women's thought here is greatly conditioned by the churches," which were antiunion.[7] Culver was replaced in late 1946 when the committee decided to scale down the drive by cutting staff and limiting office time.

Neither Bittner nor his assistant, Textile union vice president George Baldanzi, whose popularity among Southern workers was legendary, came up with a single original idea during the campaign.

Except in Daniel's South Carolina operation and in Tennessee, where Paul Christopher, a native Southern textile worker and veteran of the 1934 strike, was state director, there was no imagination behind the drive. (There was some research on industry concentration provided by TWUA's excellent Research Department and some work by its Education Department.) Even the leaflets handed out at plant gates never addressed the major concern: shop-floor issues. For example, one Cannon leaflet reminded workers: "Your Government says you can Join a Union." That refrain may have worked brilliantly in the early New Deal years, but it had long since lost its zip. Almost all the leaflets merely repeated the comparative wage argument.

In fact, by the late 1940s the wage gap between North and South, union and nonunion, was considerably narrower. Instead of cutting wages, as had been done after World War I, the mill owners understood that, by depriving the union of the wage issue, they could safeguard their union-free environment. Employees, said the owners, had little to gain, at least in their pay envelopes, by joining the union. And, given the Textile Workers' eagerness to slow the closing of union mills in the North, the union energetically promoted wage campaigns. Therefore, the more successful these campaigns were, the more remote were the union's chances of organizing the South.

The situation in South Carolina was more promising. Franz Daniel was better tuned in to workers' problems. In contrast to leaders of the North Carolina campaigns, Daniel instructed organizers to refrain from leafleting until they had formed in-plant committees, which were likely to be better informed than the organizers. Daniel was a loyal union staffer, and by following his own route he indicated the strain between the Southern Organizing Committee and the left-wing unions that had joined the drive. Nevertheless, he was not so factional that he did not appreciate successful organizing. He assisted in the campaigns of the left-wing Food and Tobacco Workers and the Mine, Mill, and Smelter Workers, but he worried that their policies of racial integration might hurt the textile drive. With the notable exception of a string of seven election victories in Rock Hill, South Carolina, involving seventeen hundred workers, and a successful Industrial Cotton Corporation strike after the company's refusal to negotiate a contract, the textile drive had little to show for its considerable efforts.[8] The Textile Workers, who effectively ran the organizing in the Carolinas, adopted a consistently defensive policy in the wake of what Daniel acknowledged was unbearable "community pressure": regular discharge of union activists, the companies' domination of the wage issue, and the union's refusal to address the leading social question of the period, racism.

Most blacks lived on the outskirts of mill villages and did not have social contact with mill workers. How, then, could the employers use the "Negro" issue to thwart organizing? One antiunion device was to allege that if the union came in, the employers would be "forced" to hire blacks on the machines and in the skilled occupations. To substantiate this charge, company literature, speeches, and news reports played up the civil rights resolutions of CIO and Textile union conventions; displayed photographs of integrated union meetings and — scandal! — interracial dancing by union officials at social affairs; and quoted the liberal statements of Philip Murray, Walter Reuther, and other unionists.

Already buffeted by the volatile cotton textile economy, which produced frequent layoffs, short-time work schedules, and plant closings, some white workers were put off by the prospect of competing with blacks, who might work for less. But the threat of social integration, with its tacit sexual connotations, played an equal role. An insecure white working class had built its sense of worth on racial superiority. It is not surprising that Bittner and the Textile union leaders were reluctant to deal with the tangled web of Southern race relations. As it turned out, the labor movement could run, but it could not hide. Employers, even Jewish textile employers, did not hesitate to use racial appeals and anti-Semitism to defeat the unions.

If textiles were the measure, Operation Dixie was an almost total failure. Despite the effort in cotton manufacturing, only 2592 textile workers in eleven elections were recruited by September, and none of them worked in mills employing more than 460, even though some mills employed more than a thousand. For the one-year period ending

June 1947, the campaign as a whole had succeeded in winning elections or recognition for fifteen thousand workers in sixty-five plants. By 1953 — when Operation Dixie finally expired — organized labor had organized 732 Southern units for total of 400,000 workers. But the Textile Workers claimed only thirteen thousand of these.

☙

The small CIO affiliate, the Food and Tobacco Workers (FTA), and the somewhat larger Mine, Mill, and Smelter Workers, together with other left-wing unions like the Packinghouse Workers and the Fur and Leather Workers, were committed to ending segregation in Southern communities and workplaces, and especially within the unions. While most anti-Communist CIO unions were ideologically opposed to racism, segregation, and job discrimination, many were hesitant to pursue these policies in the organizing campaigns in Southern locals where whites were in the majority. The Southern Organizing Committee openly renounced, on pragmatic grounds, the position of the Mineworkers and the left unions that labor could succeed only by organizing on an integrated basis. There is no doubt that these organizations were inconsistent in applying their own principles, but their practices were different from those of the Textile Workers and the Woodworkers, both of which deplored but ultimately sanctioned the practice of segregation in the mills and the community.

FTA's campaigns were "crusades," combining the near-religious fervor of the industrial unions of the 1930s and of the black freedom movement. Union issues in the narrow, company-based meaning of the term were only a part of this union's mode of operation. In Alabama and North Carolina, FTA members joined the local NAACPs, conducted voter registration drives, and held desegregation campaigns in local public places. Similar policies were pursued by Mine-Mill in Birmingham and in Bessemer, where, in the 1930s and 1940s, the union had recruited thousands of black and white metal miners, notably those in the giant Tennessee Coal and Iron Company, later to merge with United States Steel Corporation.

The left-wing unions, concentrating in industries with a considerable number of black workers, developed strong educational programs among whites on race issues, arguing that raising the wages and living standards of blacks was a condition for raising all workers' standards. Moreover, they employed black organizers and encouraged the promotion of black union leaders in newly established locals. These moves, far from being easily accepted by white workers, were also viewed with alarm by many Southern unionists and by the leadership of the CIO's Southern Organizing Committee. Nevertheless, between 1946 and 1947, FTA won eighteen elections involving more than twelve thousand workers, losing elections for about nine hundred workers; Mine-Mill won ten elections and lost one for a gain of about six thousand, including about thirty-five hundred fertilizer workers in Charleston, South Carolina. None of these victories involved more than two thousand workers in any one location, but, given the relatively modest organizing staffs of these unions, the results were impressive. FTA was beset with problems caused by the Cold War and its reflection within the CIO leadership. Among them was the union's refusal to sign the non-Communist affidavits required by the Taft-Hartley law long after the CIO unions had capitulated; its expulsion from the CIO; its lack of funds to conduct union business amid raids by AFL and CIO unions; and a small staff that was unable to cover the territory spanned by its far-flung locals.

Finally, in 1950, the FTA president, Donald Henderson, a Communist Party member, resigned so that the union could comply with the Taft-Hartley law and beat back some of the raids. After defeating an AFL raid, FTA lost its jewel, the 12,000-worker R. J. Reynolds Tobacco Company of Winston-Salem, North Carolina, to the combined efforts of a company union, the AFL Tobacco Workers, a CIO organizing committee, and "no union." In the initial vote FTA Local 22 soundly beat its union competitors but under Board rules faced a run-off with "no-union" alternative. While the CIO and AFL affiliates were eliminated from the run-off, they refused to advise their supporters to vote for Local 22. In the second ballot Local 22 lost to "no union" by 60 votes. And in 1949, shortly after its expulsion from the CIO, Mine-Mill was raided by the Steelworkers Union, which drove it out of the Birmingham mines by a racist appeal to the predominantly white workforce. The mainly black miners of Bessemer stayed with Mine-Mill.

By 1949 Operation Dixie was reduced to the Textile Workers, the Steelworkers, and a small potential challenger to FTA, the Transport Service Employees. Of the major national unions, the Textile Workers alone maintained a substantial organizing staff in the South, where, by 1951, it was representing about 20 percent of the region's textile workers. Aside from some members in small plants, it had membership in Dan River, Cone, Henderson, the dyeing and finishing plants in Rock Hill, and American Viscose, the largest synthetic fabric producer. Since these mills were concentrated in "right to work" states, the union actually represented far more workers than it had members.

Southern organizing, never the concern of the entire CIO, remained with Van Bittner, George Baldanzi, and a hired organizing staff. Bittner did his best to keep at bay the left-wing unions that participated in Operation Dixie, and his career was marked by his desire to centralize power, a cardinal feature of the Lewis legacy. No decisions to petition for an election, to file unfair labor practice charges, or to invent new tactics during a campaign could be taken without permission from his office. The organizers on the ground had almost no autonomy; they were hired and fired with little notice. After about six months of the drive, Bittner, obsessed with "keeping costs down," even questioned organizers who made long-distance phone calls. Rather than being a "crusading movement," the Southern Organizing Committee was a marginal organization. Operation Dixie neither relied on nor incorporated the militant traditions of Southern labor. It assumed that Southern workers had historical amnesia, and it proceeded as if textile workers were inherently conservative, and not only on race issues.

While the AFL did not formally undertake a coordinated drive in the 1970s, several of its major affiliates — the Meatcutters, Teamsters, Carpenters, Machinists, and Electrical Workers — were active in the region. Although statistics are hard to come by, some have estimated that the AFL's affiliates were more successful than the CIO. In wood and lumber products, food processing, tobacco, metalworking, and machine shops the two federations were in competition. The AFL organizers frequently used the Cold War rhetoric of national politics to attempt to defeat their opponents. But some of the AFL's success may have been due to its focus on more skilled workers.

A NEW BEGINNING?

Once the undisputed investment site for furniture and wood and textiles, since the 1970s and 1980s the South has become the region of choice of many industries, especially auto, electrical, and, recently, computer-based technologies. It is also the site of distribution and transportation centers. The basic explanation for this shift is the South's position in the restructuring of the American economy. It is hospitable to the corporate strategies of lowering labor costs by establishing union-free industrial environments, and of weakening environmental and health-and-safety regulations. Its state and local governments are more than willing to accommodate investors; each state has right-to-work laws, weak regulatory laws, and a sweet corporate-tax climate. Equally important, the South draws many workers from the decimated industrial regions of the North and Midwest who fear they may lose their jobs if they join unions.

So unions have their hands full. First, they must come to terms with the central position of the South in labor's and America's future. Next, they must demonstrate to Southern workers their commitment to the region and not concentrate on protecting their shrinking Northern base. And then they must dedicate their political and public relations resources to reversing the conservative Southern social climate.

They might consider a political strategy that focuses on the deleterious consequences of corporatization for the region's environment, schools, and other public services. They should build on the region's relative prosperity. If workers' jobs are secure, shop-floor and community grievances can be aired without fear. If the South is no longer an internal colony but is now in the center of America's industrial growth, there is no justification for regional wage and benefit differentials; working conditions in which safety and health are often ignored; and the neglect of the quality of life, which has been brazenly sacrificed in many communities. Unions and their allies can address all these matters.

Organized labor's official positions on issues of black equality, even those of some of its Southern affiliates, have been among the most liberal of any voluntary organization in the country. The Alabama Federation of Labor took strong positions on race issues in the 1950s, before it was fashionable. Many trade unionists throughout the South risked their jobs, in some cases their trade union careers, to defend civil rights. Nevertheless, the relation of the labor movement, in the North as well as the South, to black freedom has been ambiguous. In the South, the inability of most unions to tackle the issue of the racially based, internal, two-tier wage and occupational system within the plants provides employers with a ready-made issue to present to whites. One prominent Southern unionist told me that organizing is easiest in plants where one race or the other predominates, and is most difficult where white and black workers are at or near equal numbers.

As one gets to the shop floor or local community, both North and South, one sees that, so far, unions generally have not taken on the harder issues for fear of antagonizing their majority white membership. Until the 1970s, it was highly unlikely that any union with a substantial Southern agenda could make much headway until it was prepared to address these issues. In textiles, it was only when black workers were hired in considerable numbers to work at machines as well as cleaning jobs — after the Amalgamated Clothing and Textile Workers made explicit efforts to recruit on a nonsegregated basis — that some progress was made at the region's second largest employer, the J. P. Stevens Company.

When, in the 1970s, Southern labor, especially textile workers, began to stir again, it was largely because of the workers' resolve to address their accumulated grievances through collective organization. Also playing a role was the shift of some unions from the service model to the organizing model of unionism. This convergence produced the first victory against a textile giant since the war, the Clothing and Textile Workers' struggle to organize at J. P. Stevens. After years of legal challenges, the company agreed to recognize the union for workers in six of its eighty-five plants. The agreement was completed in 1980 with the reinstatement of Crystal Lee Sutton (the real-life Norma Rae), and labor activists looked forward to a resumption of organizing success in the South. Sadly, this did not occur. J. P. Stevens had no intention of permitting this situation in their other plants. For the union, the next two decades witnessed a substantial growth of its power in the region, even though it made no further organizing gains at Stevens.

To this day, only the Clothing and Textile Workers (since 1996, UNITE) has remained a continuous organizing presence in the region. Other unions — notably the Teamsters, the tiny but courageous Furniture Workers, and the small but persistent United Electrical Workers — have distinguished themselves as well. But most unions — the Auto Workers, Communications Workers — and the laborers have been content with episodic forays into the region. UNITE is in a different category; it has expanded its organizing activity.

In 1976, the two unions, together, had about fifty thousand Southern members — thirty thousand in clothing and twenty thousand in textiles. But since Southern states prohibited the union shop, the combined number of represented workers was closer to sixty thousand, half of them in textiles. After more than twenty years of effort, the 1997 membership was still sixty thousand. However, this is a remarkable achievement, given the extraordinary changes in apparel and textile manufacturing. In apparel, national employment was reduced from about 1.3 million in the late 1980s to less than a million in 1996. Since even $5 to $6 an hour in this labor-intensive industry could not compete with twenty-five to sixty cents offered, for example, to workers in China, the South lost many jobs in apparel. Textiles had an even steeper decline. From 800,000 workers twenty years ago, 1997 employment was just 600,000, about 450,000 in the South. Mills of all sizes have closed for various reasons: mergers and acquisitions have made some redundant; the recession of 1987–1994 hit small mills extremely hard; and, of course, as with many other sectors of the economy, computerization has taken a heavy toll.

But the prognosis for each is by no means similar. According to the union's Southern director, Bruce Raynor, the future of the apparel industries is almost certain to remain dire.[9] Although some larger chains, such as Levi Strauss, which is 50 percent unionized, perform most of their manufacturing in the United States and are technologically advanced, and the union conducts a vigorous organizing campaign among nonunion workers employed by the company, many of the union apparel producers closed their Southern plants and have shipped most of their work off-shore. But the textile employment decline reflects neither import competition nor a drop in production. Quite the contrary. It is a measure of one of the most revolutionary instances of rapid technological change in all of American manufacturing. Today, the typical textile mill — North and South — is highly computerized and is capable of turning out twice the quantity of goods it did twenty years ago. Some innovations in weaving eliminate up to 75 percent of the workers. The efficiency of textiles has been able to minimize foreign competition. In fact, in contrast to apparel, the United States is an exporter of cotton textiles.

And in the last twenty years, while real wages declined for workers in many production industries, some of them highly unionized, wages in textiles have matched or exceeded productivity increases. In 1981 textile wages averaged $5.82 an hour. Fifteen years later average textile wages had risen to almost $10, an annual increase of more than 4 percent. That wages conventionally rise with productivity is one of the reasons for this surprising statistic. But union pressure must also be factored into the equation. The union's aggressive organizing program of the last decade has put textile employers on notice that unless they share their gains, the union will march in.

The union is marching in anyway. Its Southern membership gains have been largely in textiles and in retail-clothing distribution. It has won recognition for about five thousand workers in distribution centers, most of them in key cities like Atlanta and Miami, and thousands

more in clothing and textile chains. The union gained recognition in
some cases without an election. Employers, especially those which
already deal with the union in some of their sites, are agreeing to
"card checks": the union presents evidence that a majority of the
employees in a unit have signed authorization cards. Contrary to
earlier expectations, the union has been successful in getting contracts in 95 percent of the cases. One of the factors in its success is that
the Southern UNITE region has sundered the traditional separation
of organizers and business agents. All of its staff are organizers as well
as contract negotiators and grievance handlers. And, almost alone in
the recent past among industrial unions, UNITE in the South has a
large group of volunteer rank-and-file organizers and activists. Without these activists, no professional organizers could hope to succeed
in an industry of more than 400,000 unorganized workers. More to
the point, as every good organizer knows, a member who still works in
the shop is often the most convincing organizer.

Raynor described an "organizing model" for obtaining a union
contract. In contrast to many other unions, UNITE has adopted a
policy to "never give in," no matter how long it takes to defeat employers' efforts to block the union. When the company at Coody's
Knoxville, Tennessee, distribution center dragged its feet during
1992 negotiations, the union put into place a "no holds barred"
campaign reminiscent of those employed most recently by the civil
rights movement and the more militant wing of the labor movement.
It included shop-floor campaign tactics, which Raynor described. For
instance, workers left their work stations and adjourned to the lunch-
room or cafeteria, where they held a series of prolonged prayer meetings. In a Southern community the company usually has no choice
but to wait out such a meeting. Other actions also manifested discontent and disrupted production, and then the union filed Labor Board
charges, alleging that the company had refused to bargain "in good
faith." Union members conducted mass demonstrations and pick-
eted at more than one hundred of Coody's retail stores. They ran
billboard ads appealing to the public to protest the company's refusal to address the workers' demands. After years of these actions,

the company agreed to negotiate a union contract. The union's te-
nacity again paid off at Kmart, where, after a three-year battle, the
company sat down at the bargaining table in 1996. A recent campaign at a seafood-processing plant that refused to negotiate a contract included "vigils" at the employer's home in South Florida.

But other companies remain holdouts. Raynor cited Bondo,
where eighty workers chose the union in 1989 but have not yet won
a contract. Raynor said the case was still "on the union's agenda."
Clearly, UNITE has adopted trench warfare; it has dug in for the
long haul.

To carry out its programs UNITE has enlisted about two thousand union members as volunteer organizers and activists; it also has
a full-time staff of some thirty organizers, "the largest in the South,"
half of them black and half women, a proportion corresponding to
the composition of its membership. Raynor said that the direct-action
tactics employed by the union are an effective alternative to the conventional strike, which, in his view, is "an outmoded weapon" because
"poor working people can't afford strikes," especially in an industry
where the union represents only a fraction of the workforce and has
a history of heartbreaking defeats. In rare instances, the union is
forced to strike, but it chooses its targets carefully and doesn't embark
on the strategy unless it is confident of victory.

UNITE in the South still operates on the principle that winning a
contract is its main objective. And, like most unions, it has made little
effort to broaden its strategy to a social movement model. For example, although it participates in electoral politics, even in North Carolina, where it is the state's largest union, it has not presented itself as
a force for general community change or taken its militant tactics
and resources into the community on issues such as education and
health care, which may be of concern to its members and would
likely build bridges. Nor, as a matter of policy, has it entered into
alliances with community and civil rights groups. Raynor acknowledged that its education program on "ideological issues" is relatively
undeveloped.

One can only speculate about this reluctance to engage in the

social movement, despite the union's break from hit-and-run organizing programs that, unfortunately, mark the work of most unions in
the South. As one of three or four unions with active Southern organizing programs, UNITE, whose 300,000 members nationally make it a
medium-size affiliate of the AFL-CIO, may not be in a position to
carry the burden alone. Fortunately, the Service Employees are conducting a campaign among Georgia State employees, and the Food
and Commercial Workers is organizing in a number of packing
plants. Although UNITE has taken steps to reverse the silence of
many Southern unions concerning race issues, it does not feel in a
position to move too fast, in light of its racially diverse membership and its still fragile position in the textile industry. Yet, despite
these limitations, UNITE's record indicates that, with proper support, Southern workers are willing and able to organize and win
contracts in the context of interracial campaigns.

The problem remains that, unlike UNITE, most of the unions
have not yet got the message on organizing strategies as well as social
issues. Their involvement in the South remains, on the whole, motivated by strategies to protect their existing, mostly Northern, base. An
international union like the Auto Workers will assign a staff to organize a plant, usually one that is subcontracting with a Northern employer with whom it has a contract, or one whose workers have called
on the union for assistance. After signing up a majority to union
authorization cards, it petitions for an election. If it loses, as it often
does in the South, the union usually folds its tent and goes away. The
more persistent organizations, like UNITE, will probably return, because they have linked organizing to the union's survival. Consequently, after losing a close election by 191 votes at the famous Cannon Mills — now part of the Fieldcrest chain — in 1991 among the
company's seven thousand workers, down by two thirds since 1946,
it filed a new petition in 1997. The election took place in early August, just as the United Parcel strike was launched. Having assured
workers that strikes had all but vanished from the union's arsenal,
on the eve of an election they were confident of winning the organizers found themselves in a vulnerable position. Fieldcrest manage-

ment lost little time reminding workers that unions were strike-happy, and it worked. UNITE lost the election by some four hundred votes. Although it is hard to say whether the results would have been different had the campaign handled the strike issue by acknowledging, despite its infrequent use, the strike's continued usefulness, the lesson of the Fieldcrest campaign, like Operation Dixie, is that labor cannot win unless unions embrace their most cherished and militant traditions.

For most unions, the cost of staying in the South, or emulating UNITE's style of campaigning, does not justify a long-term commitment. In too many cases union leaders act like corporate cost accountants when considering organizing. Is it any wonder that many Southern workers are suspicious of Northern-based unions? The typical union still uses the language of comparative wage advantages to describe its program. While unions have something to say to non-union workers about the superiority of union wages and benefits, in many cases the movement has fewer comparative wage arguments, because employers who can match union wages are able to stave off a union. Southern wages do not always match those in the North, but they have advanced considerably in the last decades, and in some instances wage increases have exceeded those in union workplaces.

As the work in manufacturing and services becomes more computerized, technical and professional employees are growing in number, and the number of production workers in technologically advanced industries declines. The trend, which began in the 1960s in the oil, chemical and, auto industries, has extended to nearly all Southern manufacturing. These employees are mostly salaried and in many cases are college educated, but that does not mean they are immune to union organization. To be sure, organizing them may be more difficult than dealing with low-wage workers, and any organizing drive that ignores their grievances will face the problem the oil and chemical workers faced in the 1950s and 1960s when these pioneer industries became automated. In Southern oil refineries, production workers lost their clout as the technical employees, aligned with the company, were used as efficient "replacement workers" during strikes.

The big news is that the South, the fastest growing region of the national economy, is also the fastest growing section of nonunion labor. Unions that ignore this are destined for oblivion. There is virtually no AFL-CIO affiliate that could not benefit from a consistent, well-crafted Southern drive, but it will do no good to copy the attitude of unions of the past. The South has become a leading manufacturing, distribution, and retailing center, and it will continue to grow. The growth will not necessarily be at the expense of Northern plants, because the South has become the investment option of choice for expanding capital. The real issue is whether labor is prepared to commit itself to its own survival. If so, the South remains its primary challenge.

If the unions cannot, individually, afford the cost of a permanent Southern organizing campaign, they may, by pooling their resources and working through the AFL-CIO, be able to make a real impact. In 1946 $1 million was barely enough to keep a hundred organizers in the field for six months. By the year 2000, employing twice as many organizers — still only a beginning — will probably cost at least the $20 million that the AFL-CIO has committed to its entire national organizing effort. And if the labor movement is to convince Southern workers and their communities that it is seriously interested in them, not just in the existing union members, it may consider hiring more Southern unionists as organizers and, like Operation Dixie, establishing a network of state organizing headquarters and regional offices. UNITE's organizing model may be the key to success. The existing staffs would have to devote a substantial amount of time to organizing activists found in the Southern unions themselves. Clearly the initiative for this effort would have to come from the top, from AFL-CIO president John Sweeney.

But logistical problems are more easily solved than ideological and political issues. Labor must confront the legacy of postwar union traditions. Today, most organizing is conducted for the purpose of securing union recognition and eventually obtaining a signed agreement with an employer. Workers are asked neither to pay dues nor to form a local union before a signed contract is delivered. The union supporter, therefore, who works in a plant without a union contract rarely enjoys the rights and duties of union membership. In contrast to the period before the enactment of the Wagner Act and the consequent evolution of contract unionism, the labor movement now consists of dues-paying members within specified workplaces where the union is, at the minimum, recognized by law or by the employer as a bargaining agent. Neither the unemployed worker nor the worker in a nonunion workplace is considered part of the labor movement. These circumstances do not support the thesis that unionism is a movement for all labor. On the contrary, it leads to a restrictive and exclusive meaning of the term "labor movement." Maybe it is not realistic to posit that the history of the textile union would have been different if, after the debacle of 1946–1951, the labor movement had formed locals without contracts and maintained an education campaign regardless of the immediate prospect for winning a representation election. Maybe it would have required a considerable investment by the AFL-CIO in the South without the immediate prospect of normal income. But the costs incurred by the labor movement because it did not adopt this approach proved to be considerably greater.

Of course, since the signed agreement is a legal document signifying that the employer is obliged to pay certain wages, provide specified benefits, and recognize the union as agent in negotiating job security and working conditions, it retains a vital place in labor relations. But the agreement may exceed the power of the workers and their union to enforce it. Solidarity among workers and their willingness to take action to win justice are often prerequisite to the union's obtaining the agreement. The election victory is only the first step. As often as not, the employer will not negotiate unless the workers take action to force the contract. Of course, a show of strength is no substitute for a plan. Clearly, labor must decide in which industries — and where — it should concentrate resources. If, for example, the AFL-CIO integrates its organizing with its political strategy, textiles might remain a prime target, not only because of the number of workers involved but also because Virginia, North Carolina, and Georgia still provide antilabor forces with a power base.

✍

Bill Clinton's two terms in the White House have not changed the conservative political climate; among other reasons, he is a product of postliberal Southern politics, and he shares many of its precepts. As governor of Arkansas he followed the New South policy: keep taxes low and encourage new capital investment in a union-free environment. In evaluating the Clinton presidency as well as the decline of liberal politics in the United States over the last thirty years, one must take into account the growing economic and political power of the South. With the election of John Sweeney, the House of Labor seems once more convinced that organizing is its central task. That being so, it must once again place new emphasis on the South. No other aspect of organizing will be as great a determinant of labor's future.

4 ⚄ The Working Poor:
Raising the Bottom

IT WAS MAINLY the workers, and their unions, who successfully fought poverty in America. The mass strikes, demonstrations, factory occupations, and the power of the organizations that emerged from them eventually brought to the fore the practical definition of decent living standards. Before 1936, the New Deal did two important things that addressed the urgent needs of American workers: through the federal relief program it alleviated the suffering of many and established a guaranteed income on the basis of a new official poverty standard; and, through President Roosevelt's rhetorical skill, it offered hope to millions who had abandoned hope by promising to cure the epidemic poverty, hunger, and disease that had spread in the land since the late 1920s. But it was organized labor's surge that actually raised living standards for millions of people, transformed their own and their children's aspirations and expectations, and, in effect, stimulated economic growth and technological innovation.

About a quarter of the population have, however, not shared the bounty. Official statistics show that only about a sixth of Americans are poor, but that means forty million people. Also, as we shall see, official measures are based on a miserly idea of how much income people actually need in order to live. Most poor people are coded as "white," but the poor are overrepresented among racial minorities, women, and children. In fact, in 1995 the Department of Health and

Human Services reported that by the year 2000 one of every four of America's children would be poor. And, given recessions and punitive social welfare policies, the historic decline in the proportion of poor to the population has been reversed.

During the postwar years of economic expansion, poverty was politically construed as the special problem of a few groups: blacks (sometimes coded as the "inner cities"); "depressed areas" such as the mining towns of the Appalachians and the textile mill towns of New England; and youth. Edward R. Murrow's 1960 documentary "Harvest of Shame" excited the liberal conscience in a time of unparalleled affluence and contributed to the unprecedented War on Poverty. Because of the Cold War, which put pressure on the United States to deal with its domestic poverty, and because of the military buildup in Vietnam, in which minorities played an enormous role, Presidents Kennedy and Johnson each proposed a massive effort to address the problem. Many enthusiastically agreed, and some joined the crusade to eradicate "poverty amidst affluence." But when the Vietnam War ended, the boom receded and unemployment rose.

In the 1970s and 1980s, the economic restructuring began to affect workers and a segment of professionals and managers, but it was the conservatives, not labor or the liberals, who offered explanations and solutions. Their ideas succeeded in almost obliterating what once everybody knew, that the Great Depression, with its ensuing recessions, was a failure of the market system. Instead, they attributed economic stagnation, falling wages, deindustrialization, and corporate downsizing to "big government," especially income guarantees. State intervention into the economy, they said, stifled growth by imposing heavy taxes, money that would otherwise be spent in buying goods and thereby creating jobs. That these payments made up only a small fraction of the federal government's budget failed to lessen the impact of this absurd claim. Nor did welfare critics mention that the poor spent nearly all of their meager income on necessities. These arguments were widely used in the tax revolt of the 1970s, aimed at shrinking the public sector. Categorically denying that poverty was a structural economic issue, using recycled free-market clichés, conservatives shifted the blame to the victims and to the governmental policies that addressed their suffering. Transfer payments to the poor, they insisted, should be ended, because they produced a "cycle of dependency." On the assumption that there was no shortage of jobs, they declared that the task of public policy was to help the poor become self-reliant.

Scorned as right-wing poor-bashing, these arguments at first failed to disconcert the proponents of a generous welfare state. What did the job, though, was a subtle shift in conservative ideology toward defining poverty as an individual pathology, the cure for which was imposed work. During the 1980s, some offered an even more sophisticated variant on this theme: those living on public handouts and having many children, whom the government would support, have made a "rational choice" since the government did away with any incentive to work.[1] From this followed the ideas of compulsory work programs, regardless of whether such support services as child care were available, and — the liberal solution — compulsory work with services. Under either program, the welfare recipient would have no choice.

By the time of the 1996 presidential election, "ending welfare as we know it" had become the battle cry of nearly all sections of the narrowing spectrum of American politics; liberal officials joined conservatives in espousing the doctrine of "tough love." Within a year after Bill Clinton signed welfare "reform," abrogating the sixty-year-old law providing income guarantees, hundreds of thousands of people, on penalty of losing their benefits, went to work in public agencies at minimum wages. Owing to tighter eligibility rules, a million recipients were dropped from the rolls, and many working at low-wage jobs lost food stamps and were denied partial checks.

The irony of matching poverty with social welfare is that most of the poor do work; only five million adults receive full public assistance payments. The poverty level is defined according to income criteria: $14,200 a year for a household of four and $8000 for an adult individual. A fifth of the workforce, or about 22 million workers, qualify as poor and are eligible for some federal benefits. But if under

$20,000 were taken as the realistic family poverty line, the proportion of the poor to the workforce would rise to 30 percent — or about forty million workers. Many of them earn "too much" to qualify for government programs, and their employers offer no benefits. These workers constitute the second tier of the wage system. Often, they make up much of the temporary and contingent workforce and must work two or more part-time jobs to earn even a poverty wage.

The paradox of the 1990s' rising employment is that labor short-ages have failed to appear except for a relatively narrow group in the high-skilled categories. Despite the low official jobless rate, there are still more than nine million workers waiting for jobs. This reserve labor supply dampens the chance that employed workers can reverse the steady decline of their real wages that began in 1973. The "hot" economy created three million jobs in 1996, about half of them pay-ing minimum wages (and half of those temporary or part time). As long as the labor reserves stay high, wages, especially at the bot-tom, are likely to stay low. In the short run low wages do help raise profits, which, in turn, result in investment. But if new capital is put into labor-saving technologies, investment may not produce more jobs than it destroys. And eventually wage stagnation will lead to slower growth. The combination could be deadly for the economy as well as for workers. Despite job-creation moves between 1992 and 1997, market forces were decisively on the employers' side. Without a strong labor movement to bid up wages, there is no reason to expect things to change. Only an aggressive effort to organize millions of the unorganized working poor and many others who have suffered wage erosion can reverse the sinking living standards of half the working population.

WHO ARE THE POOR?

At the turn of the twentieth century the poor consisted of practi-cally every semiskilled industrial worker and nearly all farm laborers. Even many skilled workers never had steady work; most worked in the needle trades, and construction was seasonal. Well paid for the months they were employed, they had to live on those wages during the parched season of unemployment. And the money never was enough. So some craftspersons worked "off the books" at home or in an illegal shop in order to make ends meet. (My grandfather, a clothing cutter, was a pretty good off-season card player. He said that occupation sometimes paid more than he earned in the shop.) Loggers, sawmill workers, seamen, and oilfield workers suffered the pain of casual labor. The unemployed were, in fact, working people who had not yet found a job to replace the lost one. Of course, some fell through the cracks in the labor market and, mostly to escape poverty, became inhabitants of the older underground economy. They were thieves, prostitutes, and those who labored outside the law. But domestic workers, family day-care workers (women who took neighborhood kids into their homes and were paid in cash), and many who performed casual or day labor "off the books" were also in this chronically underreported segment of the economy. For many, the legal minimum hourly wage would have been a welcome raise.

Many laborers "lacked the resources necessary to permit participation in the activities, customs, and diets commonly approved by society."[2] This conception of poverty goes far beyond the official government definition, which is based on politically contested minimum nutrition standards, a chronically out-of-date estimate of housing costs, and transportation resources in an era when mass transit is either unavailable or cost-prohibitive. The implied official-measure poverty exists only when a family has failed to earn enough to scrape by. Accordingly, under official eyes, those who have escaped the most searing version of material deprivation are "middle class," a catch-all category based on a range of income — from $20,000 to $200,000 a year — that, without distinction, absurdly embraces the majority of the population.

Poverty should not be measured by the criteria of bare survival. These standards fail to reckon what an individual or family requires to "participate" in the historical levels of material culture, where the term *historical* signifies that, in the United States, the family can afford the elements of what society regards as middle-class consumption.

What are the real measures of poverty? When people have no home of their own and, since most cities and towns in America have no rent control, are subject to eviction from their apartments or houses? When they are unable to purchase nutritionally adequate foods, such as fresh fruits and vegetables, now regarded as important health measures? When they lack means of communication and transportation, such as adequate telephone service, and are forced to drive dilapidated cars or rely on unreliable public transportation to get to work?

It is no accident that the pioneers of the labor movement recognized that raising living standards was a democratic effort. They placed the idea of reasonable wages in the larger perspective of "living standards." Yes, higher wages would enable many to put meat and butter as well as bread on the table, to buy the kids new shoes, to pay the rent on time. But, for the early unions, high wages, shorter hours, and steady work were also conditions for establishing industrial citizenship for the dispossessed and ending their disregard by society. Shorter hours would enhance workers' chances to participate in the wider world: in education, politics, cultural life, and recreation. The recent bumper sticker THE AMERICAN LABOR MOVEMENT: THE PEOPLE THAT BROUGHT YOU THE WEEKEND expresses one of the crucial elements of this vision. Raising wages was a way to end the grinding economic poverty that afflicted many factory workers; achieving shorter hours was the way to overcome cultural poverty.

THE ORIGINS OF THE TWO-TIER WAGE SYSTEM

It was after World War II that American workers came to be divided into two wage tiers. In the first tier are the millions of industrial workers and service employees who enjoy the benefits of union organization (whether union members or not) or, as professionals, are able to bid up their salaries through credentials and knowledge. Until the mid-1970s this tier comprised 70 percent of the workforce. Even though union wage leadership eroded in the 1980s and in some industries shifted to the nonunion sector, the thirty years of union dominance is still felt throughout the first tier. Factory wages, somewhat deteriorated although not lower in money terms, remain on average almost three times the minimum wage and within most industries union wages exceed those of the nonunion sector.

In the second tier are those whom the great organizing surge of the 1930s passed by: over a million farmworkers, most of whom are not migrants, as popular images have it, but stable wage workers or tenants; most of the rapidly growing retail sector; many factory workers in small shops, and, of course, most in the South, even in many large plants; domestics, day laborers, chauffeurs, taxicab drivers, and other contingent and temporary workers; the long-term unemployed, some of whom move in and out of the labor force and others who are more or less permanently unemployed because of physical or mental handicaps; age (a designation that by the 1970s meant a worker was over fifty); and youth (between sixteen and twenty-one), especially blacks and Latinos but also a substantial number of whites. Before 1965, perhaps half of public-sector, health, and social service employees in the nonprofit voluntary sector earned incomes that placed them in the second tier. As we have seen, only the great union boost among some of these groups succeeded in changing their status. Most of the working poor in the current labor market earn less than the official poverty income line for a family of four; that is, less than $50 a day, which, for a five-day week, amounts to $12,500 a year.

The two-tier system got started during the huge Southern and immigrant influx into the cities between 1950 and 1990, when good jobs were leaving and women by the millions were entering the low-wage service sectors. But unlike earlier times, when the progressive labor movement was the tribune of the poor — many of them immigrants — organized labor after the war perhaps identified with the more affluent layers of American society. From 1940 until the mid-1970s the wage gap between union members and nonunion labor steadily widened. Wage gains won by unions gave new meaning to the idea of a decent standard of living. Many industrial workers sported the appearances of the new middle class of professionals: homes, cars, appliances, and eating habits. Labor economists attributed this success to what some called the "segmented" labor market; it was the second tier that restricted opportunities for many workers, and it had few avenues of escape. They linked the secondary labor market to structural factors: lack of educational credentials, immigration, race, gender and age discrimination, and to the distinction between low-profit, highly competitive sectors and the industries controlled by a few giant corporations.

Some writers, rejecting this structural explanation, claimed that if race, gender, and age, together with lack of credentials and literacy, were barriers to good jobs, then poverty could be overcome by legislation barring discrimination. Having successfully guided a comprehensive Civil Rights Act through Congress, the Johnson administration adopted the premise that there was a "skills gap," not a shortage of jobs. With a few exceptions, it abandoned the New Deal's approach to job creation, which assumed that poverty inhered in the economic system. But legislation, training, and America's vaunted economic growth after the war could reduce the huge labor reserves by no more than half. The poor still made up about 20 percent of the population in 1969, the apex of prosperity. The War on Poverty was financed by the expanded tax and deficit income derived from the bloated war economy, but Richard Nixon gradually ended many Vietnam-era income programs, and with the economic stagnation of the 1970s and early 1980s, labor reserves rose again.

It should not be said that union practices alone are responsible for the two-tier wage system — farmworkers have suffered particular exploitation throughout U.S. history and now, too, as the flood of Latin American, Caribbean, and Asian immigrants swells the ranks of the poor. One cannot ignore labor's failure — in some cases, refusal — to organize the highly competitive sectors after the war. But the explanation based on a deficit of skills does not account for all the facts. In the late 1990s, for example, millions of workers in leading production industries and in transportation and construction, who do not have educational credentials or more than average reading ability, are earning annual incomes in excess of $40,000, some as high as $70,000. Auto workers' earnings in mass-production jobs are not linked primarily to skills; indeed, except for the skilled trades, which constitute about 15 percent of the labor force, most are classified as semiskilled and require only on-the-job training to perform their tasks.

In most instances, skills of first-tier workers are no greater than those of many in the second tier who earn half their incomes. When there is no acute labor shortage, collective organizing among workers is the decisive factor in constructing wages. In a unionized General Motors plant in Houston, say, a black assembly-line worker earns, like his white workmate, $20 an hour, yet many skilled garment workers earn between $6 to $15 an hour. A Latino woman working as a cook's helper in a unionized New York hospital kitchen makes about $35,000 a year for a thirty-five-hour week, or about $19 an hour; a worker performing the same duties in a nonunion restaurant in the same city earns $10 or less. Nor are all first-tier workers employed in industries dominated by a few large corporations. Trucking, air transportation, and construction are highly competitive even in cities where large employers predominate. What accounts for the difference? All of these workers benefit from high union densities and the state regulations achieved during the organizing phase of unionism.

ORGANIZE OR DIE

Raising wages and living standards for millions in the second tier will be a long and difficult task. If pushing up wages begins at the bottom, as the new AFL-CIO leadership has accurately declared, there will be at least four major hurdles on the move to the top. There are, as noted, the huge labor reserves poised to enter the labor force at minimum wages. Many of the low-wage jobs into which the new entrants are being pushed by welfare reform are in the public sector; these are jobs formerly held by union members earning decent wages. Consequently, public-sector layoffs have concentrated on the lowest wage categories. Second, millions employed in fast-food restaurants, department stores, hotels, and other retail trades earn the minimum wage or slightly more, and many are part-timers with no health insurance and other benefits. Their jobs are uncertain, and labor turnover is rapid and high. Third, casual and part-time jobs are increasing, and many of them are underground, that is, in the illegal economy. Most of the workers who hold these jobs are immigrants and earn wages below the legal minimum. And home work has returned to the margins of the American workplace. Some do what was once defined as office work: putting labels on envelopes, telemarketing, and word processing. While hourly wages are not always low, these are typically part-time, no-benefit jobs. Finally, the manufacturing sector, once a bastion of unionism, now employs more nonunion than union workers. In many industrial plants people work at the poverty level or below. Some once heavily unionized industries, such as apparel, auto and other machine parts, and food processing, which are vulnerable to capital flight and global competition, pay wages that have slipped in the last decade from the first to the second tier.

Unions can bid up wages through tightening labor supply, mostly by reducing hours and by legislation and organizing. As we know, the labor market is not tight now, either for low-wage jobs or for many high-wage jobs. The high-wage unionized auto, steel aircraft, and electrical industries have not increased working staff for more than fifteen years. The employers meet rising production requirements by introducing labor-saving technologies and insisting on overtime. As a result, unionized labor is often unable to keep up with even the fairly modest inflation rate, about 3 percent. But since the wage gap between semiskilled jobs in highly unionized industries and similar work in the nonunion sector remains wide — two or three to one — union wages are under siege from the growing nonunion sector.

In order to protect union wage levels, the labor movement must fight on all fronts, one of which is the federal minimum wage. In 1995, the AFL-CIO, with some success, spearheaded the fight to force a recalcitrant Congress to raise it, in two steps, to $5.15 an hour — $2 below France and $2.50 below Germany, but still a win. At the local level — in Baltimore, New York, Minneapolis, San Francisco, for example — unions, together with their allies in organizations of the poor, like ACORN (about which more later), have fought for living wage legislation, which requires companies doing business with city or country governments to pay a wage well above the federal minimum. These are important gains, but living wage legislation applies only to public contracts, so its effect is limited.

Another strategy is to force employers to increase the number of jobs. All over Europe the labor movement and its political parties have demanded shorter hours to reduce the double-digit unemployment rates. In 1997, leading a majority coalition in the legislature, the French premier, Leon Jospin, declared the thirty-five-hour week his government's policy. The largest union in Germany, the Metalworkers, has signed agreements with employers to gradually reduce the work week to thirty-five five hours, and Italian and Spanish labor have made shorter hours one of their leading demands. Thus far, despite job-destroying technologies and profound changes in work organization, which have thinned the manufacturing workforce, transformed the office, and cut deeply into professional and technical jobs, the American labor movement has not taken up the matter of shorter hours as a tool for tightening labor markets and raising wages.

The consequence is that the work week is growing longer. Despite business's lament about lagging productivity, fewer workers are producing more than ever, and corporate profits continue to climb. American labor must wage a shorter-hours campaign both at the bargaining table and in the legislature. Some workers and their unions are already demanding more hiring in companies with which they have contracts. The union successfully cracked the two-tier wage system at UPS, we saw, and GM was forced to hire thousands when workers refused to accept overtime assignments. But in many other sectors, such as retail food and department stores, the unions have allowed the growth of part-time work rather than insisting that the companies hire more full-time workers.

A third strategy is to organize the unorganized, particularly the working poor. Anyone familiar with the labor movement after World War II was probably astonished by the declaration of John Sweeney, shortly after taking office as president of the AFL-CIO, that organizing would be a high priority of his administration. For, despite some relatively modest efforts under previous AFL-CIO presidents after the 1955 merger of the two organizations, organizing has been pretty much left to the affiliates. It is true that Sweeney's immediate predecessors authorized modest (but ill-fated) coordinated organizing campaigns in the South and gave some money and political support to the California Farmworkers, but they did not commit the movement to fighting the two-tier wage system. Recognizing that the situation had become a crisis, Sweeney announced an organizing fund of $20 million, primarily to recruit workers in the lowest-paid categories, and began to keep his promise by targeting the Northern California strawberry fields and providing assistance to several campaigns organized by affiliates in food processing and among hotel workers in New York, Los Angeles, and in Las Vegas.

Of course, as the historical experience of the South demonstrates, the cost of clinging to the union's established base without undertaking organizing as the primary task, some unions in the private sector have shrunk to less than half of their membership in the last twenty-five years. Corporate mergers and computerization have taken a considerable toll on employment, as has the dispersal of production and distribution, mainly to nonunion shops. But unless unions relentlessly adopt an organizing model, eventually they will be marginalized. Beyond this consideration, union collaboration with various forms of outsourcing only exacerbates the trouble, because the little secret of the deal is that the union agrees, in effect, not to make an effort to organize the nonunion contractors. Or, in a campaign like the Auto Workers recent unionization of a leading low-wage supplier of auto upholstery, the first contract maintained the two-tier wage system.

The trouble is that most public- and private-sector unions have taken the line of least resistance. More unions in the private sector have sanctioned outsourcing in return for employers' promises not to lay off the existing labor force. In these instances, many employers continue to send out the work, so, as production expands, the unionized sector of the workforce shrinks through retirement and "buyouts." Revenue-starved or conservative local and state governments are laying off employees even as they outsource their work to

private contractors or force welfare recipients to take jobs for minimum wages on penalty of losing their checks. Some unions have
protested layoffs but many, such as District Council 37, New York's
large union of hospital, clerical, and blue-collar public employees,
went along with these practices.

There are, fortunately, exceptions to the dismal record of organizing among the working poor. The Hotel and Restaurant Employees
and the Building Trades have launched a joint drive to organize
forty-thousand low-paid workers in Las Vegas. Under the leadership
of John Wilhelm, the hotel union's secretary treasurer, who led the
successful organizing drive among maintenance and clerical workers
at Yale, it has departed from the standard practice of focusing on one
employer at a time and has avoided primary reliance on the Labor
Relations Board. Instead, like UNITE in the South, organizers have
asked employers to recognize the union by "card checks," that is,
comparing union authorization cards with the payroll. Among other
examples of aggressive organizing are the separate efforts of New
York's Hospital Workers, Service Employees Local 144, and District
Council 1707 of the State, County, and Municipal Employees. Together, they have put together collective-bargaining agreements for
thirty-five thousand low-paid home health-care workers. Cooperating with the community-based national poor peoples' organization
ACORN, Service Employees locals in Chicago and the Southwest succeeded in unionizing more than ten thousand home health-care
workers employed by the state or by companies that have contracts
with public and voluntary hospitals. And the Laborers union has
organized the two thousand workers, largely immigrants, in New
York's dangerous asbestos-removal industry. It is also undertaking
serious organizing efforts at auto parts factories in the South, most
recently in Mississippi.

WE STAND OUTCAST AND STARVING

The long, valiant fight to bring up the bottom in spite of organized
labor's indifference is illustrated by the story of an all-but-forgotten

union, the Southern Tenant Farmers Union (STFU), which pioneered the organization of farmworkers, especially in the South and
in California. Although it would hardly be considered successful by
today's measures — it failed to achieve collective bargaining in its
twenty-five-year existence, which ended in 1960 — many of its policies and practices inspired efforts by community and labor organizers, notably the United Farm Workers and ACORN. It steadfastly
insisted on building a multiracial union; it was one of the modern-day
inventors of social movement unionism, especially by its deft combination of direct action and legislative reform; and it was one of the
earliest of the grassroots democratic unions, one in which the members had the determining voice in all matters of union policy.

The interracial vision of the key leaders of the STFU — H. L.
Mitchell; Clay East, a former sharecropper; and the leading black
organizer, E. B. McKinney — prevailed over those who, for reasons of
belief or fear, argued that the union could not succeed if it disturbed
Southern traditions by remaining integrated. The success of its strikes
and demonstrations restored confidence in the union, which had
earlier been disrupted by the race issue. But its history does illustrate
the severe problems of organizing among the working poor. With
almost no money to carry on its work, the union had to be a client of
the rest of the labor movement and of the progressive middle class.
Farmworkers were, and remain, too financially strapped to support a
staff of organizers, lobbyists, lawyers, and researchers, all of which
they sorely needed to confront the power of the growers and the
federal and local governments with which farm-business interests
were usually allied. Before passage of the 1970s California Farm Labor Relations Act, farmworkers were unable to turn to government,
because liberal *and* conservative administrations alike were on the
growers' side.

When Cesar Chavez, born of a farmworker's family and himself a
sometime farm laborer, took the first steps in 1962 to organize a
union in the California fields, he was working for the Community
Service Organization (CSO), a child of Saul Alinsky's Industrial Areas
Foundation and of the Catholic Church, to which it (and he) had

strong ties. In the environment of the 1960s social movements, the chances for building a strong union among field workers rose dramatically, and Chavez formed the National Farm Workers Association, the immediate predecessor of today's United Farm Workers (UFW). With the work and enthusiasm of hundreds of student and radical activists, his group attracted a substantial supply of volunteer organizers, lawyers, researchers, and office employees. The liberal conscience — which, as Ernesto Galarza, a long-time organizer of California farmworkers, had noted, with irony and bitterness, "flickered and died down like a firefly" — was flickering again. So where earlier organizers had had to beg and borrow pennies, Chavez was the beneficiary of the social philanthropy of a number of organizations outside the labor movement.

In effect, the United Farm Workers was the semiofficial 1960s social movement of the AFL-CIO. While sharing much of the basic trade union philosophy of the mainstream labor movement — it had learned to collect dues, keep books, and sign contracts — it also shared the militant, anti-establishment direct-action tactics and the nonviolent political orientation of the radical wing of the Southern civil rights movement and of the old National Farm Labor Union; which Chavez's father had joined in the 1940s. There was much to be learned from these mentors, especially the importance of developing among the workers a grassroots leadership and a rank and file prepared to take direct action. From Galarza, both Chavez and the union's vice president, Dolores Huerta, who some believe was the real day-to-day leader of the union, learned to marshal the skills of countless volunteers to combat the growers' formidable power. From Alinsky, they learned that movements of the poor thrive on a "liberal conscience," which, through dramatic tactics that get press attention, can force the middle class to bear witness to economic suffering and social injustice. But conscience had its limits. As the workers discovered, compassion is easily exhausted and turns to pity unless there are commitments born of self-interest or social ideology.

They learned another invaluable lesson: in order to succeed against a powerful antiunion employer, they had to keep mobilizing workers and expanding the core of activists; it was not enough to get them to sign union cards. The movement had to be a calling, not a job or an avocation. Mobilization entailed using all the social movement tools: job actions, mass marches, and frequent demonstrations and rallies. The Farm Workers leadership risked internal splits in order to cultivate cordial relations with the AFL-CIO, an alliance that some feared might subject them to bureaucratic domination. Chavez and Huerta were convinced, however, that affiliation was worth the risk. The union did manifest its independence by reaching well beyond mainstream trade union networks; it found support in the emerging student movement, the civil rights movement (especially the Student Nonviolent Coordinating Committee), liberal organizations, local unions, even the powerful but outcast West Coast Longshoremens and Warehousemens union.

A major element of the UFW approach was its use of defining symbols: a flag dominated by a large spread eagle was present at every march, picket line, demonstration, and on every piece of literature; the constantly invoked slogan "*Viva la causa, viva la huelga*" signified that the union was a movement that aimed to change the lives of farmworkers, not just raise wages and improve working conditions. The *huelga* in question, the celebrated strike and boycott against California grape growers, grew to national proportions and, through the union's ability to present the struggle within the context of the 1960s political culture, attracted millions of supporters. In 1970, after defeating a grower-inspired challenge, in dozens of elections it had gathered enough strength to force a broad-based settlement with the growers, including the old farmworkers' nemesis, the DiGiorgio family. The first contract doubled the basic wage, provided housing and education funds for farmworkers, and established the union as a recognized and respected force in California agriculture.

From the beginning, Chavez and the UFW understood that, in addition to organizing the workers themselves, *la causa* required a three-pronged effort: to abrogate the growers' absolute power in the fields; to break the collaboration by various levels of government — the Immigration and Naturalization Service, politicians, and local law-enforcement agencies — with the growers; to rouse a sleeping public to the plight of the farmworkers; and to extend the movement's alliance with the Mexican as well as the mainstream United States labor movement. The leadership had to walk a thin line. On the one hand, they evoked the contradictory, semireligious symbols of revolution, especially "liberation"; on the other, they sought the support of a relatively conservative labor movement, which saw itself in the liberal rather than radical democratic tradition. Then, institutional demands and the conservative backlash, signified by the rise to national power of former California governor Ronald Reagan, overwhelmed the movement. In the last eighteen years of Chavez's reign, UFW became more like other unions. It all but ceased organizing and gradually became a business union of a surprisingly autocratic type.

Some of the change was inevitable; no social movement can maintain a frenetic level over a long stretch of time. Organizers burn out and crave a little stability in their lives and a little more money for their labors. And, of course, the Farm Workers victories did not remain uncontested. As rising labor costs threatened profit margins, and dealing with a union that had mobilized public support sapped their energies, the growers lost no time in trying to undermine the union's position. They introduced labor-saving machines that replaced many hand operations, especially picking. While the UFW had emerged from this intense organizing period with twenty-seven thousand members, ironically the Teamsters became perhaps the main beneficiary of its militancy. Although not as well organized as UFW in the fields, the Teamsters represented drivers. Nevertheless, the long struggle to establish a living wage for farmworkers had reached a new level, at least in California. And for the first time since the AFL had recognized the old National Farm Labor Union twenty years earlier, the UFW won AFL-CIO jurisdiction for workers in the fields. But the fight was not over.

Flush from a string of triumphs, the UFW, which for all practical purposes was a California organization, successfully led organized labor and its coalition partners in 1975 to push a new Agriculture Labor Relations Act through the state legislature. The law enhanced its organizing drive by guaranteeing workplace access to union organ-

izers, providing an election procedure, and, contrary to the antiboy-
cott provision of the Federal Labor Relations Act, ensuring the union's boycott rights. But the act's enforcement agent, the Agricultural
Labor Relations Board, was woefully underfunded. It was unable to
police mounting grower violations, and after 1976 the union, which
depended on the combined power of workers in the field, the law,
and a sympathetic public, began a steep decline. Until Chavez's death
in 1993, UFW sustained steady membership losses and suffered many
internal rifts, not the least of which was mass staff defections result-
ing from Chavez's surprisingly authoritarian leadership. By the mid-
1980s Chavez had lost the public's confidence. Besieged by growers' lawsuits and distracted by internal strife, he relied on a few
loyalists and cast off his long-time allies. Shortly after his death, a
new generation of activists and organizers began to revive the union's
best traditions; they have undertaken new organizing campaigns,
this time with full AFL-CIO support, to extend the union's power to
other branches of California agriculture, especially the northern
strawberry fields. Whether the momentum of this group will be
sufficient to restore the union remains to be seen. Workers in cotton,
sugar, fruit, and vegetable fields outside California and New Jersey
are still not organized. But the main strategy, social movement unionism, seems to have become widely acknowledged as the only way
forward.

WORKING TO GET A WELFARE CHECK

The separation of problems at the workplace from workers' community concerns is accepted by most union leaders as both necessary and
desirable. Typically, they contend that, though the idea of a "community union" may have merit, given limited money and staff and the
concern of adequately addressing workplace issues, such a change
might dilute a union's ability to perform essential functions. But for
unions of the working poor, the accepted doctrine of "business unionism" is losing ground, and for good reason.

Many local unions have come to understand the inseparability of
aspects of a member's life. Since the poor often consider organiza-

tions like the PTA, the local political club, and other voluntary agencies to be exclusionary, their opinions are almost completely absent in the institutions of civil society. Now, with the end of the poverty programs, they and their families are deprived of services available to middle-class and first-tier working-class people. Many union members in low-wage occupations are in the same boat as the nonunion poor: they face eviction from their homes; their children are frequently expelled or suspended from the school; and sometimes they find themselves or their children in prison. The foreign-born, fearing deportation, keep their mouths shut on the job and in the face of the landlord. Finance companies are constantly weighing them down with bloated interest rates for furniture, appliances, used cars.

Responding to these conditions — and acknowledging their inability to deliver substantial wage and benefit increases — some big-city local unions have created service organizations to address members' problems outside the workplace. These provide attorneys when members or their children are in trouble with the law; social workers to represent kids kicked out of school and to negotiate with health and welfare agencies about members' hospital admissions, bills, and food stamps, and to address unemployment and financial problems. Others, such as UNITE, the Longshoremen, and some construction unions, have for decades maintained health centers for members and their families. In recent years a number of New York unions representing public employees and the working poor, especially immigrants and minorities, have, with the assistance of state and federal funds, offered basic education, the general education diploma (GED), and English-language classes for members and their families. Today there are more than forty-thousand students in union-sponsored literacy programs all over New York. Classes are held in union halls and offices, community agencies, and workplaces.

One of the more powerful links between workplace and community is being forged by organizers for ACORN, the national poor peoples' organization. Begun in Little Rock, Arkansas, by Wade Rathke in 1970, it is devoted to community "empowerment" along the model developed by the Industrial Areas Foundation and by the Southern Tenant Farmers Union. It works in the "them against us" style, rather than seeking cooperative relationships with political and corporate establishments, and leans toward direct action instead of legislative solutions, although it pays considerable attention to electoral politics. Brandishing ACORN's slogan — "The People Will Rule" — two of its members were elected in 1994 to the Little Rock City Council on a third-party ticket. It has played an active role in living wage coalitions in many cities. Currently with headquarters in New Orleans, Washington, Brooklyn, Chicago, and Little Rock, ACORN has grown to a national organization comprising 150,000 members in a thousand chapters in nearly every large city in the country.

From the start, it has concentrated on organizing for tenants' rights, jobs, affordable housing, better schools, and other neighborhood improvements. Its strategy is to build "multiracial local organizations," led by poor people, and to foster their voices in public life. Like the Farm Workers, ACORN has learned to pay its way by combining the financial resources from liberal organizations with membership dues. Jon Kest, the chief New York organizer, proudly told me that membership dues now make up 40 percent of the organization's funds.[3] In New York, where ACORN has thirty chapters and about twenty thousand members, dues are $5 a month except for a new constituency, workers in the city government's Work Experience Program (WEP), who pay $10 a year. Most of its focus is on the city's sprawling housing projects — in the Bronx, it has organized about a thousand units — but in June 1997, ACORN made headlines when it unexpectedly filed for a representation election with thirteen thousand authorization cards for the thirty-five thousand WEP workers under the state's public employees' labor law. New York City's Office of Collective Bargaining refused to accept the cards, declaring that WEP workers were not employees under the meaning of the act, but were "trainees," gaining the experience and skills needed to enter the workforce.

How did New York ACORN, which began as a neighborhood-based organization, get involved in workplace organizing? Having put down firm roots among the poor in several Midwest and Southern states, where public employees' and other unions are either weak or absent, it was obliged to follow its members from the neighborhood to the workplace, sites of abysmal wages and working conditions. It recruited thousands of home health-care workers in Chicago, and hospital workers and other low-wage service employees in Texas, Louisiana, and Arkansas. ACORN did not itself become a collective-bargaining agent, but it negotiated an affiliation with the Service Employees (SEIU), which, as we have seen, actively sought to forge alliances with social movements. It became allied with several of the recently formed locals, particularly Chicago's Local 880, with eight thousand home health-care workers, and New Orleans's Local 100, which, before affiliating with SEIU, was an independent union of low-wage domestic workers, for whom it demanded minimum-wage compliance. Soon it evolved into a full-fledged union among hotel, catering, and service workers, with NLRB victories in New Orleans's Hyatt Regency Hotel and an overwhelming win among Tulane University's contract catering and cafeteria workers. Many workers ACORN organized pay dues to both organizations, and Wade Rathke sits on the SEIU national executive board.

The immediate impetus for organizing the New York WEP workers, which was the nation's largest experiment to undermine public employees' unionism, was serendipitous. Kest says it started in November 1996, when many of its members on public assistance were ordered by the city's Department of Social Services (which administers the WEP program) to report for work. Most of them were assigned to the Sanitation Department, where eight thousand WEP workers were employed mainly in street cleaning. Others worked in the Parks Department, the Health Department, and in hospitals. Soon members were reporting grievances: being forced to work more than the required twenty hours, being subjected to unsafe working conditions, and being badly treated by management. In some instances, they were warned not to complain under penalty of losing their welfare checks.

It was evident that DC 37, the 120,000-member public-employees' union whose members were being displaced by WEP, was not going to organize them, nor were more sympathetic unions about to get involved, aware of DC 37's clear jurisdiction. Reluctantly, ACORN decided to form an independent union and thereby risk the ire of both the city government and the powerful DC 37. Twenty-one staff organizers, half of them WEP workers, and a number of interns recruited from area colleges began getting in touch with workers, beginning at city-sponsored orientation sessions. In April 1997, the *New York Times* called the campaign the area's "most ambitious organizing drive in years." By May, it had recruited a third of the WEP workers into the WEP Workers Organizing Committee, formed committees at some three hundred sites, and conducted dozens of job actions, including sit-ins, to settle grievances, because none of the city departments was willing to establish a grievance procedure. By July, it had over fifteen thousand authorization cards.

Getting cards signed was comparatively easy; convincing workers to take action and resist intimidation proved to be more difficult. But the real challenge came in July, when, nudged by the ACORN campaign, DC 37 — which had allowed the WEP program to expand rapidly and had resisted pressure to organize the workers — announced its own organizing drive. Within weeks, the union's executive director, Stanley Hill, had an "agreement" with Mayor Rudolph Giuliani, the details of which remain vague to this day. But WEP workers still had no bargaining rights. Undeterred, ACORN held a mock election in the fall to put the question of union representation before the media and the voters. Some eighteen thousand WEP workers voted overwhelmingly for union representation. If ACORN's experience in other situations is any guide, WEP workers, with or without active cooperation from the official labor movement, will have a union. Kest has said that he does not expect to transform ACORN into a trade union, but, whatever the outcome of its unionizing efforts, it will remain on the scene as a welfare rights movement. Given the politics of New York labor — its largest locals, including DC 37, have become openly allied with the city's Republican mayor — recognition of ACORN by DC 37 is extremely unlikely.

➤

Labor has, of course, initiated major efforts to organize the poor in many other cases. It has also responded to challenges posed by others. Occasionally, a union's ability to hold the line against an employer's efforts to break it depends on whether it reaches out to community groups. One case in point occurred in the early 1980s in New York Local 23–25 of the Garment Workers, which represents workers in the sportswear industry. Many of the contracting shops were then located in Chinatown and were operated by Chinese employers. There were also some ten thousand workers in other nonunion shops. When the union contract for some five thousand workers came up for renewal in 1983, most members of the employers' association, sensing the union's weakness, announced their intention to break the agreement and run the shops on a nonunion basis. The union, whose relationships with many of its own members was, to say the least, strained, faced almost certain extinction in the community unless it got help. Fortunately, help was forthcoming from prolabor, radical community organizers, who, with the tacit support of the local union leadership, waged a campaign among nonunion workers, as well as union members, to resist union-busting. After a short strike, Local 23–25 succeeded in renewing the existing contracts and signed contracts for an additional ten thousand workers in the nonunion shops. The union-community alliance had saved and extended the union in the industry.

But the story doesn't have a happy ending. Within a few years, many community organizers were openly discontented with the union, which, they contended, was not enforcing the wage and working condition clauses of the contract. Because of the flow of imports, employers were competing with East Asian factories. Moreover, in an era of repressive immigration policy, protesting workers faced possible deportation. Under these circumstances, the union made what some regarded as a Faustian bargain: in order to keep the contracts, the union conceded wages and working conditions. By the late 1980s, child labor had reappeared in many shops, and employers were paying wages below the legal minimum, let alone the union minimum. To be sure, most employers paid into the union-administered health and welfare fund, and many workers were attending union-sponsored English classes. Clearly, the main union benefits for the workers were its services, especially health care.

The Chinatowns of America are huge tourist attractions, and their main industry is restaurants. Like the garment shop employers, restaurant employers have frequently hired undocumented workers and have fiercely resisted unionization. New York's Hotel Trades Council, whose base is in the large hotels and some high-priced restaurants, has shown little interest in organizing these workers or in defending them against the frequent raids by the Immigration and Naturalization Service. In 1988 the Chinatown Staff and Workers Association, many of whose activists had supported Local 23–25's fight a few years earlier, opened a Workers Center to address the needs of workers, not only in the restaurant industry but also in the garment shops. Bitterly critical of the established unions, the association and its Workers Center have organized against common employer antilabor practices: stealing waitresses' tips, failing to meet federal wage and hours standards, sexual and other forms of harassment, and exercising brutal authoritarian management. In 1992 the association struck Chinatown's largest restaurant and signed an agreement for its workers. Like ACORN, it is not a typical trade union; it is a community-based movement. Its six hundred dues-paying members and its small full-time staff form labor unions as one element of a large program. On a daily basis the center handles grievances against landlords as well as employers, organizes job actions and rent strikes, solves immigration problems, and conducts educational programs. The center has fiercely protected its independence but, unlike ACORN, is hostile to the AFL-CIO.

But the Workers Center is an idea whose time has come. In 1992, the Garment Workers opened three centers — in Williamsburg and Sunset Park, Brooklyn, and in Manhattan's garment district. In all of them, the union's focus is on organizing workers in shops that may be designated part of the underground or informal economy. These shops, like many in Chinatown, typically employ undocumented workers, children as well as adults, pay below-legal minimum wages, and frequently require employees to work as many as sixty hours a week. Unable to find child care for their children, many workers bring them into poorly ventilated shops, where they work alongside their parents. In 1993 the Williamsburg Workers Center conducted a highly publicized strike for union recognition; it involved some three hundred workers of the Domsey Corporation, a large reconditioner and retailer of used clothing and a member of a nonunion employers' association in the area. The struggle was a bold departure for this fairly cautious union and was the capstone of several years of organizing. The employer, with a bottomless well of undocumented workers at its disposal and support from other area employers, wasted little time in replacing the strikers, most of whom lived in the neighborhood and were Latino. Soon the picket lines dwindled, and, although the union made serious efforts to rally community backing for a boycott, within a few months the strike ended in defeat. Shortly after, the union closed its Williamsburg center.

But the Sunset Park and Manhattan centers remain open. They operate like union locals, have officers, and hold regular membership meetings. UNITE, into which the union merged, has recruited workers in these sweatshops without the immediate prospect of being able to offer them a union contract. On a Saturday afternoon UNITE's Manhattan Labor Center, located in a large, well-lighted loft space on West Fortieth Street, is teeming with people, mostly Spanish-speaking.[4] Some sit in small groups with or without an organizer, discussing problems in their shop; others wait to talk to someone about an immigration problem or another "personal" issue. According to one staffer, UNITE's strategy is to organize the entire industry before it signs a contract with a single employer. Signing an individual employer would, he said, inevitably result in the shop's closing, because raised labor costs would render the company noncompetitive. Some of the center's organizers believe the underground shops cannot be organized except through a general strike, which would either put them out of business or make them legal. As a result, the union, which has two thousand members in the center, has concentrated on helping workers settle their grievances, the most egregious of which is the frequent nonpayment of wages.

Typically, workers stage a sit-in in order to convince employers to pay them on time, to improve ventilation, or to raise piece rates. Direct action is the only way to deal with these issues, because the workers have no recourse to law. If they complain to a government agency, they risk deportation. Above all, it would be futile to strike, because the employer could easily find new workers or would close the plant if the strike succeeded. Yet in 1996 an impatient UNITE leadership did organize one shop in this market. Based on several successful job actions, the union signed a contract with the employer, who promptly closed the shop and discredited the union among the strikers. When the chief organizer of the center, an experienced and intelligent man, protested what he considered a precipitous and self-defeating gesture, he was fired from his job.

The success of unions in highly competitive industries depends, almost always, on its capacity to organize nearly all the employers into an association as much as it does on its recruitment of workers. Of course, this has been a traditional strategy of the needle trades and many other unions. Since illegal shops now make up over half the New York and Los Angeles needle trades, unions like UNITE will have to be patient, spend an inordinate amount of money before they see any appreciable dues, and tolerate considerable turmoil in the industry and among their own members. They will have to delay signing contracts until their base is large enough for them to organize the entire market. Perhaps more important, the old leadership will have to turn over power to the members. And, as in the South, they will have to rely heavily on volunteers, especially shop workers, to carry out most of the organizing work.

Some unions, like SEIU and UNITE, are learning from the social movements that have pioneered in recent years in organizing among the working poor. Others, bred in the postwar business union, often have a harder time accepting this model. The social movement model assumes no reliable alliance between the liberal state, the progressive middle class, and the union, although wherever possible activists and organizers work with government enforcement agencies and with liberal groups. Some of the reluctance to adopt the social movement model — which often entails going over to the opposition — may be traced to labor's historical fear of outsiders. And since one of the entailments of social movement unionism is radical democracy, the leaders fear losing their power. Union leaders who have no trouble supporting militancy on a tactical level are nevertheless disturbed by organizations, like ACORN, that insist that the members themselves make most of the decisions. The notion that leaders should be accountable to the rank and file — a view that remains controversial even among some progressive unions — grates on many officials, long accustomed to wheeling and dealing.

Yet again and again the most successful organizations of the working poor have evoked the symbols and often the practices of radical social change. Moreover, they have been almost consistently antiestablishment even as they negotiate with the establishment. In short, what John Sweeney learned as SEIU president is still not well accepted by most trade union officials: when labor wants to organize, it has no choice but to make alliances with radical intellectuals, activists, and community groups that may have ideologies and values different from those of the unions. And it is the radicals' initiatives that are likely to light the way for organizing those who have hitherto been excluded or marginalized in the mainstream labor movement — as well as in the American economy. For, in the main, the style of unionism that served most workers in the long duration of the regulation era may well have reached its end. Surely, as almost every discerning organizer among the poor has learned, the law, including the contract, has only limited use when employers are able to draw on huge labor reserves and on antilabor, or at least shamelessly pro-business, governments to thwart unions. To organize the millions of near and below-minimum wage workers in America will take more than money. It will require a crusading spirit and the ability to reach beyond the unions to the poor white neighborhoods, ghettoes, barrios, and Asian communities of this country. And it must touch public opinion, which, contrary to what it was thirty years ago, seems to have lost much of its liberal conscience.

5 ✍ White-Collar Workers:
Seeds of Hope?

CLERICAL WORK is the invisible glue of administration. No modern business can do without the people who maintain records, make out bills, keep accounts, sell products, and facilitate communications. As corporations relentlessly replaced family-owned businesses, between the end of World War I and the early 1980s, clerical labor became the fastest growing occupation in the economy. By 1985, there were more than sixteen million of these workers, or about one in six members of the labor force. But despite more than seventy years of continuous growth, they remain among the least unionized. Unlike events in the South and some highly visible attempts to organize the working poor, there has been no signal event to mark union efforts in the white-collar field. As we shall see, many unions have nibbled at the heels of the noncredentialed white-collar workers but have largely ceded this huge group to management.

The noncredentialed white-collar workers have essential skills, but their jobs lack glamor; they are typically performed in back rooms and factory-like environments, where, more and more, the work is subdivided. Clerks are subject to managerial technologies of control, like specialization, and much of the work consists of machine operation. While professionals like accountants (who often perform the work of management as well) enjoy a measure of autonomy, the clerical workers in a large enterprise are relegated to routine, repetitive operations in the enormous head offices of industrial corporations, insurance companies, and major sales organizations, department stores, and mail-order houses, such as Sears and JC Penney.[1]

In the smaller workplace or nonprofit institution — a university or social agency — in addition to her institutional duties the white-collar worker is expected to perform an infinite variety of personal services for the boss: making coffee, depositing his check, answering his telephone, and calling his wife or family when he works late. She may clean his desk and the area around it, make lunch and dinner and theater reservations. With the advent of the computer and voice mail, some executives have lost many of these perks, but the private secretary survives for top management.

The invisibility of clerical and sales work in American culture mirrors public disdain for bureaucracy. Although there are only about eighteen million production and transportation workers and about ten million professionals and managers, these groups maintain a relatively high profile in the American imagination. They signify our almost mystical respect for high academic credentials and, in the case of manual labor, productive work. The industrial worker and truck driver may not be loved but, given his acknowledged power, there is reason for him to be feared. But clerical labor has neither power nor aura, only a kind of grudging indispensability. And since their work is coded as "overhead" cost in an era of computer efficiency and lean corporate organization, clerical workers are being downsized faster than most other categories of employees.

In the first half-century of the corporate era, there were few mentions of the white-collar presence in the workplace or in American politics and culture. The office worker no longer corresponded to Herman Melville's Bartleby, a skilled male copyist in a mid-nineteenth-century Wall Street law firm, or to Dickens's Bob Cratchit, an all-around clerk. Instead, in the expanding corporate offices the clerk became a specialist. The skilled bookkeepers and stenographers were predominantly male, and it was they who tentatively formed unions in the first decades of the twentieth century. Then, with increasing frequency, typists and file clerks were jobs held by women. Until World

War II only 30 percent of women were wage and salary workers, and most performed factory or domestic labor. But after World War I clerical workers constituted a significant portion of women in the wage-labor force. By 1930 the office worker was likely to be a woman; but in this predominantly male work culture, she was all but excluded from power. She was typically assigned to tasks that, in the office hierarchy, were coded as semiskilled and low paid. In many cases she was subordinate to mostly male bookkeepers and accountants, who acted as straw bosses under the general supervision of the office manager.

But it was precisely because office workers were primarily women and their work was considered similar to that of industrial labor that the labor movement, dominated by skilled workers, remained indifferent to their fate. In fact, labor's legislative program tried to keep women from competing with men for some jobs by restricting women's access to certain trades and barring them from working at night. Unlike Great Britain, where important branches of the labor movement were convinced that women's rights were trade union issues, and even campaigned for women's suffrage, both the socialist and the Gompers wings of the AFL remained aloof from what they perceived to be an "upper class" women's movement. That a significant section of working women were more attracted to it than to organized labor is no surprise. The important exception was the needle trade unions, which, with the help of the Womens Trade Union League, actively recruited women sewing machine operators. Otherwise, as it had with blacks, labor remained deaf to the needs of the emerging clerical labor force.

✴

Until around 1960 the moments of glory of white-collar unions were few and far between. The early groups dwelled in the shadows of the craft and industrial unions, whose growth and rivalry dominated discussions of what was the "labor movement." According to the traditional lore, low-level, low-paid office employees were only temporarily at the bottom; they were entry-level workers destined for better things

— skilled labor, management, or, in the case of the millions of young women who streamed into corporate offices, marriage.

White-collar unionism began at the turn of the century, when a mostly male Bookkeepers and Stenographers Union was founded, with a few thousand members. But the AFL refused it admission for the reason that has marred the relations of white-collar workers and organized labor for a century: Samuel Gompers and his colleagues did not believe that most such workers were good union prospects. Although they had skills — for Gompers, a prerequisite for successful labor organization — their loyalties, he believed, tended to be with management. Record keeping and accounting remain to this day the means of providing managers with information, some of which is used against labor. Thus, that the "paper pushers of the world" could become part of the labor movement was seriously contested by most trade unionists, even as the modern corporation became more diverse, and clerical, technical, and professional jobs grew at a rate that exceeded craft and factory employment. By the early 1930s, the AFL was prepared to grant that clericals had some claim to union membership, but, because many of the early clerical unions were organized by radicals, the federation's leaders remained wary. Eventually, under pressure from insurgent white-collar workers, the federation changed its mind. Although it was willing to grant charters to individual locals, it would not agree to the idea of an international union of white-collar workers.

But at a 1936 convention attended by most of the AFL's so-called federal clerical locals — those directly affiliated with the federation — a national union took shape. It quickly gained a foothold among some social service groups and won affiliation with the independent Book and Magazine Guild. That union, unrecognized by the AFL, in 1938 moved to the CIO and remained there until it was expelled eleven years later for being under Communist domination. From the twenty-three locals, with about eighty-five hundred members, represented at the May 1937 convention, less than a year later the United Office and Professional Workers (UOPWA) claimed forty-five thousand members in seventy locals. While UOPWA never had more than fifty-five thousand members, it successfully organized some insurance employees "wall-to-wall" — from clerks to insurance agents. Met Life, Mutual of New York, sections of Prudential, and several smaller companies were under union contract in 1946. In addition to organizing the leading mail-order houses along the Eastern seaboard, UOPWA mounted a drive to unionize bank employees, and by 1947, twelve New York banks were under union contract. Some had been organized through recognition strikes.

Despite its modest numbers, at least by industrial union standards, until 1950 this union demonstrated the falsity of the belief that private-sector white-collar workers could not be organized. But with the labor movement concentrating on the unfinished task of unionizing industrial giants, it received little assistance from the CIO. The Office and Professional Workers, therefore, was a poor union, so it devoted most of its limited resources to organizing. Still, its impact on its areas was strong enough, by the early 1940s, to make the reluctant AFL leadership capitulate: it chartered a new affiliate, the Office Employees International Union (OEIU), later adding "professional" to its name. This union was formed from a combination of mainly trade union office staff and some defectors from the left-wing CIO counterpart. There was, in 1947, an effort to undermine UOPWA's victories in New York's financial district. Under the leadership of Paul Hall of the Seafarers union, the Office Employees mounted an organizing drive on Wall Street under the name of the United Financial Employees. It had modest growth in the postwar era, but, lacking resources and broad labor support, it did not thrive.

The second major group of organized white-collar workers comprised sales and stock clerks employed by department stores and other large retail stores and clerks in the rising retail food industry. From the 1930s through the 1950s the Retail, Wholesale, and Department Store Workers (CIO) and the Retail Clerks (AFL) managed to organize an estimated 400,000 retail workers. Often at each other's throat when vying to represent department store workers, the two unions nevertheless managed to unionize some of the leading retailers in New York, San Francisco, Philadelphia, and Detroit, among them Macy's, Bloomingdale's, Gimbels, Stern's, Wanamaker's, and J. L. Hudson. The victories of the Retail Clerks (now merged into the Food and Commercial Workers) in the supermarkets were even more substantial; on both coasts and in portions of the Midwest, the union succeeded in unionizing nearly all of the leading chains, although its record in rural areas and small towns is more spotty. In New York, District 65 of Retail and Wholesale was the main department store union until the store group separated in the 1960s and directly affiliated with the parent body.

The third group, tens of thousands of telephone operators and clerical workers in the Bell Telephone System, were organized in the late 1930s by a company union. The working conditions of this overwhelmingly female labor force was closer to factory labor than to the popular image of white-collar work. And since the union was organized on an industrial model, it was dominated by the male linemen and mechanics, who, although a minority of the company's employees, set the cultural norm and constituted most of the union's leadership. The low-paid, closely supervised operators worked under tremendous pressure in long rows facing boards powered by electrically driven mechanical switches, and were severely punished for work mistakes, lateness, and absences. In the early 1940s the union — which many in the labor movement believed had been formed to defeat a genuinely independent labor organization, the CIO Electrical Workers — joined the CIO and became the Communications Workers of America (CWA). Over the next thirty years this organization struggled to gain its independence from the American Telephone and Telegraph Company (ATT) and its subsidiaries. Although it had unionized the long-line workers from coast to coast, it was obliged to organize, one by one, the state and local companies. While it usually won the Labor Board representation election (except in New Jersey), in the 1950s and 1960s its members were often forced to stage strikes and job actions to convince the company that the workers were at last free of company domination. In some instances, notably in the South, California, and New York, these strikes were prolonged and bitter, frequently marked by violence and sabotage. After some confrontations with militant workers, ATT moved in the 1960s to solve the problem by getting rid of workers. The company replaced the mechanical switching system with an automated one.

The effect of automation and subsequent computerization was the elimination of tens of thousands of telephone operators' jobs. In the case of long-distance calls, "direct" dialing made the operator redundant except for collect calls, person-to-person calls, and information. Then the electronic voice took over many of these functions as well. During the postwar period, the activism of telephone company workers had thoroughly refuted the myth that women white- and pink-collar workers (pink because some were still unwilling to concede the industrial nature of their jobs but differentiated themselves from secretaries and other more privileged categories) did not really make good union members. Generally acknowledged by the union's predominantly male leadership to be stalwart in their quest for bargaining power and, although decimated in numbers since their heyday in the immediate postwar period, they have become a major force in the development of the Communications Workers into the leading communications union in the country. Through mergers with smaller unions, today the union represents employees of the major broadcasting systems, newspaper reporters, and administrative staff, some public employees, and, most recently, airline white-collar employees.

Otherwise, unionism had barely penetrated most groups of discontented clerical employees in major corporations. Even in the wake of industrial unionism in the 1930s and 1940s, organizing results were meager. In this regard, the Communications Workers is exceptional, and its success may be ascribed partly to the industrial nature of the telephone industry's work. After the expulsion and subsequent collapse of the Office Workers in 1950, the CIO did not bother to charter a union of office workers. And after the failure of the Wall Street campaign, the AFL left the weak Office and Professional Employees to limp along. Despite some limited union victories, to this day millions of white-collar and professional employees in the private sector remain outside unions. Labor as a whole has refused to put its money and its organizing capacity to work, despite evidence in the 1980s and 1990s that the recruitment of private-sector office and professional employees was almost the only bright spot in an otherwise dismal organizing era. Unions that had the foresight to focus on white-collar organizing are the fastest growing in the labor movement. As we have seen, labor's substantive gains since the war have been among largely white-collar public employees.

The 1955 merger of the two federations did not signal that the labor movement intended to reverse its drift; it was narrowing its base. And the costs of that move have been monumental. The labor movement has permitted its detractors to announce boldly that, though unions may be appropriate for factory workers and badly paid blue-collar service workers, they have no place in the office. In an era when white-collar jobs became the fastest-growing sector in the American economy, labor's failure to extend its scope may be — together with its failures in the South — the most powerful factor in its general decline. While factory employment grew by a quarter from 1948 to 1990, retail, wholesale, and white-collar labor more than tripled in the same period. All the union advances into banking, whose expansion was as great as that of insurance, were completely nullified by employer-initiated decertifications.

Since 1949 the huge financial services industry, which today employs millions of white-collar workers, has been an unreservedly open-shop bastion; the Office Employees have unionized a small group of runners in the New York Stock Exchange but almost nobody else. The extent of unionization in this growth industry is less than 1 percent. For example, after the Office Workers union was decertified in some companies, there remained only the Insurance Workers union, whose main contract is for agents of Met Life. And, except for the public sector, unionism among the two million salaried computer professionals, whose work often replaces that of clerical workers, is just about nonexistent. The only union gains in the white-collar field have been among the "old" office workers in small shops in the wholesale trades and in some retail sectors.

Since the 1950s, Teamsters locals and the West Coast Service

Employees have made significant inroads among clericals in smaller private-sector companies. And the Auto Workers, Electrical, and some other industrial unions organized plant-based office and professional workers, using the leverage gained from strong industrial workers' locals. By the 1960s these unions had recruited some 100,000 clerical and technical employees in such large corporations as the big three auto companies, GE, Westinghouse, and Sylvania, and in steel. In addition, given its huge membership in the Midwest auto and agricultural implement industries, the Auto Workers became the major union of university clerical workers in Michigan and a significant force in some Indiana universities. Recognizing the potential of this sector, during the 1970s the Auto Workers formed the Technical, Office, and Professional Department (TOP) and has devoted considerable energy to white-collar organizing by, among other measures, offering to pay for local unions an additional full-time organizer if they hire an organizer with their own funds. The task of organizing workers in private-sector financial corporate offices fell mainly to the Service Employees, whose District 925, an outgrowth of the feminist group Working Women, has made strenuous efforts, though with only modest success, to organize clericals in some insurance companies in Cleveland and upstate New York. Three types of efforts at white-collar organizing will be discussed in more detail: New York's District 65–UAW and its successor, Local 2110–UAW, which spearheaded clerical organizing in universities; and the recent victory by the Communications Workers for US Airways' passenger service staff.

☙

After 1950 some of UOPWA's units were absorbed into the new but short-lived Distributive Workers of America, whose core was New York's twenty-five thousand-member Retail, Wholesale, and Department Store Local 65. Under the visionary leadership of David Livingston, Local 65 (later District 65), poured substantial resources into industrial and clerical organizing. In the 1970s it also made a serious push in publishing, with mixed results. District 65, which disbanded in 1993 (its locals were dispersed into the Auto Workers), was one of the most unusual organizations among labor unions. Led by a coterie of college-educated clerks in New York's wholesale dry-goods industry, who had organized on the Lower East Side in the early 1930s, the union was guided by two major principles throughout its nearly sixty-year existence. Together with Local 1199 — the drugstore union that conducted the monumental hospital workers' organizing drive in the 1960s — it organized wherever possible on a wall-to-wall basis and was a "general workers'" union, meaning that it organized factory workers as well as office workers, warehouse workers as well as professionals. Its collective-bargaining strategy was to bring up the bottom through such means as the so-called solidarity wage. That is, instead of settling for increases on a percentage basis, which kept and even widened wage inequality, it negotiated across-the-board dollar increases aimed at narrowing the gap in employees' pay. In addition, it developed a union-run benefits program, which provided a comprehensive welfare plan for its members, including pension, health and drug, and dental benefits.

Although 65 organized some groups of industrial workers, the majority of its shops were in white-collar categories and employed fewer than a hundred workers each; some, fewer than twenty-five. Like the early needle trade unions, it attempted to organize the entire industry rather than individual employers. And like the apparel workers' unions, it was obliged also to organize the employers into trade associations in order to equalize wages, benefits, and working conditions and to prevent its contracts from driving some employers out of business or out of town.

Until her retirement, in 1980, my mother worked in 65 shops for twenty-seven years as a general office worker and, in the last decade of her working life, was an assistant bookkeeper in a wholesale textile firm on lower Broadway in Manhattan. She was a shop steward and, in step with 65's organizing style, spent many hours as a volunteer organizer. Often, she would rise an hour earlier than usual to go to a particular building near her job, where she would talk to workers from several shops or give out literature. Then she went to work. She was proud of her union even though she never made more than $250 a week. But her relatively low wage did not bother her, because she supported the union's 1970s strategy of building up the health and pension fund. By the late 1960s, having seen the handwriting on the wall, just before the mass migration of the industry to New Jersey or the business graveyard, the union had tempered salary increases in favor of pensions for its older members and had negotiated transfer rights for those wishing to move. My mother worked in several shops in her working career; all her jobs were obtained through the union's hiring hall, which gave her and many other office workers a fair degree of job security and, since they did not fear dismissal, helped make their voices louder in shop-floor battles. If they were fired, they simply went back to the hall and were sent out on another job.

But this was the world of the older offices. She possessed the variety of skills needed in the small office, where each employee was expected to perform several different tasks. Her union was based in the small offices that, until the 1970s, filled the city. Later, the union expanded, undertaking wall-to-wall organizing in large publishing firms and in private universities. In the 1950s it had extended its reach beyond New York City to New Jersey, Connecticut, and parts of New England. As factories and wholesale firms disappeared, David Livingston realized that white collar was the key to the union's survival. While most labor organizations were experiencing their own version of downsizing during the 1970s and 1980s, 65 grew to thirty-five thousand members, most of them in white-collar jobs.

On the East Coast, 65 pioneered by bringing thousands of university clerical workers into the labor movement. Its initiative spurred the efforts of several unions — the Teachers, Hotel and Restaurant Employees, and especially the Auto Workers, with which District 65 became affiliated in 1978. Today, clerical workers at Harvard, Yale, NYU, Columbia, Boston University, and many smaller schools are unionized, even though many managements have not accepted this fact and have fought the unions with a ferocity akin to that of the most implacable antiunion corporations. Reluctant to sign collective-bargaining agreements even after decisive union victories in Labor Board–supervised elections, university management forced some of the newly formed unions to strike in order to obtain a contract. At Yale and Columbia, management's recalcitrance made the strike weapon a staple of the bargaining process. For example, in 1983, 65 was obliged to strike to obtain three of four contracts it negotiated and conducted several strikes at Barnard College and a one-day strike at Union Theological Seminary.

The first university clericals who organized into 65 were employed at Boston University, where the union won a representation election in 1978. But, in typical fashion, the administration refused to recognize the union's NLRB victory, and employees were forced to strike for recognition. At the same time, information was sought from 65 by an independent group of mostly women employees in Harvard University's medical area. Inspired by the growing feminist movement, the organizing committee of these workers had originally constituted itself as a study group, concentrating on the problems of women working at the university. After years of seeking improvements by appealing to the corporate conscience of the university adminisration, some of the women concluded that a union was their only means of redress. Among their grievances was the lack of promotional opportunity, as well as abysmally low salaries, most of them less than $10,000 a year, even in the mid-1970s. The dedicated inside committee, expanded to include some men, soon signed up more than half the employees in the area, but, as it turned out, not enough to overcome employee turnover and Harvard's clever use of delays in the vote.[2] When the union petitioned for an election conducted by the NLRB, (some say prematurely), Harvard, through a series of delay tactics permitted under the cumbersome procedures of the Labor Relations Act, employed a series of stall tactics that delayed the election long enough to defeat the union.

Harvard's management, led by its president, Derek Bok, a well-known "prounion" labor relations expert, narrowly defeated the union again in 1981. But in 1982 it won an NLRB decision that dramatically widened the unit to include all clerical and technical staff. At the same time, the Harvard University Clerical and Technical Workers left District 65 and sought representation under the more benign sponsorship of the State, County, and Municipal Employees, which acutely understood the importance of local autonomy. Finally, buoyed by the participation of about four hundred volunteer organizers — all clerical workers — in 1988 it won an election, by forty-four votes, for the university's three thousand clerical and technical workers.

In nearly every important East Coast instance where university clericals eventually chose unionism, 65 had waged the first campaign, although it did not reap the direct benefits, except at Columbia and Boston University.

➤

Building on the earlier efforts by the Office and Professional Workers union, in the 1970s 65 conducted some important organizing drives in publishing. Already established at Harper and Row, the union achieved victories at Addison-Wesley and a few small publishers. The high point of this drive was the resounding victory at *The Village Voice.* Hard-fought struggles solidified the unity of editors and clericals, but that solidarity strategy began to fray at the edges when clerical salaries moved rapidly upward while many editors became disenchanted by their relatively weak gains. Still, the *Voice* remains one of the strongest units of the Auto Workers' New York white-collar union, 65's successor, Local 2110, an "amalgamated" organization of some twenty-six workplaces, both in private publishing and in a diverse ensemble of the nonprofits — the Museum of Modern Art, the New-York Historical Society, recently organized Mercy College, and its largest units, the complex of institutions around Morningside Heights, Columbia, Union Theological Seminary, Teachers College, and Barnard College.

The local's president, Maida Rosenstein, is a former clerical worker at Columbia who was part of the organizing committee that brought the 65 victory there. Shortly afterward, she became a full-time organizer and, on the demise of 65, was elected to head the new local. Rosenstein says that "organizing" does not stop when the union wins a representation election and procures its first contract. Universities, museums, and the publishing industry management have not, in the main, conceded that the union is here to stay. In many cases the local has tried to even the playing field by aggressively making public appeals and mobilizing other unions to support its strikes and contract demands. In 1996, AFL-CIO president John Sweeney joined the Barnard picket line, a gesture that helped settle the strike. When Columbia forced its workers on strike during the following year, the sixteen-day action was settled after the union mounted pressure through rallies and demonstrations.

Rosenstein believes that the nonprofits are easier to organize than for-profit companies but that dealing with them is not much different. Every aspect of labor-management relations is a battleground.[3] Nor, despite its contractual obligation to observe a grievance procedure, has management accepted the idea that day-to-day disputes can be settled amicably.

While employees are not required to join the union, they must nevertheless pay dues. And the workforce is constantly turning over because of the relatively low pay. Which means that new employees must constantly be organized into the union if bargaining is to remain effective. At Mercy College the union won an election in 1993 but was not certified as bargaining agent until two years later. Management continued to stall negotiations throughout 1997. Meanwhile, a chunk of employees left and the union was obliged to maintain a high level of membership mobilization under adverse circumstances. These delays have occasionally resulted in union losses. Winning an election at the Spanish Institute among its part-time teachers, for example, was not enough to get a contract and the substantial salary increases for which its underpaid staff had joined the union. After years of bargaining it became clear to employees and the union itself that despite its soft approach, management was stonewalling. Unable to strike or otherwise force management to sign, the union withdrew.

Rosenstein argues that, because there is virtually no union culture or people with a liberal political culture in the large corporate offices, there are few early prospects for success among their white-

collar groups. But neither 65 nor its successor, Local 2110, is prepared to tackle the huge insurance industry again or, indeed, the
banks. As these industries continue to hire millions of tellers, sales
representatives, and back-office clericals, whose working conditions
often approach sweat-shop standards, most unions have put their
energies elsewhere.

Many European unions have compensated for job losses in
production industries by vigorously organizing in these sectors. In
France, bank employees are among the most highly organized groups
in the country, and Britain's private-sector clerical and professional
unions have brought a million clerical workers into the labor movement in the last thirty years.[4]

American unions seem unable to emulate their European counterparts, despite the nearly seven million clerical workers in financial,
industrial, and insurance corporate offices. We know that the ranks
of full-time employees have been thinned by technological change,
mergers and acquisitions, and the transformation of many full-time
jobs into part-time and temporary work. And the office temp is no
longer an anomaly in large corporate offices but a feature of their
operations. Major corporate law and accounting firms prefer temps
to regular employees because they can save a third of the labor costs
that are allocated to health benefits. And, since the temporary employee knows the job is time-limited, there are fewer messy discharges. Moreover, office workers like many others have lost real
wages in the 1990s and they have few avenues for recourse. But the
labor movement knows little or nothing of their conditions or of
office culture. As in the South, the cost of organizing would be steep
and rewards sparse, at least for a considerable period of time.[5] Yet, in
contrast to the opinions of many male union officials, Rosenstein's
belief is that office workers make good union members because their
jobs require skills in precisely those areas necessary for building effective unions: organization and communications. As the experiences
at Columbia and Harvard made clear, they know how to form networks and how to maintain them; the office is a close-knit community often marked by a spirit of mutual aid. At US Air, the union

credibly claimed knowledge of employees' problems because many of its members in the telephone company did customer service work similar to that of employees at the airline; volunteer telephone worker organizers were at worksites to prove the point. The union has rich experience with clerical workers in large institutional settings and has a history of fighting for its independence from the most paternal of American corporations, the telephone company. It knows how to combat intimidation among white-collar employees; it knows how to deal with large service organizations. And it backed its claims with the testimonies of the trained rank-and-file organizers who were in touch with the US Air people on a one-to-one basis rather than adopting the AFL-CIO "blitz" tactic of sending a team of professional organizers into the situation. The 1997 US Air campaign was run by strong worksite committees.

Perhaps more to the point, most organizing victories over the past three decades have been among women in the white-collar field. Today, 45 percent of all union members are women. The AFL-CIO and some of its affiliates have displayed a healthy attitude toward the problems of women in the workplace and in the labor movement, but most organizers and leaders are males. This need not be an obstacle to white-collar organizing as long as unions address the cultural as well as the labor issues among these groups. As the Harvard campaign revealed, problems of wage inequality and working conditions are not the only concerns of office workers. Many are motivated to seek collective organization to achieve "dignity" at work; that is, they want to be treated with respect, they want to deal openly with sexual harassment, and they want a voice in the way the work is organized.

So far, while there are signs of change, organized labor's understanding of women's issues remains work-related, and questions such as sexuality and abortion are still unexamined — in most cases, deliberately. If labor is to convince working women that they belong in the movement, then the male-dominated unions — there are still no major national women leaders in the Auto Workers and Communications Workers — must examine their attitudes and practices. In this regard, as we saw among public employees, AFSCME has probably been in the forefront of making a U-turn in the labor culture, but many other unions remain far behind. Perhaps most important of all, unions accustomed to staff-led organizing should study closely the Harvard and US Air campaigns. Both of them were led by the white-collar workers themselves and were about democratic cultural values as much as they were about economic issues. And the fact that they were conducted by a cadre of women meeting on a weekly basis, which enabled them over time to forge close ties, is an elementary organizing lesson most trade unionists have yet to learn. There is no question that these victories would have been inconceivable without the explicit links between issues raised by contemporary feminism and those more traditionally identified with job-conscious unionism.

❦

The largest private-sector organizing victory in recent memory occurred in September 1997, when the Communications Workers of America won the nationwide election for ten thousand United Airways passenger service employees. The election was ordered when the National Mediation Board, the federal agency that administers the Railway Labor Act, found that US Airways had violated workers' rights, and ordered a rerun. However, though in 1994 the Machinists union won an election for six thousand US Air ramp workers, they still lack an agreement. And pilots and other airline employees are still in a bargaining mode. The Pilots union approved a five-year concession agreement in return for job security, and other unions are submitting to the company's give-back demands as well. After the election victory, the Communications Workers extended its drive to fourteen thousand United Airline white-collar employees, a large step toward organizing the more than forty thousand workers in this job category.

But the company, taking advantage of airline deregulation, is by no means reconciled to unionism. If it employs the delaying and intimidation tactics that marked the election campaign, the passenger service employees and their union, like the workers at Harvard and Columbia, are in for a prolonged period of permanent organizing. On the other hand, both in the organizing and the bargaining phases, the Communications union does have a major advantage: despite erosion of union power since deregulation and a series of bitter strikes in the 1980s, union culture remain strong in the airline industry. Pilots, mechanics, and flight attendants are heavily unionized among the leading carriers; only Delta is largely nonunion, and the most notoriously union-busting carrier, Continental, which defeated its unions in the 1980s, suffered a loss in 1997 at the hands of the Teamsters, who won an election for five thousand mechanics.

The style of the United Airways drive is extremely labor intensive — it requires a lot of people who must spend a great deal of time at the task. It can also entail assigning a substantial number of staff for a prolonged period, including the hiatus between the election victory and the conclusion of contract negotiations. In this organizing mode, the union treasury is sorely strained, and very few local unions are able to sustain such campaigns without strong international union support.

Under the best of circumstances, the task of organizing millions of clerical workers and other noncredentialed white-collar employees is daunting. Since unionism has failed to take root in the most strategically crucial workplaces, organized labor will need vast resources of both patience and intelligence to achieve anything. It will have to spend a lot of money on staff — mostly rank-and-file white-collar workers — without the immediate prospect of income. Unions in the field will have to combine resources, assign staff, and, for a while, surrender their jurisdictional claims. Perhaps equally important, they must allocate significant resources to research, public education, and literature tailored to specific groups. While reaching out to white-collar workers in general is no substitution for building worksite committees, considerable education may be needed along with conventional union-building tactics. An organizing drive based on a single employer may not be the best strategy.

The UOPWA bank successes and the United Financial Employees drive of more than fifty years ago should be re-examined; in each case, the successful strategy was that of organizing the industry all at once. The target might be New York's World Trade Center, Wall Street, or the Chicago and San Francisco financial districts instead of a single company. As at Harvard, the organizing committee may not have the immediate prospect of filing for an NLRB election. The committee may comprise employees from different companies in the financial services industry; its initial task will be to define the concerns of clerical and other white-collar workers, keeping in mind that only some of these concerns will be consistent with labor's usual issues. In fact, the committee could start as a discussion group. Simultaneously, a group of office temps, who are paid by agencies rather than the companies, might start discussing their problems and prospects. Since few agencies include fringe benefits in their contracts, the temp group could consider making paid health benefits an early demand, maybe offering a group plan through labor contacts as an organizing tool. And, to consolidate their position, they may explore whether and where to organize a union-run or union-sponsored independent hiring hall to compete with the agencies. Their success would depend on attracting highly qualified and reliable clerical workers and on their ability to raise the standards for the entire industry, thereby attracting office temps now working through nonunion agencies.

At the same time union researchers meeting with these committees could begin to suggest ideas of general application. One issue almost certain to be encountered is occupational health and safety. Considerable research has been done on carpal tunnel syndrome, tendinitis, and other disorders connected to typing and word processing. There is information on the effect on eyesight of video display terminals, even while many employers deny that there are deleterious effects in many aspects of office work and have opposed workers' compensation claims in this area. Since workers' compensation is administered by states, official responses to these claims are as varied as the political complexion of state governments. In addition to compensation claims, organizers would discover that employers are reluctant to institute rest periods or otherwise rotate operators away from constant exposure to word processing and other conditions that produce these disorders. Before filing for elections or asking employers for union recognition on the basis of card checks, the unions may consider opening service centers to assist office workers in filing workers' compensation claims, discriminatory discharge cases, and other problems that need the trained assistance of lawyers and counselors. Like the centers sponsored by UNITE and other groups, directed mainly to low-wage workers, the office workers' center could serve as a place for conversation and labor education over a cup of coffee.

In sum, unionists may find that organizing clerical workers will challenge their inventiveness. With few exceptions, the question of whether clerical and other office workers in the private sector are ready for unionism has not had an adequate assessment. But the broad changes in the nature of white-collar work provide hope. No less than industrial labor, office work has experienced restructuring, job losses, and other shocks. There are still some fifteen million clerical workers and the traditional "personal relationships" between boss and secretary are confined to very few; filing and stenography have all but disappeared and, more and more, jobs once done by clericals are now done by machine operators. They operate computers, photocopiers, and other office machines, are internal telephone operators or receptionists (although voice-mail is rapidly consigning this job to history) and work the telephones. In short, their work resembles that of the many members of the Communications Workers. The main differences are the power of the large corporations and the absence of union culture in the sectors in which they are employed.

Deciding to tackle these corporations would signal a clear shift in labor's organizing strategy or, to be more precise, its recognition of what has been evident for some time: that white-collar discontent is already the basis for its organizing gains. Whether the AFL-CIO and most of its affiliates are prepared to learn from the experience of the existing unions in the field, and back a bold program in the private-services sector, is still undecided. Certainly talk of a new labor insurgency is somewhat empty unless there is a significant effort among white-collar workers.

6 ⚑ Professionals and Managers: Labor's New Frontier

UNIONS FOR THE MIDDLE CLASS?

Unions are appropriate for blue-collar workers, truck drivers, grocery clerks, public employees, low-level hospital workers — but professionals and managers don't need them, right? Accordingly, labor unionism is best grasped through heroic images inherited from Émile Zola's great novel about nineteenth-century French miners, *Germinal,* John Steinbeck's grim depiction of Depression-era migrant farmworkers, *The Grapes of Wrath,* or, more recently, Carroll O'Connor's brilliant portrayal of a contemporary troglodyte, the Queens warehouse worker Archie Bunker. Lacking educational opportunity, these workers may need the benefits of labor organization, but professionals and managers negotiate by means of their credentials, which denote their talents and skills. The very definition of *professional* signifies work autonomy. Conventionally, professionals manage their own time and therefore are the true individuals of the modern era. The professions remain the ideal for those obliged to perform salaried labor, and becoming one's own boss remains the cultural ambition of many, whether they make it into the professions or not.

To be sure, professionals form and join organizations, such as the American Bar Association (ABA) and the American Medical Association (AMA). The avowed purpose of these groups is to protect their members' independence by fending off what they consider to be odious government restrictions. For example, the AMA was perhaps the nation's leading lobby against socialized medicine. Indeed, in the fights after World War II to establish some form of universal health care through congressional action, the AMA was in the forefront of the opposition. Its main argument was that the physician-patient relationship required no third party — the government or an insurance company — to mediate it. If the AMA was seen as a powerful "doctors' union," this was a metaphor that signified power at the historical moment when unions were perceived as the epitome of economic strength. The American Bar Association intervenes in the selection of judges, plays an important role in reviewing and writing legal codes, and sets ethics standards for the profession (which have a bearing on fees). But both the AMA and the ABA, as well as other such organizations, were once horrified at the prospect of genuine collective bargaining over matters concerning the economic well-being of their members.

Having obtained professional credentials, often at an exorbitant cost, from an accredited university and having passed one or more examinations administered by state and professional boards, the successful candidate is presumed to be qualified to make all determinations connected to the practice of his or her profession. For the independent professional able to hang up her shingle, joining a union would be seen as a contradiction in terms, because she would inevitably surrender some autonomy to the collective will. Unionism, after all, holds that collective action is the fundamental tool of the worker. But professionals join forces to protect their individual prerogatives *against* the collectivist colossus.[1]

The professional system has had an enduring effect on American culture. Being one's own boss occupies our fantasies as much as does hitting the lottery. The relatively easy availability of higher education — the transmission belt of the professions — remains for many the way out of the working class and lower middle class. Even if only a small fraction makes it, the ideal is crucial to the dominant belief that in America anyone with brains and the passion for hard work can be his or her own boss. Then why, despite the powerful ideology of professionalism, have the professions themselves turned to unions to address their work problems?

There are three closely related reasons. Perhaps the most important is that the world they have inhabited since the early 1970s is profoundly different from the one of their expectations and those of their parents and teachers. More and more often, they are salaried employees, not owners of their own practices, and therefore control neither their incomes nor conditions of work. While, for example, physicians' and attorneys' salaries are relatively high, they are not enough to make up for the sacrifice entailed in paying back tens of thousands of dollars in loans for professional school tuition. Physicians in private practice are no longer able to set their own rates; even if they do not work directly for a health maintenance organization, they are, in effect, employees of the payer. Some independent physicians refused to be bound by programs like Medicare, Medicaid, and most insurance plans, but one by one they discovered that, lacking a stable upper-middle-class clientele, they could not hold out. As a result, many have become affiliated with managed care organizations and submitted to reduced fee schedules. And now, all too often, the offices of once quiet private practices resemble HMOs: they are crowded, and the doctors have adopted assembly-line techniques of health care.

Second, in many instances, the cornerstone of professionalism — work autonomy — no longer exists or has been severely chipped away. Salaried physicians, accountants, and attorneys now are subject to supervision in every aspect of their work. Their time must be accounted for in a manner that would make any time-study expert proud. In the proliferating primary care corporations, which employ many doctors, cost considerations may dictate the treatment: the decision as to whether surgery is required or whether medication is sufficient for some pathologies; what kind and the length of aftercare is indicated. Even more egregious, many firms require examining physicians to meet specified quotas of patients. Many physicians are tied to computer programs, which not only assist in diagnosis but also

prescribe appropriate medication and treatment. Frequently the doctor who wishes to depart from computer-aided diagnosis and pre-
scription is required to obtain permission from management. Any
deviation from this discipline may result in discharge.

Similarly, the newly minted attorney, even one who has graduated
from a leading law school, may never get a chance to have her or his
own practice. Typically, she will keep her first job with a large or
middle-size law firm for five years. In hopes of becoming a partner,
she will typically put in a sixty-hour work week — or longer. And only
one in twenty is likely to achieve this goal. Just one of three of the
remaining group will ever have a private practice. More likely, the
attorney will get another job, one that sometimes offers less salary,
and remain an associate indefinitely. Those who graduate from sec-
ond- or third-rank institutions rarely get hired by large law firms;
instead, they may go into public service or be hired by a small neighborhood firm at a relatively modest salary.

Third, the most basic weapon of the professional, controlling
labor supply, has been undermined by professional schools, which,
for internal reasons or to accommodate to the managed care dogma
of cost-cutting, have resisted suggestions from professional associations that they lower enrollments by following more rigorous admissions criteria. The numbers of licensed doctors, lawyers, accountants,
and engineers flooding the market come at a time of relative contrac-
tion of good jobs. Among lawyers, unemployment in some regions of
the country is a grim reality. While the demand for doctors and accountants has not yet retreated to the point where there is a significant surplus, job shortages may be just around the corner. With
the rise of medical school enrollments, the decline of federal subsi-
dies such as Medicare, and the restructuring of medical treatment
from fee-for-service to managed care, doctors may soon experience a
salary and an employment crunch. And, while the four largest accounting firms and those of intermediate size still hire thousands of
accountants each year from leading business schools, whose enrollments continue to burgeon, the hiring pace slowed by as much as a
third in the 1990s.[2] In engineering, always a profession that responds

directly to market forces, computer-aided design (CAD) and other innovations have vastly increased efficiency and slowed demand in many subdisciplines. Some engineering schools have closed in recent years, and, except for computer and aeronautical engineers, there is no boom in the civil, mechanical, and electrical fields.[3]

That more professionals are prepared to depart from some of the tenets of their ideology, especially the idea that unions are pre-eminently for blue-collar people and not for them, is a subject of this chapter. Another is the prospect that some managers may be more likely to choose unions if the option becomes available.

THE TWO CULTURES OF TODAY'S LABOR MOVEMENT

Perhaps a major factor in the relative neglect of white-collar workers, especially professionals, in the lore of trade unionism was their lack of development as a social category until after World War II. Even though clerical and professional work became important with the emergence of the corporation as an institution of American business, starting in the 1890s, there were few instances of a white-collar voice being heeded in the workplace or in American politics. There were dramatic early CIO victories in companies like GM, US Steel, GE, and the rubber corporations, but in others, success proved elusive. Companies in the knowledge-based communications industries, especially IBM, ATT, and its affiliates, proved harder to crack. By the late 1930s, the CIO leaders John L. Lewis and Sidney Hillman recognized that the forward march of the labor movement required alliances with blacks, sectors of the middle class, and white-collar employees, populations they had, to put it charitably, previously ignored.

But their vision was blurred by what I call the problem of two cultures. With some exceptions, only a small group of radical unions were willing to take on the awesome task of white-collar organizing. These unions had not accepted the prevailing dogma of labor culture: that only craft, industrial, and transportation workers could be real trade unionists. Besides the conventional trade union view of professions and other white-collar employees as adjuncts of management, one of the myths of the industrializing era was that masculinity was inexorably tied to manual work. Often back-breaking, dirty, and dangerous, craft and semiskilled jobs in the giant workshops had a considerable aura. This was "real" work, as opposed to pencil pushing and paper shuffling, and it usually paid more. Many factory workers saw the engineer as an efficiency expert whose task was to put them out of a job or make them work harder. Theirs was a world in which the barroom and the union hall, the hard hat and the steel-tipped shoe, became badges of personal and cultural identity. In this world there was little room for pencil pushers, let alone women and "egg-heads."

The culture of the factory was often brutal; in many plants you shaped up or shipped out. But for those forced to spend most of their time on the shop floor, it was also a place of mutual aid. On days when you did not feel well or you screwed up on the job, you could depend on your shopmate to cover for you. Some aspired to management jobs, but, especially after the union came in, staying in the ranks became the choice. While the foreman held his job at the company's pleasure, a worker couldn't be fired except for cause, and even then a good union would come to the rescue. Then, too, workers' collective action could seriously cripple production and reduce company profits. Could white-collar employees accumulate such power?

Labor's top leadership corresponded to these images of the masculine, blue-collar worker. Its big postwar figures — George Meany, Jimmy Hoffa, and Walter Reuther — confirmed the prejudice. (Reuther was somewhat an exception, but he was a skilled tool-and-die maker.) John Sweeney and the AFL-CIO secretary treasurer, Miners union leader Richard Trumka (a trained lawyer), as well as most of the members of the Executive Council, have blue-collar origins or lead unions of industrial and construction workers. Sweeney himself stands in a transitional position, since the Service Employees, although it started as a janitor's union, now has as a majority of its members public employees, many in clerical and professional categories. Having been the leader of America's largest health care union, Sweeney understands the importance of the new sectors.

Otherwise, until recently, professional and technical organizing has been barely a blip on labor's screen. To be sure, there are signs that the environment for professional organizing is changing — indeed, the Steelworkers and Auto Workers have registered most of their recent gains in this field, and the Teamsters are not far behind. But as in the South, the AFL-CIO and most of its affiliates have been reluctant to target these employees. When asked why, union officials give two replies: the labor movement lacks the resources to organize across many sectors and must therefore choose the most likely prospects; and there is not sufficient evidence that pouring heavy resources into organizing among these relatively "privileged" groups will pay off.

One of labor's grave problems, which accounts not only for its neglect of professional and technical groups but also for a measure of the decline of its political and economic influence, is that, for over a century, it has maintained its distance from intellectuals in the broadest sense, including professionals. With few exceptions, labor leaders are practical men who view with suspicion the tendency of intellectuals to engage in visionary speculations, at times to adopt "alien" ideologies. These are not merely the leading radical doctrines of the first half of the twentieth century — socialism and communism — but the ideas of the 1960s — feminism, black nationalism, environmentalism, and radical or practiciparatory democracy. While most professional and white-collar employees are as far from these views as are trade union leaders, many became attracted to the labor movement through these doctrines. Bread and butter has never been enough for the professionals; they expect their unions to function, in part, as professional associations that address issues of knowledge as well as salaries. As a result, most white-collar and professional unions are found in the progressive wing of the labor movement. Their members have marched in civil rights, antiwar, and abortion rights demonstrations and, unlike the members of some industrial and construction unions, have tended to ally themselves with environmentalists. And they are people who are concerned with professional development.

THE THORNY PATH OF PROFESSIONAL UNIONS

Teachers, engineers, architects, and industrial scientists were the first to experience loss of professional autonomy. From the beginning of the industrial era, they were salaried employees and were subject to supervision. Driven by salary cuts, layoffs, and mass unemployment, some college-educated and professional groups became radicalized by the Depression. For example, instead of offering themselves to the industrial union drives of the day, a small group of "overeducated" clerks, such as Arthur Osman, David Livingston, and William Michelson, in New York's Wholesale Trades and Department Stores Union, chose to stay home and organize people like themselves, many of whom were unable to find jobs that matched their credentials. Similarly, Lewis Alan Berne, an engineer, worked with others to bring architects, chemists, and engineers (FAECT) into the blue-collar-dominated CIO. And professional pharmacists like Leon Davis and William Taylor managed, in the depths of the Depression, to form a wall-to-wall drug union, embracing some three thousand counter clerks and graduate pharmacists. In the public sector, mainly under the leadership of socialists, the American Federation of Teachers (AFT), founded in 1916, experienced a renaissance during the Depression. Although AFT locals hardly achieved any collective bargaining rights, many of the members became effective salary lobbyists and, perhaps equally important, were and remain a distinctive and progressive voice for educational reform.

Before World War II a particularly strong beachhead was forged among social workers in nonprofit, mainly Jewish group and casework agencies — settlement houses, the large Federation of Jewish Philanthropies, and smaller agencies in job-training and counseling, mental health, and private welfare. New York's Local 19 of the CIO's Office and Professional Workers (UOPWA) — which embraced the Federation of Architects and Engineers as well — is one of the most impressive achievements in the history of professional unionism. Unlike the Teachers, which, for the first half-century of its existence, was a craft union, this modest-size union followed the industrial union tradition: it eschewed craft exclusions by including maintenance, clerical, and professional employees within the same bargaining unit; it committed itself to upgrading black workers; and it formed coalitions with client and community groups on questions of public relief, housing, the fight for jobs and against discrimination. After UOP's demise, in the late 1940s, Local 19 became the core of today's New York District Council 1707 of State, County, and Municipal Employees, which has organized professionals and nonprofessionals in daycare centers and home health-care workers.

However, with the important exception of public school teachers — whose unions after 1960 grew to labor's highest density, about 80 percent — the first twenty years after the war witnessed setbacks for professional and white-collar organizing at a time when these categories were proving indispensable to the economy and to the workforce. Postwar labor was not tuned in to the problems of professional and technical employees, but that wasn't because of ignorance. My conjecture is that the labor movement was wary and uncooperative because many of the most active white-collar unions were under left-wing leadership.

THE SCIENTIFIC AND TECHNOLOGICAL REVOLUTION

America has always been intrigued by technology but never more than now. Our society and its culture are more often defined by various technological "revolutions" than by anything else. The late twentieth century may be designated the space age, the information era, the cybernetics era, the communications age. And of course the tool that powers all of them is the computer. These labels point to vast changes in the way we live, but for those inundated with, and somewhat numbed by, techno-hyperbole, none of them seems to describe what it was that transformed the science fiction of the turn of the century into brilliant reality. We can, however, get a clearer idea of what has happened to our economics and our culture. The core, the central factor, is knowledge, particularly the ways to apply scientific knowledge to nearly every tool of production, the production not only of goods but also of services and culture. What is new is not that science has been recruited for technologies; it is that the close link between theoretical knowledge and industrial, military, and commercial applications has been recognized as a systematic and dependent relationship. Intellectual knowledge has become the salient feature not only of the advanced industrial sectors but also of the world economy. Sciences — social as well as natural — are largely devoted to three main tasks: the development of new products; the increase of worker productivity by a reduction of labor in proportion to output; and the exploration of new methods of industrial discipline and control.

Once *style* was confined to women's clothing, cars, and some other consumer goods. But with the ubiquitous presence of the computer, technology itself has become an influence on culture. Technology can no longer be defined only in terms of its use as a tool; it is a form of life. The software system being used is a matter beyond utility; in the computer era it connotes status. Computer products are marketed with the mixture of sex and aesthetics. The leaders of the corporations that dominate the computer field have taken on the celebrity of actors and sports figures. Like fashion economists, journalists and the public closely watch the new season of computer products and derive economic forecasts from the annual technology shows. The companies, too, use these shows as occasions for making news. For example, in the summer of 1997, the Apple show was chosen as the place to announce the near-merger of the faltering computer pioneer with its imitator and arch competitor, Microsoft. When the deal was announced in August, the front page of almost every newspaper in the country featured the story, and it made the top of the news in every other medium as well. Similarly, space exploration, perhaps the most spectacular achievement of the combined disciplines of theoretical and applied physics, exemplifies for the public the marriage of science, technology, and the state.

In economic and cultural terms, the postwar era was shaped by these related developments: the technological revolution in consumer and industrial products and in the industrial and service workplace; the rise of professional and technical occupations and with them the expansion of higher education; the Cold War, which provided the justification for spending federal money on scientific and technical research and higher education; and the middle-class urban exodus, which included many industrial and transportation workers. The effects of these changes on our politics and culture are still being felt by many of our leading institutions, particularly the labor movement. For labor, the technological revolution proved a mixed blessing. There are good reasons for professional and technical employees to join unions. But there are pulls in the other direction, too.

On the one hand, the postwar boom generated millions of professional and technical jobs. But demand exceeded the usual source of recruitment for physicians, attorneys, professors, and engineers: their children. The federal and state governments, as a result, expanded the higher education system so that it could embrace working-class and farm kids. On the other hand, the emergence of the knowledge-based economy broke the continuity of industrial and service working-class jobs. In a majority of cases, the new students were the first in their family to earn a college degree. But when the children of union families entered college, they frequently acquired a new set of values, many of them not necessarily compatible with those of their parents and grandparents. As budding professionals, they were destined for the middle class, which retained its scorn for organized labor and its admiration of individual achievement.

THE DARK SIDE OF "PROGRESS"

Soon these new graduates discovered that the world they now inhabited was often different from what it had been cracked up to be. Contrary to expectations inherited from the mythology attendant on the figure of the "self-made" man, many found that they were offered salaried employment, and not always under good circumstances. American corporations, battered by a militant labor movement, relied on work reorganization, automation, and, later, computer-mediated machines to eliminate labor costs and preserve profits.

Blue-collar employment advanced only by inches, even as America's worker productivity was the envy of the world's industrializing countries. But technological jobs advanced by yards. By the late 1970s labor-saving technologies in manufacturing were taking their toll on jobs. In 1950, manufacturing accounted for 34 percent of the labor force. Between 1978 and 1993, the years of the most intense technological change and organizational consolidation, the number of production workers declined by 33 percent and were only 17 percent of the labor force. In the same period, professionals and managers rose to 9.6 percent of the labor force.

The shift is illustrated by the 1990 figures showing that employment in colleges and universities was equal to the sum of workers in the motor vehicle industries, blast furnaces, and basic steel combined. And there was a direct correlation between the rise of intellectual labor, the gain in manufacturing productivity, and the decline of blue-collar employment in the technologically advanced production industries. From the 1950s through the 1990s there was a steady increase in computer-mediated production processes, such as robots and numerical controls in metalworking, paper, food processing, and textiles, and continuous-flow technologies in oil, chemical, and rubber industries. Having reduced factory employment by a third between 1980 and 1992, many large employers trained their sights on white-collar and high-priced intellectual labor. Office computers, introduced in the 1950s in scattered workplaces, are now routinely perched on nearly every desk in small and large corporate offices. The people who once filled corporate and agency offices have been replaced by word processor operators and electronic phone voices. The file clerk belongs to the history books; the computer is the filing cabinet. Stenography is an art probably preserved in the Smithsonian Institution but rarely practiced in the contemporary office.

AREN'T MOST MANAGERS COMPANY MEN?

Several layers of management have also felt the impact of office computerization and automation. Armed with computer-mediated communications technologies, many companies discovered the virtues of consolidation. Under the watchful but benign eyes of federal regulators, many merged with their competitors, making many of the branch offices and services redundant. Computer-mediated technologies turned over dozens of managerial functions to programmers. By the end of the 1990s, managerial staffs were projected by some companies to fall by 20 percent, and there is no end in sight.

Most middle and line managers, who once had secretaries, now often do their own word processing, place and answer their own calls, communicate by e-mail, and know how to use the office photocopier. And the famed Metropolitan Life headquarters office, which eliminated the private office for most managers and was once challenged by large insurance companies and IBM, is now emulated, especially by high-tech software firms, where everyone from the clerk to the project director sits at a console in one large space, watching his or her screen. To add insult to injury, among the victims of the downsizing mania after the stock market crash of 1987 were the middle managers. Between 1989 and 1993, IBM, Xerox, Kodak, General Motors, and other corporations retired, laid off, or fired 6 to 10 percent of their managerial workforce and, despite the upturn in the mid-1990s, maintained a brisk pace of shedding managers.

The range of functions, salaries, and authority of managers is broad. At the top are those who control the important elements of the enterprise: they set company or agency policy; direct the workforce; and have the power to hire and fire. While they do not make policy, middle managers do direct workers within particular departments or sections and may or may not have the power to hire and fire. The largest group of managers assign work and are responsible for its performance but usually do not discharge or discipline employees without the approval of a higher authority.

Why would managers join unions? For one thing, line and middle managers have not reaped the rewards enjoyed by top executives. Their salaries have stayed level, and, like other professionals, some are being downsized and their positions in the organization degraded. When, in midcareer, say at age forty-five or fifty, a manager is let go by a company, re-employment may take between six months and two years. Those over fifty-five may never work again unless they are willing to change occupations and accept much lower compensation. Some managers and engineers express their discontent through their professional associations. And, as with other nonunion employees, their protests may take underground forms. What these developments have revealed is, as business publications acknowledge, that the image of the "company man" is fading. In the current business environment, middle managers are more vulnerable than ever and their future almost as insecure as that of blue- and white-collar workers. Whereas immunity to layoffs was one of the most prized privileges of all levels of management, in the last decade it has disappeared for many. Today, managers are vulnerable to some of the vicissitudes affecting workers; lacking a union, they can be fired at the will of their bosses, and are often retrenched when companies restructure or want to cut overhead.

In the Depression decade, some foremen and supervisors organized their own unions, but these were short-lived. In 1939 the Supreme Court declared managers of all sorts beyond the jurisdiction of the Labor Relations law, and Taft-Hartley later codified this decision. At the time, unions were not particularly disturbed by this development. Having been wounded by management-dominated company unions during the 1920s and early 1930s, most now viewed management with jaundiced eyes, but many industrial unions did not mind concluding union agreements that acknowledged management's right to direct the workforce and make the important production decisions. While there were good historical reasons for this bad concession, not until the advent of automation and computer-mediated technologies did its pernicious features become apparent. Sometimes when workers strike, supervisors can and do operate plants. But amending the law to remove management's exemption from union organization is not on labor's agenda, and it would surely prove controversial if it were proposed. Clearly, it is time to reconsider this, given the tendency of many companies — notoriously those in communications — to obtain strike insurance by calling former bargaining-unit employees "working" managers.

THE NEW ENGINEERING WORKPLACE

Engineering is the application of science to production. Engineers transform scientific knowledge into technology and technology into industrial practices. Once an independent professional, the engineer was swept up by the advancing industrialization and, by the turn of the century, was converted into one of the first salaried professional employees of the large corporation as well as the engineering or architectural firm. In the process, with the emergence of electrically powered machines in the factory and the office, the discipline of civil engineering yielded ground to the new fields of mechanical, chemical, and electrical engineering. And while civil engineers were, and to a large extent remain, semiprofessional, chemical, mechanical, and electrical engineering gave rise to engineering schools and the system of credentials and licenses. But scientists and engineers, once the scourge of industrial and clerical labor, found themselves beset by innovation.

Between the mid-1980s and the present, computer-aided design and drafting (CAD) had become widely accepted in the engineering and architectural workplace. The first casualties were the draftsmen, who made drawings by hand. Except for very specialized jobs, computer graphics has displaced the entire technical occupation of drafting. Now, with CAD, the engineer can combine the drafting and design functions. Where, for example, a simple switch adaptation once required twenty or more drawings, the engineer can now select from a menu of electronically simulated drawings and make the adjustments without putting pen to paper. Design productivity has swelled by an average of 800 percent in civil and mechanical engineering and industrial architecture. In addition, where engineers once devoted considerable time and effort to making mathematical calculations for routine designs, these too have been reduced to a menu of alternatives. Although the engineer still needs mathematical knowledge in order to make the correct choices, the calculations themselves are now done by the computer.

Most engineers enjoy working with CAD because they are relieved of routine aspects of the job. CAD enables them to concentrate their creative talents on design functions. And when CAD is applied to interesting projects, the work itself becomes fun. But for the more laborious tasks — that is, the work of the majority of engineers and architects — the writing is on the wall. Many are likely to suffer a fate similar to that of workers who were eliminated from production jobs. The drive by both private- and public-sector employers to reduce labor costs is not likely to abate. In addition to outsourcing much of the work ordinarily performed by full-time professionals, many employers have invested heavily in computerization, which not only eliminates a number of intellectual functions but is also a tool of what is euphemistically called "time management," a fancy term for surveillance and control. Some companies require engineers to punch a clock on the computer at the beginning and the end of a project.

Thus, the application of labor-saving technology in the professional and technical workplace has and will continue to eliminate whole technical occupations and reduce the number of professional jobs. Ironically, even as the technological threat to their jobs provides intellectuals with an incentive to unionize, it undermines their bargaining power. They can no longer claim to have irreplaceable power. On March 30, 1998, the *New York Times* reported that Microsoft and other computer corporations were using a two-tier wage-and-benefit system for programmers and other professionals. Except for a minority of engineers, computer software systems analysts, highly placed architects, and other professionals whose specialized knowledge is linked to product innovation, there is reason for many to be worried. Like physicians who have recently discovered their vulnerability to the technology and reorganization prompted by changes in government and corporate funding, computer engineers and others engaged in the labor of eliminating labor are finding themselves threatened with elimination.

THE HIGHER EDUCATION EXPLOSION

The growth of technical and professional occupations in the first third of the century was closely connected not only to the rise of new machine technologies but also to the sophisticated technologies of human control at the workplace. I do not want to deny the far-reaching functions of education, but none of them meets the dual charge of preparing a disciplined and educated workforce and of providing an "aging vat" for millions of children. At the turn of the century, child labor laws and technological advances began to drive from the factory the children, once a vital component of the labor force. The distillery metaphor should not seem surprising. From 1836, when Massachusetts instituted the first compulsory public school system, to our own day, teachers as much as administrators have been acutely aware of their caretaking functions as well as their educational responsibilities.[4] Without schools, millions of kids might roam the streets and destroy property. The schoolteacher, today a member of the largest single profession (and the most highly organized occupation) in America, has been adjured to transmit the knowledge, work habits, and "values" that are consistent with the industrial and commercial order. But in America's large cities, few teachers in public schools are spared the tasks that can only be described as monitoring and surveillance. Many have to carry out policing functions, such as enforcing classroom discipline among a school population that has little interest in much of the curriculum because they cannot imagine a future in which school knowledge would be valuable to them.

The 1945 Servicemen's Readjustment Act, better known as the G.I. Bill of Rights, was an unprecedented measure; it changed the face of American education. Among other provisions, it enabled returning veterans to complete high school and enter college. By 1950, nearly two million of them had leaped at the chance to get a government-paid formal education. Many were sons and daughters of industrial workers, farmers, and low-level service employees. And then the first baby boom led to a doubling of school-age children — and of teachers — in the 1940s and 1950s. By 1990 there were 3.5 million teachers, counselors, and other education professionals in public and private elementary and secondary schools, and more than a half-million teachers in higher education. Together, health and education formed the center of the new service economy and signaled the rise of the professional and technical worker to a new level of significance.

After graduating from high school most veterans entered clerical and sales occupations, but many of those graduating from college joined the growing ranks of the professions, technical occupations, and low-level management. During the Cold War, military research remained a major source of university funds, but other types of research played an important role: basic science, medical science, and the development of disciplines like solid state physics, which was important to the expanding electronics industry, especially computers. In addition, many universities opened or expanded schools of education, nursing, social work, and business; and they created departments of computer science, medical technology, and public administration to accommodate the demand for professionals in these new fields.

Higher education was quick to become oriented to changes in the economy. The majority of college students made their career choices during junior and senior years or waited until they got their first job. Unlike most prewar college students, who expected to spend four years exploring their intellectual and occupational interests, the new student did not have the time or the money for "self-indulgent" pursuits. Many working-class students concentrated on courses that would improve their expectations and their abilities to get jobs.

Although many college students came from blue-collar union families, some adopted the attitude expressed in a popular saying of the period: "The working class can kiss my ass; I've made the foreman's job at last." Unions might be appropriate for their parents, their siblings, and many of their friends who joined their fathers in the mill or on the truck. But, armed with an education and a degree that proved their new middle-class status, many were listening to the messages from business or conservative groups. Among them was the American tenet that the individual must depend on himself rather than on collective action to improve his standard of living; failure to achieve one's occupational and social goals was an individual's fault, not the system's. Another was that unions were ruining the economy, so their demands for higher wages should be moderated lest inflation devastate the middle class. Finally, the welfare state was putting hard-working Americans in the poorhouse.

Higher education became one of the prominent beneficiaries of the rise of the professions. By 1955 more students graduated from high school than dropped out. By the mid-1960s, half of all high school graduates went to college. In the two decades ending in 1960, attendance in institutions of higher education tripled to 4.5 million, and college graduates became the cadre for the service economy. What was unnoticed at the time was the enormous expansion of higher education as an industry in itself. After 1945 the number of colleges and universities doubled and professors became a large professional group, rivaling in number accountants and social workers. The war had transformed the university in another way; it became the place to a obtain a professional degree. After 1957, the year the Soviets beat the United States to the punch by putting *Sputnik* in space, Congress and the administration considered educational expansion a vital component of national security. For the next fifteen years, funds from the National Defense Education Act (NDEA) supported hundred of thousands of science and math students, as well as many in the liberal arts, and appropriated billions of dollars for defense-related research carried out at universities. The NDEA and similar federal programs were, in fact, the most profligate component of the welfare state, far exceeding in spending the agencies that supported individuals, veterans, and almost every other social program. Business interests, which had traditionally paid for worker training in their own facilities, were happy to support expanded public education; it relieved the firms of much of the cost of training new employees. Besides, the new knowledge-based workplace required entrants who already possessed a higher educational background than corporations could provide.[5]

For the first twenty years after the war, as we have seen, teachers were the great exception to the stable level of the professional population. Since the 1960s the restricted blue-collar notion of unions and their constituents simply has not corresponded to the trends. In the late 1970s and 1980s, when union organizing slowed to a crawl, labor unionism was catching on in, of all places, universities. And not only among clerical workers but also among professors and graduate assistants and physicians and attorneys. The untold story of the 1970s and 1980s — untold partly because it does not fit the pattern concocted by the press and believed by the public — is that the fastest-growing section of the labor movement are unions of professionals.

Since the late 1960s, some 130,000 professors and other education professionals have joined unions, mainly the AFT, the American Association of University Professors (AAUP), and the National Education Association. Unions represent a little under a quarter of full-time faculty in colleges and universities, a higher percentage than union density for the labor force as a whole. The unions have bargaining rights for faculty and staff at some of America's largest universities, such as the California State University system, the State University of New York (with the biggest professional union in the country, representing 22,000 professors and physicians, nurses, and medical technologists in the university's two medical centers), City University of New York, Wayne State, Temple, Rutgers, private universities like St. John's, Long Island, Adelphi, Hofstra, Fordham, and many small four-year and technical colleges. The greatest faculty union density has been achieved in community colleges, where unions, mostly the Teachers, represent about 40 percent of full-time faculty. But the forward motion of unionization among private school faculty was reversed in 1981, when in the *Yeshiva* decision the U.S. Supreme Court declared that, while professors in public higher education are employees, subject to the decisions of the legislature and the university administration, in private schools they are managers of curriculum, salary schedules, and other areas of policy. Under the law, managers are excluded from the jurisdiction of the Labor Relations Board, so, for all intents and purposes, *Yeshiva* ended new unionization efforts among professors in private colleges and universities.

Most professional and technical occupations remain full-time work, but there is a tendency toward part-time, temporary, and contingent work among skilled white-collar and professional workers.

Renewed public interest in higher education has focused on part-time teaching. In large cities where colleges and universities have turned to adjuncts to teach as many as half the classes, there are thousands of people with advanced degrees, including Ph.D.s, each of whom teaches a full load for $15,000 to $20,000 a year, about half the pay of a full-time assistant professor. These people are hired course by course, semester by semester; they have no continuity or job security and few, if any, benefits. Since most adjuncts are not unionized, and the supply of unemployed academics is on the rise, the pay, in some areas, for teaching a course has barely risen in twenty years.

The most important exception to the recent modest record of professional union organizing is among graduate assistants, who are not considered managers under the law. Since many senior faculty members confine their teaching to upper division and graduate seminars, or are able to buy off their teaching duties with research grants, graduate assistants are rapidly becoming the main undergraduate faculty in many so-called research universities. The part-time graduate assistants are, like the adjuncts, paid far less than beginning assistant professors. Their main complaint is that universities have recruited them as students but really want them as a source of cheap labor. Moreover, given the tightening academic job market, many suspect they will never get full-time jobs. They have unionized because they believe that, if they stay in the academy, they are destined to become permanent adjuncts, and union experience is the best way to prepare for the future.

In 1969, the first Graduate Assistants Association was formed at the University of Wisconsin's Madison campus and struck for recognition, which it won. During the next decade, the union, which had enrolled more than two thousand members, struggled to prevent the university administration from decertification as a bargaining agent and rolling back its economic gains. Facing a painfully tight job market, graduate students have helped spread unions to many leading universities — Michigan, California, Indiana, Illinois, Iowa, and some others. And they formed perhaps the country's most celebrated graduate students' union in a private university, Yale. In late spring 1996, just before final exams and grades, insisting they were adjunct instructors, not teachers-in-training as the administration claimed, thousands of graduate assistants left their classrooms in one of the highly publicized labor struggles of the 1990s. Even though the Yale administration refused to recognize the group, the Graduate Assistants Association has remained a force on campus.

Besides graduate assistants' unions, there are adjuncts' unions, especially where the AFT or the AAUP represent full-time faculty. At Rutgers in New Jersey and Nassau Community College on Long Island, adjuncts have formed separate locals and negotiate separate contracts, because they believe the full-time faculty has different interests. In other cases, they are represented by the full-timers' union and negotiate under the full-time faculty and staff agreement. But these arrangements do not take into account a rising need of adjuncts to teach in more than one institution. In many instances, the adjunct earns a living by teaching four to six or seven courses a semester in as many as three or more institutions (in California these teachers are called "freeway flyers"). Unions and the adjuncts themselves have not found the appropriate forms for addressing this situation. But there are models worth investigating. One, developed on the waterfront, in the arts, and in construction, is the hiring hall. Recognizing that the nature of the industry does not commend itself to permanent hires, unions have attempted to set wages and working conditions by controlling the labor supply. At the same time, as in other small industries, the union has encouraged employers to form their own associations, which then sign up with the union because it controls the labor.

Since most adjuncts work for more than one employer, the only way they can improve their salaries and working conditions is to organize unions across institutions. This effort would require the kind of support the Hotel and Restaurant Employees gave to the Yale Graduate Assistants Association: office space, funds for staff, and money for publicity — in short, practical organizing tools. On the whole, neither the AFT nor the AAUP has been forthcoming; on the contrary, both seem reluctant to organize part-timers lest, by improving their salaries and benefits, the associations contribute to making their situation permanent. But, despite the displeasure of the professors, who see their own situation erode, neither have they have mounted a vigorous campaign to convert part-time positions to full-time ones.

As in many other industries, the expansion of part-time work has had serious effects on the salaries and working conditions of full-time faculty and staff. For example, in the early 1980s at New York's City University, there were more than 11,000 full-time faculty members for 200,000 students. By 1996, the number had shrunk to 5300 faculty for 207,000 students. The gap was filled with part-timers. While adjuncts and other part-time teachers taught less than 30 percent of courses in 1978, by 1996 the figure had risen to 50 percent, 60 percent in community colleges. Similarly, the number of part-time faculty has grown at the California State universities, Rutgers, Wayne State, and a number of other major urban schools. Here, faculty salaries remain stagnant, and, in the shadow of the two-tier system, full-time hiring has lagged far behind vacancies. At the same time, the announced policy of administrations and the state legislatures is to accelerate faculty retirements by offering monetary incentives to those over the age of fifty-five. But in many cases rather than making room for younger full-time professors, the retiring or deceased professor takes her or his line with them.

It is hard to imagine that anyone concerned with standards in higher education can fail to be concerned about the heavy work loads for full-time faculty and the steady decline of the full-time teacher-to-student ratio in many schools. Nevertheless, almost none of the debate about the quality of America's colleges and universities has focused on this issue. The responsibility falls on the academic unions. If labor's first job is to raise the bottom, it must address unionized part-time and adjunct teachers' salaries and working conditions. Closely related is the urgent task of organizing the unorganized. The fight must be conducted on the basis of the living wage. And the result would, almost inevitably, make academic administrations realistically consider creating more full-time positions.

A WRITERS' UNION? YOU MUST BE KIDDING

The National Writers Union is one of the boldest forms of union organizing among part-time and contingent professionals. It was organized in 1981 with fewer than a thousand members among an unlikely group: free-lance writers. At first glance, there should be nothing unusual about a union whose membership is composed almost exclusively of part-time, temporary, and contingent professionals. After all, the Musicians Union and the Screen Writers, Directors, Screen Actors, and Variety Artists guilds have the same character. But in the American tradition, magazine and book writers typically make their own deals with editors and publishers; not all of them even have the services of an agent. With the exception of technical writers, the Writers Union's constituents, together with visual artists, are the preeminent creators.

The idea of a union for these people may appear futile. For one thing, the number and variety of publications for which the free lancer writes make traditional trade union standards seem difficult to attain. And the fact that few people, other than technical writers, make their living exclusively from writing books or magazine articles may be attributable to the rich supply of writers. Yet, despite these obstacles, the Writers Union, now Local 1981–UAW, has more than four thousand members in about twenty chapters in most of the country's major cities, as well as in some smaller areas. The union offers health benefits to members at group rates; conducts seminars on issues pertaining to the writers' market; has, through a model book contract, established standards it asks members to honor when negotiating; and handles grievances on members' behalf. It has run several successful campaigns to organize writers for such liberal magazines as *The Nation, Ms.,* and *Mother Jones,* and has joined with other writers' groups — notably PEN and the Authors' Guild — to protest the censorship of the work of Salman Rushdie and other authors.

NWU is a pioneer on the sensitive matter of writers' rights over work of theirs that is transmitted by magazine publishers electronically over the Internet. Union representatives have testified at hearings and the union has publicized the issue in its own and trade publications. After nearly two decades of dedicated and frustrating work, the Writers Union has become a modest but respected force in publishing. The UAW, to its credit, subsidized much of its organizing work but has recently put pressure on the local to pay its own way. The problem is that, even if dues were substantially increased, revenues would never balance expenditures. Although most writers and artists are not in the same position as most of the poor, they are not able to contribute enough for the union to maintain an adequate staff.

As with part-timers in academia, the complex issues facing free-lance writers and other artists cannot be addressed fully until the labor movement turns its attention to the professions and to the growing phenomenon of part-time and temporary labor. As the UAW discovered, organizing was easier among full-time editors and clericals in publishing, and, despite the staffing crisis, the AFT and AAUP have remained, in effect, full-time faculty and staff unions. However, despite labor's having turned its attention elsewhere, some of the most unlikely occupations are turning toward the unions. This trend will probably gather steam early in the new century as professional workers suffer some of the difficulties that have already befallen blue-collar workers.

▪

Physicians these days harbor no illusions about their position in the new world of managed care. For example, facing substantial fee reductions because of lower Medicare and insurance schedules, in 1996 a national union of podiatrists, most of whom were in private practice, was organized under the aegis of the AFL-CIO Office and Professional Employees. And only ten years ago there were exactly two unions for interns and residents — in New York and San Francisco; in 1997 the Service Employees, with which these older groups were affiliated, had eight locals of doctors, interns, and residents in hospitals in Boston, Las Vegas, Philadelphia, and other cities. In addition, several unaffiliated house staff unions were organized in New York and San Francisco. With the emergence of managed care, health maintenance organizations now employ a huge number of physicians at salaries considerably lower than what they formerly earned as private practitioners. Several organizing campaigns by AFL-CIO affiliates are under way among salaried doctors and other professionals. More than fifteen hundred lawyers employed by the Legal Aid Society and the government-funded Legal Services Corporation have organized national locals into the Auto Workers union.

Like attorneys and physicians, the more than quarter-million accountants have, until recently, been one of the last holdouts of small entrepreneurship. In contrast, the eight largest accounting firms (now reduced by mergers to six) did audits for big corporations and were the tax consultants for an array of well-heeled individuals. Two significant changes in the accounting profession have dramatically shifted the prospects for its professionals. The larger firms and a fair number of intermediate-size companies have won more business by expanding their services to financial consulting, management consulting, and investment counseling. They perform the traditional external audit for large enterprises, but now also carry out the internal audit and tax services for corporate executives and managerial staff.

Instead of hanging out a shingle, graduates of leading academic accounting programs are eager to obtain a job with one of these successful firms. They hope that, after five years, fate will smile on them and make them partners. If they don't reach that goal, they will probably shift to smaller firms. For the few who stay on, salaries will be fairly generous, but power over their work fairly small. The development of computer tax programs will, in time, enable many, if not most, individuals who now use professional consultants to perform the calculations required by tax statements. With the spread of the do-it-yourself accounting technology, prospects for the small, self-employed professional are uncertain. Yet, except in the public sector, accountants remain outside the labor movement.

A RAY OF HOPE

Many trade unionists are beginning to smell the coffee. Every rank-and-file auto, textile, and steel worker who has been around during the past twenty years has witnessed the shrinkage or disappearance of his plant. These workers don't need a guidebook to remind them that the factory of tomorrow will be as close to people-less as corporate technology can manage — or it won't stay in the United States. At the same time, their children, spouses, and some friends are scrambling to get credentials; there are virtually no good new jobs in production shops, even if the squeeze is on in most professions. The major car companies have not yet called back all laid-off workers from the last recession, and the heyday of the large steel and textile mills is over. But the great divide between intellectual and manual labor, between blue- and white-collar trade unionists, has not been closed. For most of labor, the game remains organizing people like "us."

From a strategic perspective, labor has little choice but to broaden its embrace to include those at the cusp of the new economy: knowledge producers. Just as Walter Reuther foresaw that millions of teachers were ripe for union organization — the UAW became the patron of the American Federation of Teachers, and New York's District 65 performed the same role for the great Hospital Workers union campaign of the 1960s — so contemporary labor must take seriously its responsibility to *all* who work for wages and salaries. It is more than a question of money; equally important is the recognition that the issues facing white-collar and professional employees are labor's vital concern. A beginning was made when John Sweeney walked the Yale and Barnard picket lines in the spring of 1996, and when eight physicians' unions merged with the Service Employees.

But this awareness must lead to more varied activities: not since 1983, when the AFL-CIO commissioned a study on the future of work, has the labor movement addressed the broad issues of technological changes' impact on the evolving workplace. Moreover, although health care workers face layoffs because of hospital closings and reorganizations, privatization, and reduced public funding, the AFL-CIO has not intervened in the debate or used its lobbying muscle to publicize and fight the catastrophic national health care situation. Instead, its two major health care employees' affiliates are left with the task of picking up the pieces at the bargaining table.

There is no pat formula for organizing the two million engineers and computer programmers who are outside labor's ranks. There is almost no active organizing taking place among these groups. Nor do working scientists seem eager to explore unionization. Nonetheless, only at its own peril will labor persist in ignoring the importance of knowledge and the knowledge workers. Here is a purely defensive example. In 1962, the Oil, Chemical, and Atomic Workers struck a fully automated oil refinery complex, employing thirty-six hundred workers, in Port Arthur, Texas. For a solid year, the Shell Oil Company maintained 100 percent of the plant's production with six hundred nonunion supervisors and staff, many of them engineering professionals. The union lost the strike. In this and many other branches of the oil and chemical industries, strikes have become outmoded, because, in the era of high technology, it is the managers and professionals who control production.

So the question is whether the labor movement is capable of spreading its arms wide enough to take in all of labor. The answer will provoke another question: Can unions absorb and utilize the new ideas that today propel the economy, work processes, and the modern cultural elements linked to science, medicine, and technology? And, once it does grasp the future, will labor exhibit the same strategic ingenuity among the knowledge producers as it did when it campaigned to organize the working poor? The task can be accomplished only by people with a fresh vision, trade unionists who can address educational issues, work autonomy, issues of gender, race, and sex discrimination, and, last but certainly not least, the corporate conception that managers are an extension of themselves and not a form of labor.

In the last thirty-five years, at the national level only the late Albert Shanker and the Teachers have shown that their vision extends beyond bread-and-butter unionism. While many of Shanker's ideas were controversial even in trade union terms — his advocacy of national educational standards to secure the professional status of classroom teachers, for example — he was one of the few union leaders to express his views on the national platform. Like Reuther, he became a public intellectual as well as the voice of his own members, and helped make classroom teachers a visible component of the national culture. One may disagree with much of what he said, but his legacy should be carried on by the current leadership — even of the Teachers union. Where, now, are the visionaries of the knowledge classes? Labor cannot afford to concede the mantle to the likes of Bill Gates and Steve Jobs — two of the moguls of the late-twentieth-century nonunion workplace — lest it vindicate the grim prognostication of its adversaries: that unions are destined to irrelevance.

7 ✒ Labor and American Politics

> The union member is first and foremost a citizen
> of his community. — *AFL-CIO Constitution*

> The labor movement can only be effective if it
> becomes less an economic movement and more a
> social movement. — *Walter Reuther*

WITH ALL ITS MONEY and vast membership, the labor movement has been unable to advance its legislative and political
program. It has not won government-financed universal health care,
got minimum wages equal to those of other advanced industrial societies, or retained progressive taxation. Many corporations and wealthy
individuals pay little or no taxes, while workers bear the brunt of
them. Unions have not even taken up the cause that labor movements
in all the European countries know is central in the battle against
unemployment and the spread of part-time jobs — legislation mandating shorter hours. In this period of massive economic restructuring real wages have stagnated and labor has been unable to maintain
the living standards of a large chunk of its own members, let alone all
working people.

Contrary to much expert opinion and the way labor itself tells the
story, it is not numbers or union density that accounts for the weakening of labor's political clout. As the Canadian and French experiences
demonstrate, it is possible for labor movements with fewer financial
resources and even lower densities than the American movement to

have consistent and enduring effects on the political climate of their societies. In those countries, the right, as it has done in the United States, embarked on pernicious programs, but the effectiveness of resistance abroad is much higher than here, so, despite some erosion of the social wage, the conservative programs of the American "model" has been stalled in Germany, Italy, and France.

There is no doubt that labor's organizing policy is at odds with its political strategy. As we saw in chapter four, the Sweeney administration has provided the most aggressive and unapologetic support for unionizing efforts among the working poor in the postwar history of American unions. But it is as if there were two AFL-CIOs. Labor has begun to come alive as an economic movement; but with regard to its social and political policies, the AFL-CIO seems cemented into positions that are directly opposed to its organizing agenda. Saddled with a Republican Congress, labor is reluctant to make an active effort to rescind many of the onerous provisions of Taft-Hartley, especially its approval of replacement workers, the ban on secondary boycotts and sympathy strikes, and the eighty-day cooling-off period. Nor has it held the president and congressional Democrats to a rigorous pro-labor standard either on labor reform legislation or on social wage policies.

Rather, accommodation and compromise with a conservative Democratic Party ultimately undermine labor's urgent tasks. For example, labor needs Labor Relations Act amendments that restrict the employers' right to a Labor Board–supervised election to determine representation. It needs punitive sanctions against employers who violate workers' rights. And in the wake of the weakening of Occupational Safety and Health law enforcement, labor must mount a public campaign to protect workers on the job. Moreover, if the experience of farm and hospital workers is any guide, organizing the working poor must take the form of a crusade, and part of that crusade's purpose should be to make poverty a public issue and thereby gather legions of allies among students, women, and middle-class organizations. Such a coalition would campaign for the repeal of the bipartisan welfare reform of 1996 and for dramatic raises in the minimum wage as part of a comprehensive policy for a new political realignment.

As demonstrated by the 1997 Teamsters strike against the United Parcel Service, when unions take on the two-tier wage system through direct action, they are, in effect, opposing the program of a large segment of corporate America and its bipartisan political supporters. The Carey affair shows that unions would be naive to underestimate what labor's enemies are prepared to do to cut off the movement at the knees. Even if the next Congress does not enact yet another round of anticorruption measures directed at the labor movement, we have not seen the last of the attacks. Although I believe that Carey brought grief upon himself and upon the labor movement, there is plenty of evidence showing that whenever labor raises its voice, established power has lowered its noise.

The reason for the current bind in its political and legislative policy is that, unlike the right, American labor does not function as a political party. Instead, AFL-CIO is a faction of the Democratic Party but without a public voice of its own. Some labor leaders are reluctant to speak in behalf of all working people, fearing that some union members will object to parts of labor's program. For example, one could speculate that AFL-CIO's reluctance to publicize its opposition to the 1996 welfare reform package was motivated, in part, by such fears. Many union members have been influenced by the media's echoing the conservative mantra that welfare recipients are "cheats" and that single parents, especially mothers, are sexually irresponsible and ought to pay for their sins. Indeed, very little positive information about the poor comes from any quarter of organized labor. With the abortion issue, the Executive Council stood by in embarrassed silence; and now, an audible utterance on the question of public assistance seems beyond the will of labor's spokespeople.

Compromised by political myopia and a short-sighted assessment of its political options, labor, for the past twenty years of conservative dominance in politics, has offered no offensive strategy. On Capitol Hill it continues to backpedal. There is little reason, then, for the press or the public to pay attention. In fact, there is little reason for the public to believe that labor's political beliefs are any different from those of the Clinton administration. Of course, if one examines convention resolutions, the labor press, and some of Sweeney's speeches, one can see the difference, and if the labor movement took the matter seriously, it could make that difference politically significant. While, as I indicated earlier, there is considerable room for improvement, especially on gender and race issues — and these are no small matters — there is enough in the programs of the federation and most of its affiliates to form the core of a new party of labor. The main problems are lack of political will and the fear of many in the top leadership that such a course would mortally wound the labor movement by isolating it from mainstream America.

But American labor has another unacknowledged problem. When critics, including this writer, argue that unions are more like insurance companies than movements, the statement should not be taken as a metaphor. For historical reasons, many unions are health and life insurers, and some do recruit members on the basis of these benefits. Some unions, like the needle trades, as we saw, are staunch supporters of universal health care, but others stayed on the sidelines during the 1993 health care fight, because they felt the plan was not in their interest. Many labor organizations have a lot to lose by risking the union's treasury and other resources on confrontational activities like strikes. The burden of labor's complex institutionalization, such as its deep legal entanglements in insurance, federal management, and reporting requirements, exert conservative pressure on even some progressive union leaders.

One sign of the failure of labor's nerve is that the AFL-CIO has made no appreciable effort to correct one of the crucial deficiencies in its approach to political education. Labor's near blackout in newspapers, on television, and on radio has done nothing to increase its visibility. For example, since the 1950s, when the AFL sponsored a nightly radio news broadcast, there has been no regular presentation of labor's views on network television or radio. Nor are there plans afoot to implement one of the long-held dreams of the progressive labor movement: a national labor daily. In short, if to *be* is to be *seen*, in the public sphere there is no labor movement.

Moreover, while conservative and business-oriented think tanks supply hordes of "experts" to talk shows, the thirteen-million-member AFL-CIO does not support a broadly based institute to compare with the Heritage Foundation, American Enterprise, Manhattan, and Cato, all of which regularly deliver the religion of free enterprise and conservative social and economic policy to the news media. Right-wing business interests and their intellectuals dominate the public conversation with their ideological message; they have a well-directed philosophy of untrammeled capitalism that informs their positions on nearly every political and social issue. In contrast, unionists, true to their pragmatic traditions, which worked only during the regulation era, have been content with piecemeal reform. The media announce this doctrine as the "American Way," but it is a leftover from a bygone era. The AFL-CIO has espoused organizing, collective bargaining, and human rights, and has thoroughly argued against bipartisan free-trade policies. But it has not directly addressed the basis of these policies, that is, the ambition of global transnational corporations — and their agencies, such as the World Bank and the International Monetary Fund — to make the world safe for capital.

Of course, to take on the transnationals, labor would need its own form of internationalism, and to forge such a program, it would require a fully dimensional estimate of the degree to which business interests have melded with those of the government and the political parties. Nor is it only a question of the huge corporate contributions to election campaigns (which in 1996 beat those of unions by twenty to one). It would have to understand and acknowledge that the insiders' joke about Bill Clinton being the greatest Republican president of the twentieth century is not at all funny. Both political parties are in the thrall of business and, in contrast to its traditional populist stance, the Democrat Party today makes no bones about it. It competes with the Republican Party for the label "probusiness."

One of the myths about labor is that the difference between the craft and industrial unions was that the AFL engaged in "pure and simple" unionism, in contrast to the CIO, which was committed as much

to political as to industrial action. On the contrary. Even as it trum-
peted its nonpartisanship for most of the twentieth century, organized labor has entered partisan politics, mostly in behalf of Democrats. Although this alliance was informal and, on a few occasions,
strained, it was never sundered after 1912, when the AFL supported
Woodrow Wilson's bid for the White House. By the time of the New
Deal, organized labor was firmly in the party's fold. And for the last
forty years, labor's political machinery has been an indispensable
component of national and most state Democratic organizations. In
major industrial states, in fact, Democratic victories hinge on strong
labor support. For this reason, the labor movement is afraid to publicly oppose a Democratic administration's policies, let alone lead the
charge against them.[1]

That is what made remarkable the AFL-CIO's spirited campaign
against the 1993 North American Free Trade Agreement. Labor's
opposition to NAFTA was even more extraordinary in that it was
undertaken during the watch of Lane Kirkland, a loyal acolyte of
George Meany. That Kirkland should have taken issue with NAFTA,
an agreement first negotiated by the Bush administration and then
adopted as a cornerstone of Clinton's foreign policy, was not entirely
because of the treaty's probable harm to American jobs. The labor
movement in the past had not taken serious issue with most of the
practices of free trade even though they led to the loss of workers'
jobs. On the contrary, with only a few exceptions — mainly textiles,
apparel, and auto parts — labor showed little inclination, even under
Republican administrations, to put pressure on Congress when it
considers tariffs and import quotas.

The AFL-CIO under Kirkland, and its conservative allies, came
close to sinking NAFTA, which Clinton, after some hesitation, had
finally embraced, and it came under terrific pressure from some affiliates. Those unions, in the 1980s, had seen large segments of their
membership melt away, and they tended to blame the corporate policies of runaway shops and other forms of capital flight for most of
their losses. Mistakenly, as it turned out, they saw a chance for a
reversal of fortune with the new Democratic presidency. Indeed, Clin-

ton himself had been skeptical about the treaty, but in the end he backed the deal because, among other reasons, he foresaw, correctly, little chance of political condemnation from organized labor. In the administration's calculus, labor had no place to go. On the other hand, major business groups were clamoring for the treaty, and Clinton knew they could ruin his re-election chances if he bowed to labor.

John Sweeney, whose relationship to the Clinton administration is closer than Kirkland's was, obviously believes that labor's home is the Democratic Party. He has made no public moves, therefore, to slow or reverse the administration's pursuit of free trade, despite considerable evidence that in its first three years NAFTA has cost American workers more than 100,000 jobs. Like the welfare reform and the balanced budget debates, which became occasions for drastic cuts in social wages, labor's legislative strategy on foreign trade has been to work within the lines drawn by the administration. While, in 1997, labor did oppose the president's having so-called fast track powers, which would limit Congress's function only to voting trade treaties up or down, the federation leadership confined its intervention to dealing with free trade's effect on specific industries and groups of workers. As on most issues, the federation was fated to remain a behind-the-scenes player.

American labor's relationship to electoral politics has always been ambivalent. Apart from a small group of radicals, who have inconsistently urged the movement to adopt an independent stance, mainstream labor is most effective when it engages in defensive politics. Despite years of political action, many unions remain bastions of contract unionism. The tradition of holding political action at a distance may be traced to the origins of the AFL, where Samuel Gompers laid down the doctrine that workers and their unions should not seek redress from government. The labor movement was to be independent of both major political parties and concern itself with legislation only to the extent that the gains to be made could not be achieved at the bargaining table. According to one writer, labor's creed was "only for maladies beyond the reach of collective bargaining ought workers seek political cures. Wages and hours were no proper matter for legislators. The union, not the state, was to be looked to for insurance against unemployment, ill-health or old age."[2]

For Gompers, the best plan was to control the market for skilled labor and to carry out collective bargaining with employers. For this reason, what Theodore Roosevelt dubbed the mainstream of "organized labor" did not join the political opposition of its day: the populist movement and the socialists. Nevertheless, from its inception, the AFL did enter politics, but only to protect skilled-labor monopolies or to encourage a political climate favorable to economic organization. That is why the AFL favored legislation to restrict immigration, ban goods made by convict labor, curb female labor, and abolish child labor. And, since most government employees were denied collective bargaining, labor advocated in legislatures in their behalf. After 1896 the AFL maintained a National Legislative Committee in Washington and gradually assumed the main coordinating function of its affiliates' legislative agents. But in a reversal, in 1908 the AFL made its first presidential endorsement, of the Democrat William Jennings Bryan, and by the time of Woodrow Wilson's successful run in 1912, the federation was well on its way to an active and partisan role in electoral politics.

Why did Gompers and other AFL leaders depart from their earlier practice of steering clear of partisan politics? At the turn of the century, major corporations were taking a direct role in the operations of government, and capital had become inextricably linked to the state. The AFL, saddled with a craft-union base, was rapidly being marginalized, so Gompers acquiesced to the entreaties of radicals to organize unskilled and semiskilled workers. That endeavor called for a favorable political environment to neutralize the corporations' power to thwart the union. Now, rather than viewing government as captive, labor saw the state as an essentially neutral agent which, given proper circumstances, might support labor's cause. In return, the AFL had to abandon its antipathy to political involvement. Some trade unionists, alarmed by brazen corporate power at the workplace, formed revolutionary unions. But Gompers took the line that if you can't fight 'em, join 'em. He was named a member of the executive committee of the business-led National Civic Federation, which sought to ameliorate the conditions that produced militant industrial actions and achieve class peace through dialogue between capital and labor.

During World War I, when the AFL collaborated with several wartime labor and production boards set up by the Wilson administration, Gompers pledged to suspend the use of the strike for the duration, and he gained the president's good offices in securing employer recognition of several unions engaged in organizing workers. In 1924, confronted with a conservative Democratic contender, John Davis, a corporation lawyer (later the defense attorney for the segregationists in *Brown* v. *Board of Education*), labor supported the Progressive Party standard bearer, Robert LaFollette, on a third-party ticket that Gompers, from his deathbed, blessed. But this episode did not signal a change of course. After the election, the AFL declined to work with these voters to form a new political party.

What did labor's involvement in politics mean on the ground? Not much. For the first half-century of its existence, the AFL maintained no political apparatus by which to educate its members. It was not until the New Deal that labor jumped with both feet into the political arena. In 1935, facing what many believed would be a tough re-election, Roosevelt aggressively solicited the active support of the new industrial unions on the basis of his pledge to support many of labor's legislative goals. Already involved in the New Deal, if not the Democratic Party, the needle trades' unionists Sidney Hillman and David Dubinsky led an exodus from the Socialist Party, which had refused to collaborate with the Democrats. To support Roosevelt, John L. Lewis, a lifelong Republican, abandoned his party (as it turned out, only temporarily); the Communists were motivated by their search for a broad antifascist front to hop aboard the Roosevelt coalition; and many other trade unionists became convinced that labor required a friendly government to secure its interests. A new era in modern labor history had begun.

But it was not until World War II that, under Sidney Hillman's guidance, the CIO built the first genuinely effective political organization of labor. The CIO's Political Action Committee (PAC), organized on a national, state, and local basis, employed a full-time staff to work with state and local councils on congressional and state campaigns and, of course, in behalf of the national Democratic ticket. Although the committee was ostensibly nonpartisan, it was, in fact, the Democratic Party's labor arm. This relationship was sealed in 1948, when, despite its reservations about Truman, the CIO refused to endorse Henry A. Wallace's third-party campaign and suppressed its suspicion that, despite his veto, Truman welcomed most of the Taft-Hartley provisions. Labor plunged into the president's re-election bid and played a significant role in his come-from-behind victory.

When the AFL and CIO merged in 1955, it combined its two political operations into the Committee on Political Education (COPE), modeled on PAC. The structure calls for a national director, who reports to the AFL-CIO president; a full-time staff of regional representatives, who work with state and local federations of labor; and COPE organizations within international and local unions. While the Executive Council makes policy and determines AFL-CIO political strategy, the tactics are directed by COPE's Operating Committee, made up of representatives from leading affiliates, most of whom are COPE directors for their respective unions. In any presidential or midterm election, it is the Operating Committee that makes decisions about which campaigns to concentrate on and how much union money to put into television ads, phone banks, and staff resources. Labor's organization for political action became, ironically, the model for the corporate and conservative PACs in the 1970s and 1980s. While COPE is still capable of delivering for the Democrats, it is today outgunned and outspent by the probusiness groups.

Meanwhile, both the AFL and the CIO streamlined their Washington legislative operations. After the war, labor developed a program to raise unemployment benefits, the minimum wage, public housing, and universal health care. By 1948 labor's lobby was as well financed and potent as any in Washington. After the merger, the AFL-CIO had a staff of legislative lobbyists led by Andrew Biemiller, a trade unionist and former representative from Wisconsin, and most major unions maintained their own Washington staffs, which cooperated with the federation's Legislative Department. In the division of labor, the AFL-CIO Legislative Department called the shots in Congress, but the affiliates were responsible for lobbying the individual government agencies whose jurisdiction bore on a particular trade or industry. The Communications Workers was concerned with the regulation of telephone rates and other matters before the Federal Communications Commission; the Teamsters acted on such matters as freight rates, which came before the Interstate Commerce Commission; and the Oil, Chemical, and Atomic Workers, led by Tony Mazzocchi, the legislative director, became one of the powers behind the enactment and enforcement of the Occupational Safety and Health Act.[3]

During the Kennedy-Johnson era, unions reached the zenith of their postwar influence in national politics. As crucial players in the electoral scene, and fervent supporters of the administrations' unpopular Southeast Asia military intervention, they had ready access to the White House and were able to push some cherished proposals through Congress and the White House. Kennedy's 1962 executive order granting federal employees collective bargaining was perceived by many as opening the gates to public employees organizing also at the local level. In 1965 Congress passed legislation providing medical care for the aged and people on public assistance. Medicare and Medicaid perhaps crowned labor's legislative achievement and were viewed as a prelude to universal health care.

Under George Meany's leadership the AFL-CIO maintained some of the trappings of independence, exemplified by Meany's refusal to support George McGovern's 1972 presidential bid, even when he became the Democratic candidate. During the primary season that year, the AFL-CIO had led the charge for Washington State's Senator Henry Jackson, an outspoken war hawk, who was whipped by a coalition of reform and antiwar Democrats, including some dissident unions, like the Auto Workers, the Machinists, and the State, County, and Municipal Employees. The insurgents not only succeeded in nominating their man, but also were able to change the party rules to give feminists, minority groups, and environmentalists more power on the DNC. Organized labor never forgot or forgave the humiliating defeat of 1972. After Richard Nixon beat McGovern in the general election by a margin that exceeded Johnson's victory over Barry Goldwater eight years earlier, the AFL-CIO joined with the Democratic congressional leadership and powerful party organizations in New York, Illinois, and the South to drive the heathen from the temple. Within a few years the old rules — and the old guard — were back.

The McGovern insurgency marked a low point in the relations between labor and the social movements that had developed in the 1960s. Meany's support of U.S. foreign policy, his reluctance to back the militant wing of the civil rights movement, and the union hierarchy's hostility to left activists was, as we have seen, contested more and more by the rank and file. Yet many activists were prone to making summary judgments that, in the vernacular of the period, unions were "part of the problem, not part of the solution." And some in the New Left dismissed the industrial working class and the labor movement as relics. It may be that capitalism had abolished material deprivation in the advanced industrial societies, but the working class was hopelessly "integrated" by affluence — it had lost its fighting spirit except when seeking "more" from the system.[4] Proponents of this view suggested that social change would come from blacks, women, youth, and the Third World. For a decade, they were the loudest voices on the left, obscuring the fact that others were building new unions, organizing for older unions and forming caucuses that campaigned inside labor for union democracy.

By Meany's lights, the party in 1974 was back on track. Although two years later Jimmy Carter came from left field to capture the Democratic Party's nomination over the heads of AFL-CIO and most of the established party leadership, Meany and his colleagues felt safe again. The voices of antiwar activists, feminists, militant blacks, and dissident public officials had briefly been heard above those of conservatives and conventional liberals, but they were now muted, if not entirely silenced. Sobered by the setbacks sustained during eight Republican years, even some on the party's left fell in line behind Carter, who went on to narrowly defeat Gerald Ford.

✄

Labor's involvement with the federal government is now complex and broad. The AFL-CIO and its affiliates are invited to testify on pending legislation and are generally more potent in opposition to some measures than they are in behalf of their own. Labor representatives are regularly consulted by the Democratic congressional and administration leadership on top appointments to agencies, many departments, and regulatory commissions of vital interest to unions. During Democratic administrations, dozens of labor leaders and staff are appointed to top- and middle-level management positions in these and other agencies. For example, the Carter administration appointed the Clothing and Textile Workers' vice president Howard Samuel to be deputy assistant secretary of labor for international affairs, and Ray Marshall of the University of Texas — perhaps the most prolabor labor secretary since the department was founded in 1913 — became his boss.

The Carter presidency, however, witnessed a decline in labor's legislative and political effectiveness. Setting its sights on labor law reform, especially the infamous section 14b of Taft-Hartley, which gave states the right to ban union and agency shop agreements, AFL-CIO lobbyists were spectacularly unsuccessful. And their relationship with the president was never warm. Unlike Kennedy and Johnson, who knew how to court labor leaders even while demurring on some of labor's key demands, an introspective Carter held the unions at arm's length. And, sensing the president's ambivalence, a rightward-drifting Democratic congressional majority was in no mood to revise the National Labor Relations Act, let alone enact a single major piece of labor-backed legislation. Instead, in 1978 the Democratic Congress passed the most sweeping business deregulation legislation since the Sherman Antitrust Act, which established the framework for federal jurisdiction over business mergers, trans-

portation and communications rates, and other commercial activities. After deregulation, transportation unions, which had thrived on
regulation, were scrambling to keep up with the wave of mergers,
acquisitions, and bankruptcies that accompanied the transformation.
And, of course, the airline unions were thrown on the defensive as
corporations demanded wage and benefit concessions.

In the ensuing decade, stunned by the effects of deregulation,
many unions were forced on the picket line to defend their gains. In
some cases, notably Continental, Eastern, and some regional airlines,
the issue was the very existence of the unions. Continental, for example, succeeded in routing the unions and, until the Teamsters reor-
ganized its 4800 mechanics in 1997, operated on an entirely open-
shop basis. The unions thwarted a similar move by Eastern, but only
at the cost of the airline's demise. The AFL-CIO gave perfunctory
support to these unions but, in the case of trucking, failed to oppose
deregulation legislation. Only the Teamsters offered some resistance,
but they were ignored. Since 1979 the union has lost nearly a million
members to mergers, leasing arrangements whereby drivers become,
ostensibly, owners of their own rigs, and bankruptcies among the
smaller carriers. Much of the decline is attributable directly to deregulation. Many new trucking companies have sprung up in the last
twenty years and operate on a nonunion basis. Unperturbed by deregulation, labor's leaders were nevertheless distressed by Carter's
embrace of the politics of austerity and the administration's lacklus-
ter backing of their legislative program.

But these leaders were not sufficiently exercised by Carter's conservatism on domestic issues to back Ted Kennedy's unprecedented
challenge to a sitting president of the same party in the spring 1980
primaries. Kennedy attacked Carter for his scorn of workers' interests, especially his fiscal conservatism, the partial dismantling of the
remnants of the antipoverty program, and his inability or unwillingness to address the problem of long-term unemployment through a
vigorous job creation program. Kennedy's challenge was the last gasp
of the party's liberal wing.

The 1980 presidential primaries might have provided organized labor with an opportunity to forge a new majority within the Democratic Party. To win, it would have had to become allied with some of the same forces it had fought during the McGovern insurgency, especially the feminists and ecologists, and the coalition might also have had to include the black freedom movement. It might have been obliged to support abortion rights, despite the reservations of part of its large Catholic membership, and to seek alternatives to job losses that might result from environmental regulations. But in the face of the new centrism within the Democratic Party, which was ideologically unsympathetic even to labor's most modest programs, the labor movement chose to close ranks behind the party establishment, and that helped seal the fate of liberal democracy for years.

As a powerful voice within a chronically minority party, labor was able to preserve at least one element of the legacy of Sidney Hillman. Even though organized labor might not have been be able to name the party's presidential candidate, through its still formidable membership, campaign contributions (in some elections about a third of the Democrats' total expenditures), and its ability to field an army of campaign workers, the AFL-CIO had built up a sufficient presence to veto any objectionable contender. At the same time, its criteria of acceptability slowly veered to the right. While some perennial contenders for the Democratic presidential nomination, such as Missouri's Dick Gephardt, were closer to the labor movement on some issues than was Clinton, union chiefs, tired of roaming in the wilderness during the Reagan-Bush years, were only too happy to welcome the avowedly centrist Arkansas governor as their own.

The AFL-CIO has been an integral — and disciplined — component of the Democratic leadership. This relationship, forged during the dark days of the Reagan reign, was codified in 1988, when the federation accepted fifteen seats on the Democratic National Committee. Labor's strategy of political integration has had many consequences. A natural corollary of its becoming a constituent of the party, rather than a strategic ally or an independent critic, is that trade union leaders tend to think and act as Democrats. For example, having decided that an alternative to Clinton was unthinkable even as, in 1995, he appeared to capitulate to Gingrich and the Republican congressional majority, privately and publicly many labor leaders and liberal politicians assured one another that Clinton was really on their side; his ideological centrism and his tactical backpedaling were merely ways to save his presidency and close ranks against the Republicans. After all, they reasoned, didn't he run in 1992 on a program of job creation, universal health care, and renewed federal aid to education? In a time of apparently deepening Republican recessions, wasn't he making the economy the central campaign issue?

But in office Clinton has proved that he meant what he said: he was a free trader in foreign economic policy and, by his embrace of the Republican balanced budget doctrine, proved that he was a conservative on domestic issues. It wasn't only that the administration's tepid health care plan, which handed the wolf — large insurance companies — the task of guarding the chicken coop, went down to ignominious defeat, or that its job creation program was whittled into oblivion even before being taken up by a rebellious Congress. Or that Clinton responded to the 1996 pilots' strike against American Airlines by using both the Taft-Hartley eighty-day cooling-off injunction and the sixty-day Railway Labor Act against the union. He has been unable to draw any line in the sand, especially after the Republican 1994 midterm sweep. Instead, he quickly co-opted the two main planks of the Republican platform, welfare reform and the balanced budget, while assuring his shrunken liberal flank that he meant well.

⚑

Whether the AFL-CIO's current political and legislative policy did once serve labor's interest, growing evidence shows that it no longer does. In its classic formulation a party is distinguished by two salient features: it openly proclaims its distinctive interest in behalf of a social group or groups, and it is prepared to act as an independent force up to and including taking power in its own name.

In the first place, the party of labor must decide whether it can tolerate capitalist dominance of every itch and scratch of American life, especially within the two major parties. Where, in 1908, Gompers was invited to join in the corporate celebration, today's trade unions are often treated as pariahs. So the option of collaboration, touted by some as labor's preferred strategy, may not exist. For labor to define its difference, it may not be necessary for it to delineate a program for the construction of an alternative economic system. But certainly it would not be excessive if it exposed the rampant, shameless, and bold corporate takeovers of politics, culture, government, and the workplace. Labor could point out that what leading corporations want for the country is not necessarily good for most of us. It could show how large corporations have broken the social compact that sustained American prosperity and have replaced it with the law of "winner take all." By enunciating a doctrine of political and social difference, labor could take the first steps toward defining a new majority.

A party of labor can take many forms: together with its allies it can constitute a third major electoral force in American politics, as it did, briefly, during the 1924 presidential campaign; it can remain within the Democratic Party but as a full-fledged alternative to the prevailing party establishment; or it can leave the Democratic Party. If labor finds that its best interests are no longer served by a government seemingly intent on stripping working people of their gains, the last option may be justified. It would entail restoring the early injunction to remain outside the formal apparatus of the party system. But it would not prevent labor from conducting, on behalf of its program, the campaigns of those running for Congress and other legislative bodies, and putting up its own candidates in congressional, state, and local elections. Labor would be free to decline endorsing a presidential candidate; and by refusing to commit itself to the party apparatus, it could use its independence to draw a prospective candidate toward its positions.

The party of labor is a concept, not an institution. In my view there is no principle involved in the formal founding of a labor party that considers putting up a full slate of candidates for public office, including Congress and the presidency. In this respect, for example, the AFL's decision not to form a new electoral party or become affiliated with an existing one was not necessarily consistent with anti-politics. It was an expression of what Vivian Vale has termed "conservative syndicalism." Gompers's early philosophy was to confine trade union-ism to the economic movement on the conviction that any entangle-ment with the state would compromise labor's interests. Suppose, for argument's sake, that the labor movement, assessing the last fifty years of its collaboration with the political system, decides that both the government and the two-party system are firmly in the pocket of the transnational corporations that call the policy tune. If this were to be determined as a working idea, labor might disengage from the Democratic Party and proceed on the determination that labor is a social movement, not a collaborator in the system of power. It could declare that a real democracy entails a transfer of power in many areas of public life, from corporations to working people.

In the new century, the point of labor's political program should be to renew the perception that the movement has the intention, the power, and the will to change the face of America. At the bargaining table labor would demand the end of the two-tier wage system, sup-port measures to bring up the bottom, shorten working hours, and provide a substantial social wage. What are the irreducible political demands corresponding to these economic demands? Without a clear articulation of such demands the labor movement cannot at-tract a new generation of workers to its ranks. Its efforts will remain confined to shop-by-shop, workplace-based incremental organizing, which at best can help labor to tread water. If labor were to fulfill the hope expressed by Walter Reuther and by John Sweeney, that it be a social movement, it would have to embrace the whole range of work-ers' needs, social as well as economic. The labor movement could not remain tied to corporate capitalism; it would have to acknowledge that its goals are, in the main, opposed to those of the large corpora-tions and their political retainers in both major political parties. At the minimum it would have to:

1. Elaborate what labor means by a decent standard of living for all Americans. One of its components would be a dramatic boost in the minimum wage and guaranteed income for all. Second, as the wave of General Motors strikes for shorter hours in 1996 and 1997

revealed, many working people believe they are working too hard and want to be relieved of the oppression of long hours. Moreover, because technological change is destroying many good working-class jobs and replacing them with part-time and temporary work, the AFL-CIO must put its weight behind shorter-hours legislation. Shorter hours is also a job creation program, because it forces employers to hire more workers. Third, labor must be the loudest voice against poverty, because low wages and chronic joblessness drag down the working conditions of all workers, not just the poor. Regardless of the Clinton administration's relationship to a Republican Congress, labor should fight for a federal job creation program at a living wage with decent benefits to replace workfare or, as an alternative, insist that workfare jobs be converted into real jobs at the prevailing wage. Recognizing that there is no point in forcing people on the job market in a time of chronic job shortages, labor should fight to have the welfare law amended, making work for welfare recipients a voluntary program. Until that happens, the government should not be allowed to force parents to work unless it provided adequate day care.

2. Vigorously pursue the goals of economic and social equality at all levels of life. This would oblige labor to insist on a more progressive system of taxation and to oppose the current trend of heaping more of the tax burden on the backs of working people, including the poor. On issues of social equality, the AFL-CIO, if not its affiliates, has made important strides. Sweeney was instrumental in forming a Womens Affairs Department and naming Karen Nussbaum, a powerful fighter for womens' rights, to head it. Bill Fletcher, the AFL-CIO education director, is a fervent advocate of black and minority rights. However, as many trade union officials now recognize, labor cannot take the fight for equality into the public arena unless its own house is in order.

The problem of taking the spirit of social equality to the affiliates is complex. As president of a loose federation of autonomous affiliates, Sweeney and each of his successors will have little more than a bully pulpit to influence organizations like the Building Trades. But Sweeney has not yet used his pulpit to rid the labor movement of its

own inequalities. Thirty-five years after the first confrontations between the civil rights movement and the Building Trades, women and
minorities are still severely underrepresented in the lucrative area of
commercial construction. In some cities, locals of the Plumbers, Electricians, and Riggers are almost lily-white. Among Carpenters, blacks
are de facto segregated in locals that have little access to good jobs.
And in order to fulfill guidelines requiring minority representation
on federally funded projects, many construction trade unions and
contractors shuttle the few minority craftspersons from job to job,
without allowing them to accumulate seniority. But the Building
Trades are not the only culprits. Minorities have trouble breaking
into other skilled crafts, as well.

3. If labor were an independent force, the AFL-CIO could de-
velop and publicize its own foreign policy, based on the principle of
international labor solidarity. The first element might be a trade policy that balances the interests of American workers with those of
workers in other countries. For example, labor would question GM's
shifting its production facilities from North America to off-shore
sites. Currently, the company is building four large offshore assembly
plants.[5] Its aim is to increase the share of foreign plants from 20
percent to 50 percent of its total production. Labor could revive the
concept of domestic content, according to which a fixed proportion
of every car or truck must be built in the United States. And it could
insist that transnational corporations like GM observe decent labor
standards and dramatically raise wages in its offshore locations. Labor
could oppose granting favored-nation status to countries that have
been guilty of human rights violations, both those having to do with
fair labor standards and those having to do with the right of people to
political dissent, organize free trade unions and political opposition
groups.

It is true the new AFL-CIO leadership is sensitive to these issues
and has, from time to time, expressed reservations about the Clinton
administration's alliances with countries that ban free trade unions,
jail trade unionists, and repress all forms of political opposition. And
unions like UNITE have, together with the National Labor Commit-

tee — an independent labor and human rights organization — addressed the issue of foreign sweatshops with militancy and skill. But the AFL-CIO has been slow to intervene in many instances where trade union and other human rights have been trampled, allowing the Clinton administration to pursue its probusiness trade policy with almost no opposition.

The International Department of the AFL has taken steps to separate itself from the Cold War nationalism of its predecessors. It is reducing its commitments to such organizations as the Agency for International Free Labor Development (AIFLD) and the Foundation for Democracy. Both of them have worked with government intelligence agencies in pursuit of U.S. policies. At the same time it is extending its hand to European labor movements in the hope of strengthening cooperative relationships in collective bargaining with transnational corporations, supporting the social charter of the European Community, which AFL-CIO officials say they would like to extend to the United States and to the Americas, and, perhaps, seeking membership in European labor coordinating organizations. Unfortunately, these steps are not visible on the political and legislative face of the labor movement.

4. Which leads to the final point in assessing labor's relationship to American politics: the problem of its visibility on many issues of concern to working people. Except for the flurry of press attention that accompanied the victory of the Sweeney slate in the fall of 1995, the political presence of the AFL-CIO is today barely a blip on the news screen. In major metropolitan dailies, strikes and other labor developments are still routinely treated as business news; in fact, the *Wall Street Journal* devotes more space to labor than the *New York Times* or the *Washington Post.* One of the reasons for labor's invisibility may be its unwillingness to take a firm stand against many of the Clinton administration's conservative policies. Also, since Sweeney took office, the only major affirmative legislative campaign the administration conducted was for the modest minimum wage increase. For the most part, the AFL-CIO has been a faithful supporter of the administration by coming to its defense, but it spent most of its energy on

putting out conservative fires rather than promoting its own program. This fails to comply with the slogan "the best defense is a good offense." Where is labor's promotion of positive programs?

As we have learned from past experience, there is no reason to believe that failure breeds change. Organizational habits have a logic that outlives their feasibility. In the political and legislative sphere, the labor movement is tragically tied to the past. It refuses to comprehend that state power is not being wielded in behalf of working people. For the past quarter-century its strategy has depended on the outmoded assumption that the Democratic Party and the liberal state will once more become the means for meeting workers' needs. But it is plain to see the state has been hollowed of its compassionate functions. Brick by brick, the edifice of social concern and publicly funded benefits that the industrial and public employees' unions built after 1936 is being taken apart.

It may be time to fashion a new doctrine of *democratic* syndicalism, wherein the labor movement remains distant from both the state and the party system while focusing on the vigorous promotion of legislation with direct consequences to working people, running its own candidates in selected races, and allying itself with independent political formations and social movements. It would be a democratic rather than a conservative syndicalism, because it would rely on solidarity, the main weapon of all mass workers' movements. Above all, the labor movement would lend its considerable, albeit latent, power to the fight for all working people, union members or not. More than pious appeals to abstract ethical principle, concrete acts of solidarity with the working poor, women, and minorities as well as others, such as professionals and managers who are more vital to labor's objectives than its cherished hope for labor law reform. For what labor lacks now in terms of organizing is the kind of visible power and boldness that marked the drives of yesteryear.

Perhaps the main problem is labor's eagerness to become part of the middle class. Like many of their constituents, labor leaders crave this respectability as much as they do the material comforts that come with it. In the immediate postwar years they reveled in signs of acceptance by those who occupied the pinnacle of political power. In time, at the political level as well as at the bargaining table, the labor leaders became, as C. Wright Mills reminded us almost fifty years ago, the "new men of power," but in a restricted sense. In an era of unparalleled prosperity, union leaders turned their collective backs on ideologies and became devoted to pragmatic reform. In the bargain, they imperceptibly surrendered the autonomy to chart their own course. Nonetheless, for many a union official, rubbing shoulders with celebrities, powerful politicians, corporate leaders, and even the President of the United States is bound to be heady stuff. Lewis and Hillman were relatively immune to such enticements, because they were accustomed to being outsiders. And Reuther, too, remained his own person. The House of Labor they rebuilt from ruins was sturdy enough to allow these leaders the illusion that nothing, not even a tornado, could blow it down. But this may be exactly what is happening, and labor would be well advised to build a new foundation lest, like the welfare state, it is soon cleared away by the demolition crew.

8 🏴 American Labor and America's Future

After fifteen years of taking it on the chin . . . this is a victory not only for the Teamsters but for all American working families.

— *Teamster president Ron Carey*

For it's my union. I built this union.
If you want to know who owns it, I'm the guy.
No matter what they say, the union's here to stay,
And I'll fight for the union 'till I die.

— *Labor song*

IN THE 1990s America took giant strides to shed vestiges of its traditional espousal of the ideal of economic and social equality. The gap between rich and poor is growing. Statistically, U.S. income inequality is the widest in any advanced industrial country; the ability to pay now overshadows merit and social criteria for college admissions; the newspapers are filled with celebratory stories of fantastic salaries for CEOs and other executives in a time of wage stagnation. And major media have treated the entrepreneur as a cultural hero and held him up to the world as someone worth emulating. In every form of public communication we are fed the revival of the rags-to-riches legend of the late nineteenth century. The businessperson's rise from obscurity to fame has replaced the Western as the narrative of popular culture, and business values are our national ethic. Now the corporate mogul is the messenger of the new world and adorns the covers of daily newspapers and weekly magazines and is a coveted guest on talk shows; the successful small-business owner occupies the space of the imagination; and the lotto winner is everyman. When the marketplace becomes judge and jury of all social and economic activity, no one is spared. Even as individualism remains official doctrine, we are advised to get with the program. No social institution, not even the family, can be exempt from the demand to put money first.

The public is no longer repelled by revelations of boundless individual wealth and outsized corporate profits. Since the modern corporation dominates all aspects of economic life, even the tiniest business aggressively seeks investors. The prospective investor in nearly any business demands a return that competes with that of Microsoft. Even marginal enterprises like publishing, which was once the playground for "gentlemen," or normally low-profit trades like apparel, are under the gun to produce high revenues. That the manufacturer is obliged to turn to child or sweated labor in order to deliver maximum profits is of no concern to the investor. In fact, chances are that the identity of the worker from whom this bounty is sweated is carefully hidden. The bottom line is the bottom line. What disturbs is not the saga of corporate life but our having become accustomed to it.

Of course labor cannot remain indifferent to a cultural shift that devalues it. It must fight constantly to prevent wages from sinking, but it must also oppose the culture that produces the circumstances supporting inequality. To be sure, there is a heartening rise in labor activity against some prominent corporations that exploit child labor and other forms of near-slave labor. But unlike similar circumstances at the turn of the twentieth century, when labor conducted a public struggle against the capitalist values that underlay such practices, contemporary American unions choose to fight these battles on a case-by-case basis. In this respect the 1990s resemble the 1920s, except that there is no antitrust movement, nor are there tribunes of the popular interest except the populists of the right.

Management claims that what some perceive as "irresponsibility" is an inevitable consequence of our nation's becoming globally competitive and capital's insistence that every social and economic institution adopt for-profit principles and procedures remain largely unquestioned. Not only corporations but also education and health care must bow to business efficiency. College and universities increasingly hire retired private-sector managers as their CEOs (still called presidents or chancellors, but this too shall pass). With the assistance of business consultants, some universities, "reform" their curricula to correspond to what they believe are corporate requirements. Health maintenance organizations and universities refer to patients and students as "customers" and undertake marketing and advertising campaigns to sell their "product."

Who will contest the prevailing ethic that ours is a business civilization? The few radicals who oppose the drift are shouting in the wilderness. As a result, it falls mainly to the labor movement to protest. To maintain the momentum, labor must place itself in the forefront of the challenge to corporate power and especially its dictum that, in Margaret Thatcher's words, "there is no society," only individuals. The answer to the question "Can and will labor rise to the task?" will determine the future not only of the United States, but of the world.

▨

Some at the helm of the AFL-CIO are shedding part of their attitude of subordination to corporate America and displaying signs of independence. In this regard, labor is obliged to learn the lesson of the UPS strike, in which, for the first time since the plague of concessionary bargaining, labor addressed the two-tier wage system. It was a visionary challenge, because it took on the whole system and proposed a different model. The union was determined to make the company stop relying on part-time contingent labor. The rank and file, convinced that this was a fight about principle, rose to the occasion. And the union understood that reaching out to labor and to the public was as vital as stopping the delivery of packages.

But no sooner had the ink dried on the UPS contract than the monitor appointed by the court to oversee Teamsters elections voided the 1996 election. Although the scandal surrounding Ron Carey's campaign associates' tampering with dues was brewing before the strike, the conjunction of the public disclosures and the victory over UPS may not have been accidental. Nor can labor expect to avoid congressional inquiries, media bashing, and repeated predictions of its imminent demise. The next period is likely to see an acceleration of the right-wing campaign to put the labor movement in its place. Labor must recognize this as merely the latest in a fifty-year series of conservative attacks on the movement, beginning with the link between the great 1946 strikes and the Taft-Hartley Act.

But this is also a time for reflection. The lesson of UPS and of Carey's fall is that there is no easy path to labor's revitalization by the heroic acts of talented leaders beloved by many. The new labor movement will come to pass only if unions once more belong to their members. This means that labor must rebuild from the ground up and avoid the temptation to take short cuts. Carey's errors were much more grave than the legal question of whether he knew of the dealings of the consultants who had raised money through laundering Teamster funds. More relevant is why he reversed his bold statements during his first election campaign — that he would accept no outside funds and that only the rank and file could save the union from corruption.

In the aftermath of the scandal some critics argued that the explanation for Carey's indiscretion is that he was a business unionist. Or, defenders claim, he had no choice but to take extraordinary measures to defeat a better-financed opponent. Maybe so. But more to the point, he fell victim to insiders' disease, a virus that strikes liberal politicians as well as trade union functionaries. Carey, or his surrogates, confronted the need to raise about $1 million to defeat the challenge by James P. Hoffa, who had the advantage of being the son of the famed (and beloved) Teamsters leader.

How to raise this huge sum from a rank and file that was still severely demobilized after fifteen years of concessions and cynicism born of years of leadership malfeasance? After all, reasoned some of his advisers, Carey had won with a plurality of the votes in the last election against two discredited representatives of the old guard. And the rate of voter participation was only 29 percent of the members. So he or his surrogates called on friends on the AFL-CIO Executive Council and in liberal advocacy groups. He believed they could save him from almost certain defeat. The wrong question is the one that some Carey defenders have asked: Could he have won without the shenanigans? The right question is what kind of labor movement do workers need and deserve? Do Carey's acknowledged virtues justify the use of any means to keep him in office?

If independence from employers and freedom from debilitating political entanglements are primary conditions for a real labor movement, so is democratic unionism. Carey made a beginning, but his and his helpers' infractions against union democracy indicate that the labor movement remains burdened by its past. Even many of the most progressive unions have been ruled by plebiscite and consent. The leadership proposes and the membership agrees or disagrees and asks for a new proposal. In either case, the policymakers are the elected leaders, who do not yield office except by death, indictment, or an occasional electoral insurgency. Even a new broom rarely sweeps clean, because the new bureaucrats soon learn to protect their perquisites. Later I will discuss a different concept of democratic unionism. First I want to argue that one of its components, membership involvement, is the basic condition of labor's chance to extend its purview beyond its shrinking base.

≥

Previously, I pointed out that broadening unionism to millions in newer categories — white-collar workers and professionals, production and service workers in the burgeoning South, and the working poor — must succeed if labor is to defy predictions that it will represent an ever-narrowing group of privileged workers. Rather than remaining a junior partner in the prevailing power structure, labor must mount efforts beyond its remarkable but defensive efforts, such as the recent fight against fast-track legislation, and fashion a bold new program. Unions should reach beyond the specific interests of their members and speak boldly to the interests of all working people. Next, they should craft an imaginative program to link labor with America's future. And they cannot turn back from the tentative steps toward defining the movement in international terms. Rather than adopting nationalist slogans like "Buy American," labor should focus on supporting workers' struggles for human rights all over the world. If labor recognizes that equalizing wages and working conditions is the key to ending capital flight, it should support such struggles as the 1997 hunger strike of Hyundai parts workers in Tijuana, Mexico, which resulted in a victory for the union, and the fight against Kathie Lee Gifford's line of apparel when the National Labor Committee showed it was being made in sweatshops.

But labor's problems reach into the core of the old social compact itself: the virtual disappearance of collective bargaining. Although the 1930s' legal framework for union representation is still in place, despite the economic restructuring and rightward political shift of the last quarter-century, genuine bargaining has suffered considerable deterioration. Bargaining still works in a few industries and corporations where, like UPS and the auto industry, the union remains powerful and the membership is mobilized to resist some of management's initiatives and even, on occasion, to impose its will. But in most production sectors, the once mighty fortresses of unionism have become weak and fragmented. And public-sector bargaining is in serious disrepair. Under these circumstances the idea of the "bargain" that implies a level field upon which adversaries deal has all but disappeared.

Buffeted by low-wage competition at home and abroad, by job insecurity and by the shortsighted belief that cooperation with management's program of "flexibility" is better than conflict, labor's tolerance for confrontation has weakened. Employers who have badgered and cajoled workers to keep their noses to the grindstone are taken aback by the scattered instances of genuine militancy. Despite brave words, these instances have become rare. Three years after the election of the slate headed by John Sweeney, labor remains on the defensive.

Which makes more urgent the task of applying the UPS lesson. At every level, unions should renounce concessionary contracts. And labor must declare that it is prepared to take on the fifty-year agreement to concede to management the unilateral right to make investment decisions. Management must know that no agreements are secure as long as unions represent a counterforce. However dormant it has been in the past, local union leadership can come alive on such issues as enforced overtime and outsourcing, as happened at GM plants in 1996 and 1997. And the union must challenge one of the most important of management's prerogatives: determining how many workers are needed to do the job and under what circumstances the company can deploy labor. When unions do their job, they can interfere with capital's "flexibility" in directing the workforce and "allocating its resources to maximize efficiency," phrases that mean enforced overtime, hiring mainly part-time and contingent workers, and investing according to the criterion of lower labor costs and a "favorable business environment," a euphemism that signifies the foreign government is prepared to intimidate, jail, or even kill recalcitrant workers.

Even when unions concede employers' requirements and cooperate with measures like just-in-time production, a two-tier wage system, and unrestricted technological innovation, the rank and file must keep its reputation as the wild card. They are the workers who can reject negotiated concessionary agreements and stage job actions and walkouts against what they consider intolerable conditions. And they can join hands with workers in other countries to limit or thwart a corporation's efforts to pit one group against another, domestically as well as internationally. In management's language, these actions contribute to an "unstable investment environment." In the case of the Flint, Michigan, Buick plant, where in 1996 workers successfully struck against compulsory overtime in favor of hiring more workers instead, the walkout provided the excuse for the company's decision to close the plant.

The new leadership of the AFL-CIO has made a start on the way forward. But now it must articulate the most hopeful aspects of its strategies. That John Sweeney, a loyal member of the team that

guided American labor down the road to decline and marginaliza-
tion, smelled the coffee and led a coalition that is attempting to halt
labor's slide has inspired thousands of embattled trade unionists,
intellectuals, and a considerable section of the general public.
Sweeney and his colleagues were able to take the scales from their
eyes and see farther than many others, to defy the forecasts of many
that unions are inappropriate in the global workplace.

But it will take more than the professionals and administrators to
overcome the hurdles erected by labor's enemies — and by a substantial fraction of labor itself. The recognition by Sweeney and others
that the social compact of the postwar era was broken by employers
is a tremendous step toward a full grasp of the crisis. And labor must
be stronger if it is to sue for a new compact, given its weakened state.
Even if this remains a long-term objective of the leadership, its
achievement presupposes that labor acts as if it aims for power, not
compromise.

Compromise was possible when there was room for change
within the economic and political system. Labor could share American prosperity, but only when it was prepared to disobey authority
and to force capital to make a place at the social bargaining table.
Since 1975, when the Vietnam War ended and public deficits became a sin, capital was unwilling to compromise its own unsubsidized
profits. Instead, business invited workers to accept less in their pay
envelopes, even as it told government that business needed tax cuts in
order to survive.

Labor's ability to regain the initiative depends on a conception of
the good life that is radically different from prevailing conservative
ideas; and the capacity to mobilize millions of workers, their families
and like-minded intellectuals, civic organizations, and social movements to resist moving backward to the nineteenth century. Neither is
easy to accomplish, most of all because organized labor has openly
renounced what other labor movements take for granted: that ideological moorings are the basis for their program. The contemporary
conservative vision of the future is heavily soaked in images of human
evil. Their ideology begins with the statement that people are not

only imperfect but are sinful, and accuses those who hold to the possibility of general happiness of being authoritarians. On the contrary, since the idea of happiness veers toward pleasure, it is, like budget deficits, a sin and should be banished. From this cardinal precept it follows that happiness plays no role in the idea of the Good. We should pay for our profligate habits such as sex, excess consumption, which leads to high personal debt, and laziness by putting our noses to the grindstone. Conservatives never tire of extolling the virtues of sacrifice and hard work as penance for our original or acquired sins.

The best traditions of the labor movement have insisted on labor's major goals — freedom from unpaid unemployment, free time for personal development, and a secure future for one's kids. Even if we take the old trade union adage that the only goal of labor is "more," this simple and apparently anti-ideological statement recognizes no inherent limit to satisfaction, which in a time of austerity retains considerable radical resonance. At its best, the labor movement has always shunned the conservative doctrine of permanent scarcity, which has become the basis of capital's rejection of its demands.

The real consideration behind issues like overtime, two-tier wages, and the wage freeze is what workers will accept. Or, put another way, how the labor movement can change the cultural environment that limits workers' sense of possibility. When unions refuse to paint the vision of the good life, informed by the idea of freedom and abundance, they forfeit the chance to inspire the rank and file. And they defeat their own goal of restoring equity to the polity and to the workplace.

How can union leaders persuade the membership to donate time and energy for labor's cause, when for years most of them have bent considerable effort to keep the membership at bay? While the AFL-CIO's program of placing emphasis on organizing is admirable, the leadership cannot achieve the ambition of bringing millions of workers into the labor movement without a reactivated rank and file. Professional organizers may be necessary but they are not sufficient.

As every successful organizer knows, workers organize themselves with help from other workers and their unions. At best the good organizer is an educator and an adviser, and does not substitute for an in-workplace committee. As we saw, unions made substantial organizing gains when they learned that they achieve success by joining with social movements and with communities in which workers and their families live.

The chance that people will turn to unions to help address their economic needs are greatest when they have experienced deterioration in their wages and working conditions; when, like professionals, they have suffered diminished expectations; or, as in the case of farmworkers and janitors, when unionization becomes a mission, a crusade for liberation and justice. In the very act of organizing lie the seeds of democratic unionism. The organizer's job is to show how self-organization can overcome the sense of powerlessness that first prompted workers to seek unionization. The organizer knows that "leadership" means assisting people to lead themselves.

Similarly, lobbyists are useful to carry labor's message to lawmakers and the public, but the strategic deployment of television ads is no substitute for the one-on-one organizing that thousands of volunteers can do to help a political or legislative campaign. Ask the hundreds of Democratic legislators and governors who have benefited from union volunteers what helps them most. But if members are disaffected because they believe the union leaders are doing the boss's bidding, or if they have been fed the idea that their union is a bank or insurance company that dispenses services and benefits, they are unlikely to respond to appeals to become involved in organizing, let alone in political campaigns.

The fundamental condition for active members is their perception that there is hope for real change, and the belief that they, not the leaders and staff, own the union. The obstacles are some of the entrenched practices of the unions themselves. For example, to combat the union hierarchy's arrogant refusal to place power in the membership to elect its own officers directly, Teamsters for a Democratic Union, temporarily putting aside its doubts about state interference in internal union affairs, called on the federal government to compel direct elections. Even some progressive unions, notably the Auto Workers, still elect their officers at conventions, not by direct membership vote. Others rig the rules to make it difficult for insurgents to win. Even when there is a direct membership vote for national officers, opposition slates are still fairly rare, although their number is growing. At Flint's Buick plant some full-time union representatives threatened members with the prospect that the plant would shut down unless they voted out the incumbent, who was affiliated with the opposition New Directions caucus. They did, and the company promptly announced it was closing it down anyway.

But most union leaders hesitate before calling on the members to do anything beyond confer their consent. The reasons for this reluctance are not difficult to fathom. They do not want to risk the emergence of new, potentially opposing forces within the union. With some exceptions, rank-and-file and other opposition groups have difficulty gaining equal access with the leadership caucus to the union's newspaper and mailing lists, and often are forced to make complaints to the Labor Department or to conduct lawsuits to bring the leadership to heel. Even when there are good reasons to involve the rank and file, leaders often say that the membership is "apathetic" or does not have the time to participate. These excuses have some justification, given the fact that many members are working more than one job or large chunks of overtime, but one suspects the underlying reason is the leaders' self-protection.

UNION DEMOCRACY AND LABOR'S REVITALIZATION

In a democratic society individuals are free to express their views and have the power to shape the decisions affecting the polity without fear of being coerced or losing their jobs. They are most effective when they act in concert with others to advance proposals that may be in conflict with those of the party in power. Competition between unions and ideologies is inherent in the European system of labor relations. It doesn't work perfectly, but it does provide rank-and-file members with alternatives. The American system discourages political differences within the labor movement. A single union wins exclusive bargaining rights, and its officials come to feel that they have exclusive power over union affairs.

Nor have American unions taken seriously the proposals that would cancel bargaining as the exclusive right of unions. For example, in many European countries the labor law guarantees bargaining rights to employees of enterprises employing more than a specified number of workers. Unions compete for representation on works councils or workplace committees, but a single union cannot be the exclusive bargaining agent, because representatives are elected on a proportional basis. If a union receives 20 percent of the vote, it has a fifth of the members of the council. In turn, people join the union voluntarily. In the United States, work councils historically were identified with company unions and incurred the enmity of most independent trade unionists. But where collective representation is a right for nearly all workers, by law the unions are freed from most of the tasks associated with bureaucratic administration. The union becomes almost completely a means for mobilization and political struggle.

American labor representation is established on a workplace-by-workplace basis; workers do not have the statutory right to representation. Union representation is a privilege reserved for those who choose a union by majority vote against "no union." If "no union" wins, workers are deprived of the legal right to collective representation. And the law, like our electoral system, recognizes winner-take-all representation. This construction of industrial relations was advanced by the New Deal, with the approval of large corporations. In the interests of labor stability, these companies wanted to deal with a single representative, who, in principle, could control an often unruly rank and file. Most unions strongly supported the main embodiment of this system, the Wagner Act, and have defended its provision that a single organization will have exclusive bargaining rights within a legally defined bargaining unit.

Under these circumstances the only reasonably firm assurance of continuous practice of union democracy is to encourage the forma-tion of two or more permanent political parties within the union. The existence of opposition groups may not always protect individual rights, lead to genuine collective bargaining, or even succeed in "un-ionizing the organized." But the experience of the Teamsters, New York's Transport Workers union, Teachers, and the most famous and effective of them all, the official two-party system in the Typo-graphical union, demonstrates the value of an institutionalized oppo-sition. Under penalty of being ejected from power, the leadership is more responsive to members' needs, generally more militant at the bargaining table, and its tendencies to trample on members' political rights are tempered if not entirely suppressed.

The difficulty is that most national unions are one-party regimes. Opposition waxes and wanes at the local union level, especially when the officers negotiate weak contracts or are incompetent administra-tors. But apart from "getting a better contract," most insurgents have few ideas about how to prevent the sins of their predecessors from being repeated. Consequently, the most democratic of the local un-ions experience more or less frequent leadership turnover.

Many national unions treat successful local insurgencies as if they were violations of sacred rights. As Carey did in nearly eighty Team-ster union locals, the national union is right to impose penalties on local affiliates for corrupt practices, financial irregularities, and bla-tant incompetence in fulfilling reporting requirements or adminis-tering national agreements. But the line between malfeasance and rebellion is often crossed by union administrators. As we have seen, Sweeney's great strength as the Service Employees union president was to let the locals "do their thing," but he was not beyond placing trusteeships on rebellious locals. Full-time representatives are often assigned to make sure that the local union stays in line and may intervene in a local union election in behalf of the incumbent leader-ship or to dislodge an insurgency that has won office.

In order to free full-time staff for organizing, I previously advo-cated that unions undertake an extensive education program to train stewards and local union officers in the control of grievances and most contract procedures. There are two further consequences of this proposal: it rebuilds the union's base by transferring real power to shop-level leaders, and it can help recruit volunteer organizers. Most certainly education of this kind would undermine the service model of unionism by narrowing the functions of full-time representatives to organizing and assistance in the last stages of contract negotiations. Placing power over the most basic union functions in the hands of rank-and-file leaders would democratize union politics by raising the stakes of participation and the ability of the membership to run its own affairs. In time, self-perpetuating bureaucracies would be more difficult to sustain, and that might encourage the union to confront its complex problems. However irksome to the leaders, there is no better cure for inertia than a group of discontented firebrands determined to turn the world upside down.

American unions mimic American politics in that holding fulltime office is a vocation rather than an assignment. While one may have sincere reservations about term limits that ensure the dominance of legislatures and the political parties by large corporate donors, the modest proposal of term limits for union leaders is eminently democratic. It would go a long way to breaking up bureaucratic hierarchies in the labor movement, minimizing the problem of nepotism, and reducing, if not eliminating, corrupt practices. I am not naive enough to believe that career union officials are likely to embrace this or any other proposal that would transform the nature of the unions. It would have to be placed on labor's agenda by an out-of-power caucus.

This is not just a question of giving up perks like high salaries, cars, daily allowances, and the notorious practice of accepting two salaries. Most union officials simply do not want to return to the shop. Few leaders of major national unions or of large locals come from jobs they would willingly resume. They are no longer comfortable with the routine tasks associated with most blue- or white-collar work; even many who were in skilled trades or professions, like teaching, engineering, and social work, would require considerable upgrading of their own skills in order to go back. The leaders' interest in maintaining their positions, then, is entirely understandable.

Yet career office-holding has widened the gap between leaders and members, especially the growing numbers of women and minorities. And since most officials and staff are in their fifties and sixties, and have been in office for decades, it is difficult to banish the image of the labor movement as a geriatric home. In this regard it is important to note that, since the industry has done little hiring for the past fifteen years, the average age of auto workers matches the age of their leaders. But teachers, communications workers, hotel and restaurant workers, and public employees are considerably younger, and only with few exceptions have younger leaders taken the helm of those unions.

Has labor gone far enough in remaking itself? I wish I could confidently predict that the odds are better than even that the labor movement will pull up its socks and help lead working people and America to a different future from that offered by transnational corporations and the political establishment. I would like believe that a "let us go forth" conclusion is justified by the experience of the recent past. And there are some grounds for hope: a reinvigorated AFL-CIO leadership that understands the dire consequences of maintaining business as usual; signs that the number of rank-and-file activists is growing; an expanding organizing activity; and the renewed interest and involvement of some workers.

But there is little discussion of new ideas within the labor movement. Few unionists are asking whether the old system of collective bargaining needs to be replaced; even fewer are exploring other possibilities. Why, for example, does the American system of labor relations, including union contracts, view the employee as guilty until proven innocent? Why have workers in nonunion workplaces virtually no rights unless they can prove race, gender, or age discrimination for a limited number of issues? Why haven't more complained that labor's voice remains muted on a range of issues of importance to the country, like the environment, and on the national discussion about race in America? The bare fact is that, despite an atmosphere of remarkable openness in some quarters, the labor movement as a whole still lacks a vision for America to offer as a justification for its claim to leadership.

Until labor decides that America's future belongs in the hands of working people, it will not seriously entertain alternatives to its current practices, let alone transform itself into a social movement. Until labor frankly addresses the bewildering changes in economic, political, and cultural life, openly condemns the gallop toward an age of corporate hegemony, and proposes an alternative path, its power will continue to fade. But social movements cannot be brought into being by fiat. If the task exceeds the capacity of the current union leadership, new forces will have to emerge to take up the burden. Perhaps, as has happened before, a new labor movement may grow outside the official ranks. For now, what is needed is public debate about the future of working people and their organizations. Ideas must be put on the table and seriously discussed by all in the labor movement and their allies. For, contrary to common sense — which views ideas and action as separate spheres — the labor movement desperately needs the imagination to act and the courage to think the unthinkable.

Notes

INTRODUCTION

1. C. Wright Mills, "The New Left," in *Power, Politics and People*, edited by Irving Louis Horowitz, New York, Oxford University Press, 1963, p. 248.
2. Ulrich Beck, *Risk Society*, London, Los Angeles, and New Delhi, Sage Publications, 1992.
3. Terri Mizrachi, *Getting Rid of Patients*, New Brunswick, N.J., Rutgers University Press, 1986.
4. For example, Richard B. Freeman in the *Wall Street Journal*, June 23, 1991.
5. Thomas A. Kochan, Harry C. Katz, and Robert B. McKersie, *The Transformation of American Industrial Relations*, New York, Basic Books, 1986.
6. Steven Greenhouse, "Militant Is Elected Head of AFL-CIO," *New York Times*, October 26, 1995.
7. Steven Greenhouse, "New Fire for Labor," *New York Times*, October 26, 1995.

1. RIDING THE WAVE OF POSTWAR
PROSPERITY AND DECLINE

1. For the best account of labor's wartime compromise, see Nelson Lichtenstein, *Labor's War at Home: The CIO in World War 11*, Cambridge, Cambridge University Press, 1982; see also Martin Glaberman, *Wartime Strikes*, Detroit, Bewick, 1980.
2. Jeremy Brecher, *Strike* (second edition), Boston, South End Press, 1997.
3. For Reuther's postwar economic philosophy, see Nelson Lichtenstein, *The Most Dangerous Man in Detroit: Walter Reuther and the Fate of American Labor*, New York, Basic Books, 1995, pp. 221–226.

4. For a detailed account of the 1970 General Motors strike, see William Serrin, *The Company and the Union.*

5. "Comparative Wages in Europe and the United States," International Labor Organization World Labor Report, 1997.

6. For an analysis of the energy crisis of the early 1970s, see Stanley Aronowitz, *Food, Shelter and the American Dream,* New York, Seabury Press, 1974.

7. William Julius Wilson, *When Work Disappears,* Cambridge, Harvard University Press, 1996.

8. For the most complete history of the rise of 1199, see Leon Fink and Brian Greenberg, *Upheaval in the Quiet Zone,* Urbana, University of Illinois Press, 1989.

9. The most extensive discussion of this concept is Paul Johnston, *Success While Others Fail,* Berkeley and Los Angeles, University of California Press, 1994.

2. THE RISE AND CRISIS OF PUBLIC EMPLOYEES' UNIONS

1. Daniel Bell, *The End of Ideology,* Glencoe, Ill., The Free Press, 1960.

2. See especially Richard B. Freeman, "Unions Come to the Public Sector," *Journal of Economic Literature,* vol. xxiv (March 1986).

3. There are two excellent studies of comparable worth: Sara M. Evans and Barbara J. Nelson, *Wage Justice: Comparable Worth and the Paradox of Technocratic Reform,* Chicago, University of Chicago Press, 1989; Linda Blum, *Between Feminism and Labor: The Significance of the Comparable Worth Movement,* Berkeley and Los Angeles, University of California Press, 1991. The "paradox" of the comparable worth movement was, according to Evans and Nelson, that it unwittingly fostered tighter managerial control of the workplace. While Blum does not deny the contradiction, in my view she correctly argues that the movement's contribution to pay equity outweighed its dubious results.

3. LABOR, THE SOUTH, AND AMERICAN POLITICAL CULTURE

1. David Brody, *Workers in Industrial America,* 2nd ed., Oxford University Press, 1993.

2. For the outstanding study of the populist movement, see Lawrence Goodwyn, *Democratic Promise: The Populist Moment in America,* New York, Oxford University Press, 1976.

3. Janet Christine Irons, *Testing the New Deal: The General Strike of 1934,* Ph.D. dissertation, Duke University, 1988.

4. Ibid., p. 427.
5. Ibid., p. 478.
6. *Operation Dixie Archive,* Fletcher Library, Duke University, box 53.
7. Dean Culver to North Carolina Director William Smith, ibid., box 53.
8. Franz Daniel, "Report to George Baldanzi," ibid., box 87.
9. Bruce Raynor, interview with the author, May 14, 1997.

4. THE WORKING POOR: RAISING THE BOTTOM

1. For example, Lawrence Mead, *The New Politics of Poverty,* New York, Basic Books, 1992.
2. Peter Townsend, *Poverty in the United Kingdom,* quoted in Michael Harrington, *The New American Poverty,* New York, Penguin Books, p. 74.
3. Jon Kest, interview with the author, July 26, 1997.
4. My thanks to Professor Immanuel Ness of Brooklyn College for making possible my visit to this center and for sharing with me his work on workers' centers and home health-care workers.

5. WHITE-COLLAR WORKERS: SEEDS OF HOPE?

1. For a superb history of twentieth-century office work, see Sharon Hartman Strom, *Beyond the Typewriter: The Origins of Modern American Office Work 1900–1930,* Urbana and Chicago, University of Illinois Press, 1992; also the classic study by C. Wright Mills, *White-Collar America's Middle Classes,* New York, Oxford University Press, 1951.
2. For a thorough examination of the Harvard clerical workers' campaigns, see John Hoerr, *We Can't Eat Prestige,* Philadelphia, Temple University Press, 1997.
3. Maida Rosenstein, interview with the author, November 1997.
4. Clive Jenkins and Barrie Sherman, *White-Collar Unionism: The Rebellion of the Salariat,* London, Routledge and Kegan Paul, 1979; Roger Lumley, *White-Collar Unionism in Britain,* London, Methuen, 1973.
5. For a pioneering study of part-time work, see Veronica Beechey and Tessa Perkins, *A Matter of Hours,* Minneapolis, University of Minnesota Press, 1987.

6. PROFESSIONALS AND MANAGERS: THE NEW FRONTIER

1. Magali Larson, *The Rise of Professionalism,* Berkeley and Los Angeles, University of California Press, 1977.
2. Stanley Aronowitz and Tony Tinker, "Changes in Accounting as an Occu-

pation," Report to Research Foundation, City University of New York, 1997.

3. Stanley Aronowitz and William DiFazio, *The Jobless Future: Sci-Tech and the Dogma of Work,* Minneapolis, University of Minnesota Press, 1994, chapter four.

4. For a fine history of the origins of public education in America, see Michael B. Katz, *The Irony of Early School Reform,* Boston, Beacon Press, 1968.

5. For an able history of American higher education, see Christopher Lucas, *American Higher Education: A History,* New York, St. Martins Press, 1994.

7. LABOR AND AMERICAN POLITICS

1. Vivian Vale, *Labour and American Politics,* New York, Barnes and Noble, 1971.

2. Ibid., p. 32.

3. The story of the Occupational Safety and Health Act (OSHA) has yet to be fully told. I worked with Anthony Mazzocchi in the late 1960s, when I was with the Oil, Chemical, and Atomic Workers, and Mazzocchi was a member of the union's executive board. Tony was always interested in safety and health at the workplace, but our focus at that time was on the nuclear fuel and weapons industry, some of whose workers were in our union. Tony established working relations with Dr. Irving Sellikoff of Mount Sinai Medical School, who developed criteria for determining safe levels of radiation ingestion for workers in nuclear plants, and with Leo Kaplan, then of the AFL-CIO staff. In a series of discussions, testimony before the Atomic Energy Commission, and campaigns at Kerr McGee in Tulsa, Oklahoma, and Northern Nuclear Fuels in New Haven, Mazzocchi was the key figure in the development of the approach that led to the enactment of OSHA. Without his persistence and vision, it would never have seen the light of day.

4. Herbert Marcuse, *One-Dimensional Man,* Boston, Beacon Press, 1964. This text was extremely influential among the new left. Among its many theses, none was more powerful than the idea that the working class had been fully co-opted by late capitalism.

5. "GM to Build Plants Abroad," *Wall Street Journal,* August 4, 1997.

Index